Practical BASIC
Programs

TRS-80™ Level II Edition

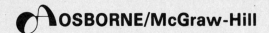OSBORNE/McGraw-Hill

Practical BASIC Programs

TRS-80™ Level II Edition

Edited by Lon Poole

Staff Writers:

Steven Cook
Martin McNiff
Robert Thomson

Contributors:

Richard E. Beckwith
Samuel H. Westerman

**Converted to TRS-80
by Karl Koessel**

Published by
OSBORNE/McGraw-Hill
630 Bancroft Way
Berkeley, California 94710
U. S. A.

TRS-80 is a trademark of Tandy Corporation.

For information on translations and book distributors outside of the
U. S. A., please write OSBORNE/McGraw-Hill at the above address.

PRACTICAL BASIC PROGRAMS — TRS-80^{TM} LEVEL II EDITION

1 2 3 4 5 6 7 8 9 0 MLML 8 7 6 5 4 3 2 1

ISBN 0-931988-67-5

Special thanks to Cynthia Greever and Pamela Phillips for their technical assistance.

Cover design by Joseph Mauro.

Disclaimer of Warranties and Limitation of Liabilities

Acknowledgments

Steven Cook, Martin McNiff, and Robert Thomson conceived, designed, wrote, and tested many of these programs, and prepared the final write-ups and program listings for publication in the original Osborne book, *Practical BASIC Programs.*

Samuel H. Westerman provided the concepts, designs, and initial program listings for 18 of the original programs: Income Averaging, Continuous Interest Compounding, Depreciation Switch, Apportionment by Ratios, Profit Sharing Contributions, Statistical Estimation Theory, Statistics, Unbiased Estimator of Standard Deviation, Chi-Square, Data Forecasting Divergence, Newtonian Interpolation, Lagrangian Interpolation, Sums of Powers, Factorials, Temperature Conversion, and Musical Transposition. He also provided source material for the write-ups for the 18 programs.

Richard E. Beckwith provided the concept, design, program code, and write-up for the program Swedish Machine (Queuing Theory).

George M. Blake suggested programs Accrued Interest on Bonds and Current Value of a Treasury Bill.

The programs were converted to the TRS-80 by Karl Koessel.

Contents

Preface   xi
Introduction   xiii

Income Averaging   1
Current Value of a Treasury Bill   14
Accrued Interest on Bonds   16
Continuous Interest Compounding   19
Rule of 78's Interest   21
Present Value of a Tax Deduction   23
Future Value of an Investment (Uneven Cash Flow)   25
Net Present Value of an Investment   27
Lease/Buy Decision   29
Syndicated Investment Analysis   32
Depreciation Switch   37
Apportionment by Ratios   39
Internal Rate of Return   42
Financial Management Rate of Return   45
Financial Statement Ratio Analysis   49
Profit Sharing Contributions   55
Checkbook Reconciliation   59
Home Budgeting   62
Critical Path Method (CPM)   77
Program Evaluation and Review Technique (PERT)   82
Transportation Algorithm   89
Swedish Machine (Queuing Theory)   99
Markov Analysis   105
Nonlinear Break-Even Analysis   111
Payoff Matrix Analysis   114
Bayesian Decision Analysis   119
Economic Order Quantity   123
Economic Production Quantity   126
Statistical Estimation Theory   128
Statistics   132
Unbiased Estimator of Standard Deviation   139
Chi-Square   141
Data Forecasting Divergence   145
Newtonian Interpolation   148
Lagrangian Interpolation   151
Sums of Powers   155
Factorials   157
Temperature Conversion   159
Numeric Base Conversion   162
Musical Transposition   165
Appendix   168

Preface

We collected the programs in this book to address the continuing need for readily available and easy-to-use computer programs that do something useful. The supply of such programs has not kept pace with the demand. The number of computer users is growing at an astounding rate, thanks chiefly to the availability of inexpensive small computers. An increasing number of these people, many of them first-time users, are interested only in the practical aspects of computing. Today, those who view the computer solely as a means of entertainment are few and far between. While more practical programs are now available, many contributed by new users, there just aren't enough. And those that do exist are hard to find. So, we brought together in this book 40 relatively short programs covering a wide range of practical applications.

Introduction

Purpose

Considering all the small computers people have bought in recent years, it should be easy to find practical computer programs. This is especially true since few users still consider their computer just a diversion. But practical programs are not readily available. The purpose of this book is to help fill that void. All forty programs in this book are useful computer applications. The Basic program listings are included. Type them into your computer and they are ready to run. Both the programmer and the nonprogrammer benefit from this; neither has any programming to do. All of which saves everyone time; the nonprogrammer needn't learn programming and the programmer has more time to write programs no one else has written.

While you don't have to be a programmer to use this book, you must understand the subject matter of the programs you wish to use. It is beyond the scope of this book to explain how, when, where, or why you would use any of them. This does not mean you must be a tax accountant in order to use the Income Averaging program, or a management science professional to use the Transportation Algorithm program. There are sample runs and practice problems for each program. Chances are you can figure out the program's applications from them. And if you understand the applications to some extent, but would like more information, you will find further reading suggested in the References section of many programs.

This book has a secondary purpose as well, and that is to show by example the wide range of subjects that lend themselves to computerization. All too often, computer users who have cut their teeth on entertainment computing have trouble coming up with ideas for practical computing. So even if you don't see a program in this book that is exactly what you need, you may find it easier to invent your own practical applications after studying some of these.

As you look through the programs in this book, you may discover that you can use pieces of the programs or some of the programming techniques in your own work. For example, embodied in these programs is a function for rounding arithmetic calculations to the nearest cent and a subroutine for pausing at the end of each full display screen. For that matter you may be able to use an entire program as a component part of your own larger, more complex program. Some of these programs themselves make use of programs from the book *Some Common BASIC Programs, TRS-80™ Level II Edition,* also published by Osborne/McGraw-Hill.

Organization

These programs find their primary applications in four general areas: financial, management decision, statistics, and mathematics and science. This arbitrary classification has no bearing on the utility of the programs per se. Clearly, the question is not what label we have applied to a program, but rather how it can be used.

Towards this end, each program includes a complete write-up in addition to its listing. Each write-up begins with a discussion of its subject matter, its required inputs, and its resultant output. In some cases, there are limitations in the algorithm the program employs, or in the applicability of the program. These are described next. Following this in many programs is a Program Notes section. It tells you how to make minor program changes that make the program operate in a slightly different way, accommodate more or less data, and so forth. These changes may make the difference between the program being convenient or difficult for you to use. The Program Notes section also explains any complex or tricky aspects of the way the program itself is written. Generally speaking, it addresses the technical aspects of implementing the application with a computer program.

Following this narrative material is an example of the program in use. Wherever possible, we set this example in a more or less real-life situation. An example which states a situation that can be resolved by using the program is more instructive than a list of raw data which you can plug into the program. The point of doing this is not to exercise our imaginations in concocting these situations, but to exercise your imagination in visualizing potential uses of the program. The examples demonstrate as many program features as they can in a problem of reasonable size. We provide the correct answers to the unknowns of the example. The answers may be in narrative form, or they may be an inherent part of the sample run, which comes next. The sample run shows the dialogue that occurs between the user and the computer when the program is used to answer the questions posed in the example. Compare the user's inputs and the computer's outputs in the sample run with the problem stated in the example. You should be able to determine how you would use the program to solve a similar problem.

Practice problems follow each example. Use them to gain more familiarity with different ways you can use a program. Generally, we provide only the answers to these practice problems and not sample runs.

The complete Basic program listing comes next. The listings are documented with in-line remarks. The remarks make it easier for you to figure out how the program works, if you are so inclined. The remarks (which always begin with the Basic command REM) are not essential to program operation but they will facilitate your understanding of it.

Finally, we list references for most programs. Investigate these books, articles, etc., if you wish to read more about the subject matter of the program.

Data Files

None of these programs requires a mass storage device — disk or tape — for storing data. Of course you will want to store the programs themselves on a tape or disk once you have typed them in. But this is a fairly straightforward procedure which is adequately described in your computer owner's manual.

How to Use These Programs

Follow the steps listed below to use any of these programs.

1. Read the program write-up and familiarize yourself with how the program works. Read the cited references if they will give you a better understanding of the subject matter which the program addresses. Be sure the program does what you need it to do before going any further.

2. Type the program listing into your computer. Since the remark statements (those that begin with REM) are not essential to program operation, you need not type them in. By doing so, you will save time and programs will take less space (on most computers), and the programs may even run marginally faster. But if you plan to modify a program extensively, you may be better off including its remarks, since they can be very helpful in tracing program logic flow during debugging.

3. Check your program listing carefully for accuracy. Compare it line-by-line and character-by-character with the published listing. Correct any discrepancies.

4. Save the program on tape or disk. Do it now, before you run the program. That way you can easily retrieve it in the event that anything happens while you are running it.

5. Run the example exactly as shown in the sample run. If you have done everything right to this point, the results should be the same as those published.

6. If your answers differ markedly from ours, or your program does not run at all (i.e., you get some sort of error message), it is time for some detective work. First, double-check and triple-check your listing against the published one. We cannot overemphasize the importance of this scrutiny. Check for missing program lines and incorrect line numbers. Make sure you have entered the right letter or digit. It is often easy to confuse zeros and O's, ones and I's, two's and Z's, fives and S's, and U's and V's.

By now, your programs should be running correctly. If not, have someone else look over your program. Often another set of eyes can see things that you will miss repeatedly. Try putting the program aside for a while and coming back to it. After a short break, errors you didn't see before may be glaringly obvious.

7. As a further test of your program, run the practice problems. Compare your answers with those in the book.

8. The programs in this book end in a routine allowing the operator to choose between rerunning the program or returning to the command mode. These make use of the TRS-80[1]'s 'INKEY$' function and therefore do not print the character that was input on the screen.

Throughout the program listings, the character 'ʟ' is the "up arrow" character. The printer uses this character for the ASCII Code 91 while the TRS-80 uses the '^' on the display screen.

All progams in this book have been tested, run and listed on a TRS-80 Model I Level II computer system. The sample runs and listings in this book were printed on an Epson MX80[2] printer. The sample runs represent program output as it would apper on a display screen.

[1]TRS-80 is a trademark of Tandy Corporation.

[2]MX80 is a trademark of Epson Incorporated.

Income Averaging

This program calculates U.S. federal income tax using the income averaging method (Form 1040, Schedule G). It determines whether a taxpayer qualifies for income averaging, and if so, it displays the entries to complete Schedule G. The program is based on 1980 tax forms, tax rates, and tax laws. It is devised to be used for as many years in the future as the law, rates, and forms remain the same as in 1980.

To use the program, you must enter the taxpayer's name, the taxable year, and the taxpayer's filing status that year — i.e., single, married filing jointly, married filing separately, unmarried head of household, or qualifying widow(er). You then enter the taxpayer's base period income — the four years preceding the taxable year. For 1977 and later, this is the amount from line 34 of Form 1040, or line 11 of Form 1040A (line 10 on the 1977 and 1978 Forms 1040A). You must also enter the number of exemptions for each year 1977 and later, when the program asks for them. For any years of the four-year base period before 1977, you enter the taxable income directly. We should emphasize that you should enter an income figure — even a negative figure — for each year, and you should enter the total number of exemptions claimed each year (when requested), *even though the taxpayer had no net income or even though it was a negative taxable income.*

Note that even though Schedule G directs that line 3 may not be less than zero, whenever the Internal Revenue Service has been confronted with the legislative history of the applicable section of the Internal Revenue code, it has backed off, and permitted a negative figure on line 3; this program takes advantage of that fact. One the other hand, note that line 6 on Schedule G may not be less than zero, and the program takes account of that, too.

The program then asks you for other applicable income amounts (e.g., excluded foreign income) and the taxable income from Schedule TC for the taxable year. It then determines whether income averaging is permissible. If so, it displays the amounts you need in order to fill out Schedule G (1980 format).

Program Notes

The program rounds all outputs to the nearest penny. Some taxpayers prefer to work only to the nearest dollar. To put whole dollar outputs into effect, change lines 39 and 40 as shown below, and when the program asks you to enter dollar amounts, enter them in whole dollars only.

39 REM 'PRINTUSING' STRING TO ROUND OFF OUTPUT
40 PU$="$$####,####,####,####"

The 1980 Schedule G reproduced below shows how the elements of array A( ) correspond to the lines and columns of Schedule G, from A(1), the taxable year in the upper right corner, to A(44), the computed tax amount. Note that variables A(5), A(9), and A(14) are in hatched boxes (the I.R.S. intends that they remain blank in 1980). For 1980, the program accounts for that by making them all zero. As years pass, the hatching will pass off to the right, and entries will be required in those boxes.

Example

John and Mary Brown are filing a joint tax form. They have one dependent. Line 34 of their 1979 Form 1040 is $16,699.00. Line 34 of their 1978 and 1977 1040 Forms shows $10,270.00 and $12,600.00. Their taxable income for 1976 was $11,133.00. Their foreign income for 1979 and 1976 was $5,300.00 and $5,000.00. They have no penalty under section 72(m)(5) and no community income. Their taxable income for 1980 was $37,900.00. How would you use this program to help fill out their Schedule G for 1980?

SCHEDULE G
(Form 1040)
Department of the Treasury
Internal Revenue Service

Income Averaging

►See instructions on back.
► Attach to Form 1040.

A(1)

21

Name(s) as shown on Form 1040

Your social security number

Base Period Income and Adjustments	(a) 1st preceding base period year **1979**		(b) 2d preceding base period year **1978**	(c) 3rd preceding base period year **1977**	(d) 4th preceding base period year **1976**	
1 Enter amount from: Form 1040 (1977, 1978, and 1979)—line 34 Form 1040A (1977 and 1978)—line 10 Form 1040A (1979)—line 11	A(2)		A(3)	A(4)	A(5)	
2 a Multiply $750 by your total number of exemptions in 1977 and 1978	/////		A(7)	A(8)	A(9)	
b Multiply $1,000 by your total number of exemptions in 1979	A(6)		/////			
3 Taxable income (subtract line 2a or 2b from line 1). If less than zero, enter zero . . .	A(10)		A(11)	A(12)	A(13)	
4 Income earned outside of the United States or within U.S. possessions and excluded under sections 911 and 931	A(16)		A(17)	A(18)	A(19)	
5 On your 1980 {2 or 5 enter $3,200} {in column} Form 1040, if {1 or 4 enter $2,200} {(d)} you checked box {3 enter $1,600 . .}	/////		/////	A(14)	A(15)	
6 Base period income (add lines 3, 4 and 5) .	A(22)		A(23)	A(24)	A(25)	

Computation of Averageable Income

7 Taxable income for 1980 from Schedule TC (Form 1040), Part I, line 3 . . .	7	A(26)		
8 Certain amounts received by owner-employees subject to a penalty under section 72(m)(5) .	8	A(20)		
9 Subtract line 8 from line 7	9	A(27)		
10 Excess community income	10	A(21)		
11 Adjusted taxable income (subtract line 10 from line 9). If less than zero, enter zero	11	A(28)	
12 Add columns (a) through (d), line 6, and enter here	12	A(29)		
13 Enter 30% of line 12	13	A(30)	
14 Averageable income (subtract line 13 from line 11)	14	A(31)	

If line 14 is $3,000 or less, do not complete the rest of this form. You do not qualify for income averaging.

G

Computation of Tax

15 Amount from line 13	15	A(32)	
16 20% of line 14	16	A(33)	
17 Total (add lines 15 and 16)	17	A(34)	
18 Excess community income from line 10	18	A(21)	
19 Total (add lines 17 and 18)	19	A(35)	
20 Tax on amount on line 19 (see caution below)	20	A(36)	
21 Tax on amount on line 17 (see caution below)	21	A(37)	
22 Tax on amount on line 15 (see caution below)	22	A(38)	
23 Subtract line 22 from line 21	23	A(39)	
24 Multiply the amount on line 23 by 4	24	A(40)	
Note: If no entry was made on line 8 above, skip lines 25 through 27 and go to line 28.			
25 Tax on amount on line 7 (see caution below)	25	A(41)	
26 Tax on amount on line 9 (see caution below)	26	A(42)	
27 Subtract line 26 from line 25	27	A(43)	
28 Tax (add lines 20, 24, and 27). Enter here and on Schedule TC (Form 1040), Part I, line 4 and check Schedule G box	28	A(44)	

Caution: Use Tax Rate Schedule X, Y or Z from the Form 1040 instructions to figure your tax on lines 20, 21, 22, 25 and 26. Do not use the tax tables.

Answer:

```
INCOME AVERAGING

TAXPAYER'S NAME IS:
? JOHN AND MARY BROWN

TAXABLE YEAR:
? 1980

ENTER FILING STATUS--
 --1 FOR SINGLE
 --2 FOR MARRIED/JOINT
 --3 FOR MARRIED/SEPARATE
 --4 FOR HEAD OF HOUSEHOLD
 --5 FOR QUALIFYING WIDOW(ER)
? 2

ENTER THE INCOME FIGURE CORRESPONDING
   TO LINE 34 ON FORM 1040, OR ON FORM
   1040A, CORRESPONDING TO LINE 11(1979)
   OR LINE 10(1977-1978).....
FOR THE YEAR 1979
? 16699

HOW MANY EXEMPTIONS CLAIMED THAT YEAR?
? 3

ENTER THE INCOME FIGURE CORRESPONDING
   TO LINE 34 ON FORM 1040, OR ON FORM
   1040A, CORRESPONDING TO LINE 11(1979)
   OR LINE 10(1977-1978).....
FOR THE YEAR 1978
? 10270

HOW MANY EXEMPTIONS CLAIMED THAT YEAR?
? 3

ENTER THE INCOME FIGURE CORRESPONDING
   TO LINE 34 ON FORM 1040, OR ON FORM
   1040A, CORRESPONDING TO LINE 11(1979)
   OR LINE 10(1977-1978).....
FOR THE YEAR 1977
? 12600

HOW MANY EXEMPTIONS CLAIMED THAT YEAR?
? 3

ENTER TAXABLE INCOME FOR YEAR 1976
? 11133

MOST TAXPAYERS DON'T HAVE EXCLUDED
   FOREIGN INCOME, PENALIZED AMOUNTS
   UNDER CODE SEC 72(M)(5), OR EXCESS
   COMMUNITY INCOME. DO YOU HAVE ANY
   OF THESE ITEMS?  (Y/N)
```

```
? Y
EXCLUDED FOREIGN INCOME--YEAR 1979
? 5300
                        SAME--YEAR 1978
? 0
                        SAME--YEAR 1977
? 0
                        SAME--YEAR 1976
? 5000

ENTER PENALIZED AMOUNTS, SEC. 72(M)(5)
? 0
ENTER EXCESS COMMUNITY INCOME
? 0

ENTER TAXABLE INCOME FOR YEAR 1980
? 37900

FOR JOHN AND MARY BROWN, 1980 TAX
USING INCOME AVERAGING,
COMES TO                $7,718.70

THE FOLLOWING REPRESENTS THE FILLED IN
SCHEDULE G, USING THE 1979 FORMAT:


************* SCHEDULE G **************
JOHN AND MARY BROWN -- 1980
FILING STATUS: MARR./JOINT

ENTER 'C' TO CONTINUE? C
BASE PERIOD INCOME AND ADJUSTMENTS
LINE 1 -        1979 :              $16,699.00
                1978 :              $10,270.00
                1977 :              $12,600.00
                1976 :                   $0.00
LINE 2A-        1978 :               $2,250.00
                1977 :               $2,250.00
LINE 2B-        1979 :               $3,000.00
LINE 3 -        1979 :              $13,699.00
                1978 :               $8,020.00
                1977 :              $10,350.00
                1976 :              $11,133.00
ENTER 'C' TO CONTINUE? C
LINE 4 -        1979 :               $5,300.00
                1978 :                   $0.00
                1977 :                   $0.00
                1976 :               $5,000.00
LINE 5 -        1976 :               $3,200.00
LINE 6 -        1979 :              $18,999.00
                1978 :               $8,020.00
                1977 :              $10,350.00
                1976 :              $19,333.00

ENTER 'C' TO CONTINUE? C
```

```
COMPUTATION OF AVERAGABLE INCOME
     AND COMPUTATION OF TAX
LINE   7 :                 $37,900.00
LINE   8 :                      $0.00
LINE   9 :                 $37,900.00
LINE  10 :                      $0.00
LINE  11 :                 $37,900.00
LINE  12 :                 $56,702.00
LINE  13 :                 $17,010.60
LINE  14 :                 $20,889.40
LINE  15 :                 $17,010.60
LINE  16 :                  $4,177.88
LINE  17 :                 $21,188.48
ENTER 'C' TO CONTINUE? C
LINE  18 :                      $0.00
LINE  19 :                 $21,188.48
LINE  20 :                  $3,549.77
LINE  21 :                  $3,549.77
LINE  22 :                  $2,507.54
LINE  23 :                  $1,042.23
LINE  24 :                  $4,168.92
LINE  25 :                      $0.00
LINE  26 :                      $0.00
LINE  27 :                      $0.00
LINE  28 :                  $7,718.70
********** END OF SCHEDULE G **********
ENTER 'C' TO CONTINUE WITH NEXT TAXPAYER? N
READY
```

Practice Problems

1. Hester Prynne is single, head of household, and has one dependent. Line 34 of her 1979 Form 1040 is $13,988.39. Line 10 of her 1978 Form 1040A shows $12,650.10. Her taxable income for 1977 was $9,212.58; for 1976 it was $8,775.34. In 1979, she had $1,996.50 excluded under section 911. Her taxable income in 1980 is $25,300.17, and she has $1,100.00 subject to penalty under section 72(m)(5). How should she fill out her 1980 Schedule G?

Answer:

```
FOR HESTER PRYNNE, 1980 TAX,
USING INCOME AVERAGING,
COMES TO                $5,115.79

THE FOLLOWING REPRESENTS THE FILLED IN
SCHEDULE G, USING THE 1979 FORMAT:

************** SCHEDULE G **************
HESTER PRYNNE -- 1980
FILING STATUS: UNM. HEAD OF HOUSEHOLD

ENTER 'C' TO CONTINUE? C
BASE PERIOD INCOME AND ADJUSTMENTS
LINE 1 -       1979 :          $13,988.39
               1978 :          $12,650.10
               1977 :           $9,212.58
```

```
                          1976  :                       $0.00
LINE  2A-                 1978  :                   $1,500.00
                          1977  :                   $1,500.00
LINE  2B-                 1979  :                   $2,000.00
LINE  3  -                1979  :                  $11,988.39
                          1978  :                  $11,150.10
                          1977  :                   $7,712.58
                          1976  :                   $8,775.34
ENTER 'C' TO CONTINUE? C
LINE  4  -                1979  :                   $1,996.50
                          1978  :                       $0.00
                          1977  :                       $0.00
                          1976  :                       $0.00
LINE  5  -                1976  :                   $2,200.00
LINE  6  -                1979  :                  $13,984.89
                          1978  :                  $11,150.10
                          1977  :                   $7,712.58
                          1976  :                  $10,975.34


ENTER 'C' TO CONTINUE? C

COMPUTATION OF AVERAGABLE INCOME
    AND COMPUTATION OF TAX
LINE  7 :                 $25,300.17
LINE  8 :                  $1,100.00
LINE  9 :                 $24,200.17
LINE 10 :                      $0.00
LINE 11 :                 $24,200.17
LINE 12 :                 $43,822.91
LINE 13 :                 $13,146.87
LINE 14 :                 $11,053.30
LINE 15 :                 $13,146.87
LINE 16 :                  $2,210.66
LINE 17 :                 $15,357.53
ENTER 'C' TO CONTINUE? C
LINE 18 :                      $0.00
LINE 19 :                 $15,357.53
LINE 20 :                  $2,568.96
LINE 21 :                  $2,568.96
LINE 22 :                  $2,031.25
LINE 23 :                    $537.71
LINE 24 :                  $2,150.84
LINE 25 :                  $5,599.06
LINE 26 :                  $5,203.06
LINE 27 :                    $396.00
LINE 28 :                  $5,115.79
********* END OF SCHEDULE G **********
ENTER 'C' TO CONTINUE WITH NEXT TAXPAYER? N
READY
```

2. Billy Budd is single and has no dependents. Line 34 of his 1979 Form 1040 is $45,130.75. Line 34 of his 1978 Form 1040 is $48,968.20. In 1977 and 1976, his taxable incomes were $37,500.00 and $38,105.05. He had $10,000.00 of excludable foreign income in 1979, $3,000.00 in 1978, $2,500.00 in 1977, and $2,000.00 in 1976. He has no excess community income and nothing subject to section

72(m)(5) penalty. His income for 1980 is $57,762.53. How would he complete Schedule G, if he is eligible for income averaging?

Answer:

```
BILLY BUDD
DOES NOT QUALIFY FOR AVERAGING
AVERAGABLE INCOME FOR  1980
IS $1691.33 - WHICH IS $3000 OR LESS
ENTER 'C' TO CONTINUE WITH NEXT TAXPAYER? N
READY
```

Program Listing

```
9 REM ///// INCOME AVERAGING /////
10 DEFDBL A-Z : DEFINT I,J,K,F : DEFSNG R,C
18 REM A() HOLDS SCHEDULE G AMOUNTS
19 REM C() AND R() ARE FOR TAX RATE SCHEDULES
20 DIM A(45),C(4,16),R(4,16)
29 REM READ TAX RATE SCHEDULES
30 GOSUB 6900
39 REM 'PRINTUSING' STRING TO ROUND OFF OUTPUT
40 PU$="$$####,####,####,####.##"
49 REM CLEAR SCHEDULE G FOR NEXT TAXPAYER
50 FOR I=1 TO 15
60 A(I)=0
70 NEXT I
79 REM CLEAR SCREEN
80 CLS
90 PRINT "INCOME AVERAGING"
100 PRINT
110 PRINT "TAXPAYER'S NAME IS:"
120 INPUT Z$
130 PRINT
140 PRINT "TAXABLE YEAR:"
150 INPUT A(1)
160 PRINT
170 PRINT "ENTER FILING STATUS--"
180 PRINT " --1 FOR SINGLE"
190 PRINT " --2 FOR MARRIED/JOINT"
200 PRINT " --3 FOR MARRIED/SEPARATE"
210 PRINT " --4 FOR HEAD OF HOUSEHOLD"
220 PRINT " --5 FOR QUALIFYING WIDOW(ER)"
230 INPUT F
240 IF F<1 OR F>5 THEN PRINT "PLEASE, 1 THROUGH 5 ONLY":GOTO 170
250 PRINT
256 REM
257 REM **** BASE PERIOD INCOME AND ADJUSTMENTS ****
258 REM
268 REM ENTER INCOME AMOUNTS--
269 REM PROCEDURE IS DIFFERENT BEFORE 1977
270 FOR J=1 TO 4
280 IF A(1)-J>1976 THEN 330
290 PRINT "ENTER TAXABLE INCOME FOR YEAR";A(1)-J
300 INPUT A(J+9)
```

```
310 PRINT
320 GOTO 570
330 PRINT "ENTER THE INCOME FIGURE CORRESPONDING"
340 PRINT "   TO LINE 34 ON FORM 1040, OR ON FORM"
350 PRINT "   1040A, CORRESPONDING TO LINE 11(1979)"
360 PRINT "   OR LINE 10(1977-1978)....."
370 PRINT "FOR THE YEAR";A(1)-J
380 INPUT A(J+1)
390 PRINT
500 PRINT "HOW MANY EXEMPTIONS CLAIMED THAT YEAR?"
510 INPUT B
520 PRINT
528 REM EXEMPTIONS ARE $1000 EACH 1979 AND AFTER
529 REM $750 EACH BEFORE THAT
530 A(J+5)=1000*B
540 IF A(1)-J>1978 THEN 560
550 A(J+5)=750*B
560 A(J+9)=A(J+1)-A(J+5)
570 NEXT J
866 REM 5. FROM FILING STATUS, DETERMINE ZERO
867 REM      BRACKET AMOUNT FOR 1975 AND 1976
868 REM IF TAX YEAR IS 1981 OR LATER, IGNORE
869 REM ZERO BRACKET AMOUNTS
870 IF A(1)>1980 THEN 1000
880 ON F GOTO 890,910,930,890,910
889 REM SINGLE OR HEAD OF HOUSEHOLD
890 A(15)=2200
900 GOTO 940
909 REM MARRIED/JOINT OR WIDOW(ER)
910 A(15)=3200
920 GOTO 940
929 REM MARRIED/SEPARATE
930 A(15)=1600
937 REM 1975 SAME AS 1976
938 REM IF TAX YEAR IS 1980, IGNORE 1975
939 REM ZERO BRACKET AMOUNT
940 IF A(1)=1980 THEN 1000
950 A(14)=A(15)
1000 PRINT "MOST TAXPAYERS DON'T HAVE EXCLUDED"
1010 PRINT "   FOREIGN INCOME, PENALIZED AMOUNTS"
1020 PRINT "   UNDER CODE SEC 72(M)(5), OR EXCESS"
1030 PRINT "   COMMUNITY INCOME. DO YOU HAVE ANY"
1040 PRINT "   OF THESE ITEMS?   (Y/N)"
1050 INPUT W$
1060 IF W$="N" THEN 1210
1070 PRINT "EXCLUDED FOREIGN INCOME--YEAR";A(1)-1
1080 INPUT A(16)
1090 PRINT "                    SAME--YEAR";A(1)-2
1100 INPUT A(17)
1110 PRINT "                    SAME--YEAR";A(1)-3
1120 INPUT A(18)
1130 PRINT "                    SAME--YEAR";A(1)-4
1140 INPUT A(19)
1150 PRINT
1160 PRINT "ENTER PENALIZED AMOUNTS, SEC. 72(M)(5)"
```

```
1170 INPUT A(20)
1180 PRINT "ENTER EXCESS COMMUNITY INCOME"
1190 INPUT A(21)
1200 PRINT
1209 REM ADD UP BASE PERIOD INCOME COLUMNS A-D
1210 A(22)=A(10)+A(16)
1220 A(23)=A(11)+A(17)
1230 A(24)=A(12)+A(18)+A(14)
1240 A(25)=A(13)+A(19)+A(15)
1248 REM BASE PERIOD INCOME CANNOT BE NEGATIVE
1249 REM IN ANY YEAR
1250 FOR I=22 TO 25
1260 IF A(I)>0 THEN 1280
1270 A(I)=0
1280 NEXT I
1286 REM
1287 REM **** COMPUTATION OF AVERAGABLE INCOME ****
1288 REM
1289 REM 7. TAXABLE INCOME FROM SCHEDULE TC
1290 PRINT "ENTER TAXABLE INCOME FOR YEAR";A(1)
1300 INPUT A(26)
1310 PRINT
1319 REM 9. SUBTRACT LINE 8 FROM LINE 7
1320 A(27)=A(26)-A(20)
1328 REM 10. EXCESS COMMUNITY INCOME IS A(21)
1329 REM 11. ADJUSTED TAXABLE INCOME
1330 A(28)=A(27)-A(21)
1339 REM LINE 11 CANNOT BE NEGATIVE
1340 IF A(28)>0 THEN 1360
1350 A(28)=0
1359 REM 12. TOTAL BASE PERIOD INCOME
1360 A(29)=A(22)+A(23)+A(24)+A(25)
1369 REM 13. 30% OF LINE 12
1370 A(30)=A(29)*.3
1379 REM 14. AVERAGABLE INCOME
1380 A(31)=A(28)-A(30)
1390 IF A(31)>=3000 THEN 1460
1400 PRINT Z$
1410 PRINT "DOES NOT QUALIFY FOR AVERAGING"
1420 PRINT "AVERAGABLE INCOME FOR "; A(1)
1430 PRINT "IS "; : PRINTUSING "$$###.##"; A(31);
1440 PRINT " - WHICH IS $3000 OR LESS"
1450 GOTO 2240
1459 REM 15. AMOUNT FROM LINE 13
1460 A(32)=A(30)
1469 REM 16. 20% OF LINE 14
1470 A(33)=A(31)*.2
1479 REM 17. TOTAL (ADD LINES 15 AND 16)
1480 A(34)=A(32)+A(33)
1488 REM 18. EXCESS COMMUNITY INCOME IS A(21)
1489 REM 19. TOTAL (ADD LINES 17 AND 18)
1490 A(35)=A(34)+A(21)
1499 REM 20. TAX ON LINE 19 AMOUNT
1500 S=A(35)
1510 GOSUB 6000
```

```
1520 A(36)=T
1529 REM 21. TAX ON LINE 17 AMOUNT
1530 S=A(34)
1540 GOSUB 6000
1550 A(37)=T
1559 REM 22. TAX ON LINE 15 AMOUNT
1560 S=A(32)
1570 GOSUB 6000
1580 A(38)=T
1589 REM 23. SUBTRACT LINE 22 FROM LINE 21
1590 A(39)=A(37)-A(38)
1599 REM 24. MULTIPLY LINE 23 AMOUNT BY 4
1600 A(40)=4*A(39)
1608 REM -IF THERE'S NO SECTION 72(M)(5) PENALTY
1609 REM -INCOME, SKIP TO LINE 28
1610 IF A(20)=0 THEN 1690
1619 REM 25. TAX ON LINE 7 AMOUNT
1620 S=A(26)
1630 GOSUB 6000
1640 A(41)=T
1649 REM 26. TAX ON LINE 9 AMOUNT
1650 S=A(27)
1660 GOSUB 6000
1670 A(42)=T
1679 REM 27. SUBTRACT LINE 26 FROM LINE 25
1680 A(43)=A(41)-A(42)
1689 REM 28. TAX (ADD LINES 20, 24 AND 27)
1690 A(44)=A(36)+A(40)+A(43)
1692 REM
1693 REM **** PRINT SCHEDULE G ****
1694 REM
1700 PRINT "FOR ";Z$;",";A(1);"TAX,"
1710 PRINT "USING INCOME AVERAGING,"
1720 PRINT "COMES TO"; : PRINTUSING PU$; A(44)
1730 PRINT
1740 PRINT "THE FOLLOWING REPRESENTS THE FILLED IN"
1750 PRINT "SCHEDULE G, USING THE 1979 FORMAT:"
1760 PRINT
1770 PRINT "************* SCHEDULE G **************"
1780 PRINT Z$;" --";A(1)
1790 PRINT "FILING STATUS: ";
1800 ON F GOTO 1810,1830,1850,1870,1890
1810 PRINT "SINGLE"
1820 GOTO 1900
1830 PRINT "MARR./JOINT"
1840 GOTO 1900
1850 PRINT "MARR./SEP."
1860 GOTO 1900
1870 PRINT "UNM. HEAD OF HOUSEHOLD"
1880 GOTO 1900
1890 PRINT "QUAL. WIDOW(ER)"
1900 PRINT
1909 REM WAIT FOR OPERATOR CUE TO CONTINUE
1910 GOSUB 5800
1920 PRINT "BASE PERIOD INCOME AND ADJUSTMENTS"
```

```
1929 REM PRINT LINES 1, 2, AND 3
1930 FOR I=2 TO 10 STEP 4
1940 IF I=6 AND A(1)=1980 THEN GOSUB 5700 ELSE GOSUB 5600
1950 NEXT I
1960 GOSUB 5800
1969 REM PRINT LINE 4
1970 I=16
1980 GOSUB 5600
1989 REM PRINT LINE 5, IF IT'S APPLICABLE
1990 PRINT "LINE 5 - ";
2000 IF A(14)=0 THEN 2020
2010 PRINT ,A(1)-3;": "; : PRINTUSING PU$; A(14)
2020 IF A(15)=0 THEN 2040
2030 PRINT ,A(1)-4;": "; : PRINTUSING PU$; A(15)
2039 REM PRINT LINE 6
2040 I=22
2050 GOSUB 5600
2060 PRINT
2069 REM WAIT FOR OPERATOR CUE TO CONTINUE
2070 GOSUB 5800
2080 PRINT
2090 PRINT "COMPUTATION OF AVERAGABLE INCOME"
2100 PRINT "    AND COMPUTATION OF TAX"
2110 PRINT "LINE  7 : "; : PRINTUSING PU$; A(26)
2120 PRINT "LINE  8 : "; : PRINTUSING PU$; A(20)
2130 PRINT "LINE  9 : "; : PRINTUSING PU$; A(27)
2140 PRINT "LINE 10 : "; : PRINTUSING PU$; A(21)
2150 FOR J=11 TO 17
2160 PRINT "LINE";J;": "; : PRINTUSING PU$; A(J+17)
2170 NEXT J
2179 REM WAIT FOR OPERATOR CUE TO CONTINUE
2180 GOSUB 5800
2190 PRINT "LINE 18 : "; : PRINTUSING PU$; A(21)
2200 FOR J=19 TO 28
2210 PRINT "LINE";J;": "; : PRINTUSING PU$; A(J+16)
2220 NEXT J
2230 PRINT "********* END OF SCHEDULE G **********"
2238 REM WAIT BEFORE ERASING SCREEN FOR
2239 REM NEXT TAXPAYER
2240 PRINT "ENTER 'C' TO CONTINUE WITH NEXT TAXPAYER";
2250 INPUT W$
2260 IF W$="C" THEN 50
3000 END
5597 REM
5598 REM *** SUBROUTINE TO PRINT ALL OF LINE 1,2,3,4,OR 6 ***
5599 REM
5600 PRINT "LINE";INT((I-2)/4)+1;"- ";
5610 FOR J=0 TO 3
5620 PRINT ,A(1)-J-1;": "; : PRINTUSING PU$; A(I+J)
5630 NEXT J
5640 RETURN
5699 REM *** SUBROUTINE TO PRINT OUT LINES 2A AND 2B
5700 PRINT "LINE 2A-          1978 : "; : PRINTUSING PU$; A(7)
5710 PRINT "                  1977 : "; : PRINTUSING PU$; A(8)
5720 PRINT "LINE 2B-          1979 : "; : PRINTUSING PU$: A(6)
```

```
5730 RETURN
5795 REM
5796 REM *** SUBROUTINE TO WAIT FOR OPERATOR CUE
5797 REM      TO CONTINUE SINCE ENTIRE SCHEDULE G
5798 REM      WON'T FIT ON ONE SCREEN
5799 REM
5800 PRINT "ENTER 'C' TO CONTINUE";
5810 INPUT W$
5820 RETURN
5897 REM
5898 REM *** SUBROUTINE TO CALCULATE TAX ON AMOUNT S ***
5899 REM
5999 REM INITIALIZE TAX TO ZERO
6000 T=0
6009 REM SINGLE HAS 16 BRACKETS, ALL OTHERS HAVE 15
6010 K=15
6020 IF F>1 THEN 6040
6030 K=16
6039 REM DETERMINE WHETHER TO USE SCHED. X,Y, OR Z
6040 I=F
6049 REM WIDOW(ER) SAME AS MARRIED/JOINT
6050 IF F<5 THEN 6070
6060 I=2
6069 REM START WITH ZERO BRACKET AMOUNT
6070 J=1
6079 REM IS INCOME <= ZERO BRACKET AMOUNT?
6080 IF S<=C(I,J) THEN 6160
6089 REM IF INCOME > THIS BRACKET'S CEILING?
6090 IF S>C(I,J+1) THEN 6120
6098 REM FOUND MAX TAX BRACKET--
6099 REM --TAX BALANCE OF INCOME
6100 T=T+(S-C(I,J))*R(I,J)/100
6110 GOTO 6160
6119 REM ACCUMULATE TAX FROM THIS BRACKET
6120 T=T+(C(I,J+1)-C(I,J))*R(I,J)/100
6129 REM PROCEED TO NEXT BRACKET
6130 J=J+1
6140 IF J<K THEN 6090
6149 REM TAX BALANCE OF INCOME AT HIGHEST RATE
6150 T=T+(C(I,J)-C(I,J-1))*R(I,J)/100
6160 RETURN
6897 REM
6898 REM ***    SUBROUTINE TO READ TAX RATES    ***
6899 REM
6900 RESTORE
6909 REM FIRST SCHED. X
6910 FOR J=1 TO 16
6920 READ R(1,J),C(1,J)
6930 NEXT J
6939 REM THEN SCHEDS Y & Z
6940 FOR I=2 TO 4
6950 FOR J=1 TO 15
6960 READ R(I,J),C(I,J)
6970 NEXT J
6980 NEXT I
```

```
6990 RETURN
6991 REM
6992 REM ***** 1979 TAX RATE SCHEDULES X,Y, AND Z *****
6993 REM
6994 REM FOR EACH TABLE BELOW, GET RATE AND
6995 REM CUT OFF DATA PAIR FROM THE RIGHTMOST TWO
6996 REM COLUMNS OF THE APPROPRIATE SCHEDULE
6997 REM
6998 REM ----SCHEDULE X----
6999 REM
7000 DATA 14,2300,16,3400,18,4400,19,6500,21,8500
7010 DATA 24,10800,26,12900,30,15000,34,18200
7020 DATA 39,23500,44,28800,49,34100,55,41500
7030 DATA 63,55300,68,81800,70,108300
7037 REM
7038 REM ----SCHEDULE Y (JOINT/WIDOW)----
7039 REM
7040 DATA 14,3400,16,5500,18,7600,21,11900,24,16000,28
7050 DATA 20200,32,24600,37,29900,43,35200,49,45800,54
7060 DATA 6000,59,85600,64,109400,68,162400,70,215400
7067 REM
7068 REM ----SCHEDULE Y (SEPARATE)----
7069 REM
7070 DATA 14,1700,16,2750,18,3800,21,5950,24,8000,28,10100
7080 DATA 32,12300,37,14950,43,17600,49,22900,54,30000
7090 DATA 59,42800,64,54700,68,81200,70,107700
7097 REM
7098 REM ----SCHEDULE Z----
7099 REM
7100 DATA 14,2300,16,4400,18,6500,22,8700,24,11800,26,15000
7110 DATA 31,18200,36,23500,42,28800,46,34100,54,44700,59
7120 DATA 60600,63,81800,68,108300,70,161300
9999 END
```

References

U.S. Internal Revenue Service Code, Sections 1301-1305.

U.S. Public Law 91-172, Section 311(b) amending Internal Revenue Code Section 1302.

U.S. Treasury Department, Internal Revenue Service. *Income Averaging,* publication number 506.

U.S. Treasury Department, Internal Revenue Service. Regulations, Sections 1.1301-0 to 1304-6, especially the last sentence of 1.1302-02(b)(1).

Current Value of a Treasury Bill

Treasury bills differ from other investment vehicles in that they are bought and sold at a discount from their face value. The rate will vary as the bill approaches maturity. Also, discounts are figured as if a year were 360 days; the annual percentage rate, or yield, is calculated using a 365/366-day year.

To use this program, enter the T-bill's face value, issue and maturity dates in MONTH, DAY, YEAR format, using one or two numbers for each value (be sure to separate each value with a comma). Then enter the current date and current price bid. The program provides the current value as a dollar amount.

Example

A $10,000 T-bill was sold 1/10/80 to mature on 4/10/80. On 1/17/80, government securities dealers were quoting a bid price of 12.09%. How much was the bill worth?
Answer: The bill was worth $9,717.90

```
CURRENT VALUE OF A TREASURY BILL

                   FACE VALUE ($)? 10000
          ISSUE DATE (MM,DD,YY)? 1,10,80
       MATURITY DATE (MM,DD,YY)? 4,10,80
        TODAY'S DATE (MM,DD,YY)? 1,17,80
          CURRENT PRICE BID (%)? 12.09

CURRENT VALUE =                   $9,717.90

WOULD YOU LIKE TO RE-RUN THIS PROGRAM USING NEW DATA   (Y/N) ?
READY
```

Practice Problems

1. A one year bill issued 2/16/80 with a face value of $50,000 was sold on 4/10/80 at a 7.35% discount. What was the selling price?
Answer: The bill sold for $46,815.00.

2. Diego bought a $1,000,000.00 bill on 1/25/80 that matures 7/25/80. On 4/10/80 he noted that dealers were offering 15.54% on his issue. How much could Diego sell his bill for on that day?
Answer: The bill was worth $954,243.33.

Program Listing

```
10 CLS : DEFDBL A-Z : DEFINT D,Y,M,X,A,I
20 PRINT "CURRENT VALUE OF A TREASURY BILL"
30 PU$="$$####,####,####,####.##"
40 PRINT
50 PRINT "                        FACE VALUE ($)";
60 INPUT P
```

```
70 PRINT "                  ISSUE DATE (MM,DD,YY)";
80 INPUT M,D,Y
90 GOSUB 310
98 REM -- X3 = ABSOLUTE NUMBER OF DAYS FROM IMAGINARY DATE
99 REM --     00/00/00 TO ISSUE DATE
100 X3=A4
110 PRINT "               MATURITY DATE (MM,DD,YY)";
120 INPUT M,D,Y
130 GOSUB 310
139 REM -- X4 = TOTAL NUMBER OF DAYS IN PERIOD
140 X4=ABS(X3-A4)
150 PRINT "                TODAY'S DATE (MM,DD,YY)";
160 INPUT M,D,Y
170 GOSUB 310
179 REM -- X3 = NUMBER OF DAYS FROM ISSUE TO TODAY
180 X3=ABS(X3-A4)
190 PRINT "               CURRENT PRICE BID (%)";
200 INPUT B
209 REM -- X4 = NUMBER OF DAYS LEFT UNTIL MATURITY
210 X4=X4-X3
220 PRINT
230 PRINT "CURRENT VALUE = ";
240 PRINTUSING PU$; P-P/1D2*B*X4/360
250 PRINT
260 PRINT "WOULD YOU LIKE TO RE-RUN THIS PROGRAM USING NEW DATA
    (Y/N) ?"
270 Z$=INKEY$ : IF Z$="" THEN 270
280 IF Z$="Y" THEN 40
290 IF Z$="N" THEN 390
300 GOTO 260
306 REM -- SUBROUTINE TO DETERMINE NUMBER OF DAYS BETWEEN
307 REM -- IMAGINARY DATE 00/00/00 AND MM/DD/YY USING 365/366
308 REM -- DAY YEAR.       REF. ACCOUNTS PAYABLE & ACCOUNTS
309 REM -- RECEIVABLE (WANG), P. 255
310 RESTORE
320 DATA 0,3,3,6,8,11,13,16,19,21,24,26
330 FOR I1=1 TO M
340 READ A4
350 NEXT I1
360 A4=A4+Y*365+INT(Y/4)+1+(M-1)*28+D
370 IF INT(Y/4)=Y/4 AND M<3 THEN A4=A4-1
380 RETURN
390 END
```

References

U.S. Department of Treasury. *Information about Treasury Bills Sold at Original Issue,* Form PD 800-D (rev. June 1978).

U.S. Federal Reserve. *Marketable Securities of the United States Government — U.S. Treasury Bills, Notes, and Bonds,* circular No. LLM 185.

Accrued Interest on Bonds

This program computes accrued interest to date on a bond. The program performs calculations using either a 365/366-day standard year, or a 360-day year method (used by some federal agency notes and bonds). Sometimes a bond is issued after the first period has begun. Because this results in a first coupon payment of less than the normal amount, some issues skip that payment and include it with the second period's payment. In this case, you would respond "Y" for Yes when the program asks if this coupon involves a long first period, and enter the additional dates requested.

To use the program, select the type of year the bond calculations will use, then enter the coupon rate and the number of coupons per year. If this coupon involves a long first period, enter a "Y" and enter the date the first period began, the date the bond was acquired, and the date the first coupon would normally have been paid had this not been a long coupon. If this coupon is normal or short, enter "N" and then enter the beginning date for this period. For both long and normal or short coupons, you now enter the date the current period ends, and the settlement date. The program will output the accrued interest in percent of par value.

Example

What is the accrued interest for settlement on 9/10/79, for an 8.25% note due on 8/31/81 and issued on 8/29/79, with a long first coupon? The coupon dates are 2/28 and 8/31. The first period began on 2/28/79. (1980 is a leap year, so the end of the current period is 2/29/80.)

Answer: Accrued interest is 0.271485% of par value.

```
ACCRUED  INTEREST  ON  BONDS

COMPUTE  USING:
                    1)  360  DAY  YEAR
                    2)  365/366  DAY  YEAR
                    3)  END  PROGRAM

             WHICH?  2

        COUPON  RATE  (%)?  8.25

 NUMBER  OF  COUPONS  PER  YEAR?  2

DOES  THIS  COUPON  INCLUDE  A  LONG  FIRST  PERIOD  (Y/N)?  Y

   BEGINNING  OF  FIRST  PERIOD  (MM,DD,YY)?  2,28,79
              ISSUE  DATE  (MM,DD,YY)?  8,29,79
        FIRST  COUPON  DATE  (MM,DD,YY)?  8,31,79
    END  OF  CURRENT  PERIOD  (MM,DD,YY)?  2,29,80
         SETTLEMENT  DATE  (MM,DD,YY)?  9,10,79

ACCRUED  INTEREST  IS  .271485  %  OF  PAR.

WOULD  YOU  LIKE  TO  RE-RUN  PROGRAM  WITH  NEW  DATA  (Y/N)?
READY
```

Practice Problem

What is the accrued interest for settlement on 6/3/80, of a Federal Home Loan Bank Bond at 7.375% due 8/25/82? The coupon payment dates are 2/25 and 8/25. (FHLB bonds use a 360-day year for calculations.)

   Answer: 2.00764% of par.

Program Listing

```
10 CLS
20 PRINT "ACCRUED INTEREST ON BONDS"
30 PRINT
40 PRINT "COMPUTE USING:"
50 PRINT "                        1) 360 DAY YEAR"
60 PRINT "                        2) 365/366 DAY YEAR"
70 PRINT "                        3) END PROGRAM"
80 PRINT
90 PRINT "                   WHICH";
100 INPUT T
110 IF T=1 THEN 140
120 IF T=3 THEN 710
130 IF T<>2 THEN 90
140 PRINT
150 PRINT "         COUPON RATE (%)";
160 INPUT I
170 PRINT
180 PRINT " NUMBER OF COUPONS PER YEAR";
190 INPUT N
200 X1=0
210 PRINT
220 PRINT "DOES THIS COUPON INCLUDE A LONG FIRST PERIOD (Y/N)";
230 INPUT Z$
240 IF Z$="N" THEN 380
250 IF Z$<>"Y" THEN 220
259 REM -- SKIP THIS SECTION IF FIRST PERIOD IS NOT LONG
260 PRINT
270 PRINT "  BEGINNING OF FIRST PERIOD (MM,DD,YY)";
280 GOSUB 570
290 X2=A4
299 REM -- ISSUE DATE IS DATE CURRENT BONDHOLDER OBTAINED BOND
300 PRINT "                ISSUE DATE (MM,DD,YY)";
310 GOSUB 570
319 REM -- X1 = NO. OF DAYS FROM ISSUE TO END OF PARTIAL PERIOD
320 X1=ABS(X2-A4)
330 PRINT "           FIRST COUPON DATE (MM,DD,YY)";
340 GOSUB 570
341 REM -- X2 = TOTAL NUMBER OF DAYS IN FIRST PERIOD
350 X2=ABS(X2-A4)
360 X1=(X2-X1)/X2
370 GOTO 410
380 PRINT
390 PRINT "BEGINNING OF CURRENT PERIOD (MM,DD,YY)";
400 GOSUB 570
408 REM -- X3 = ABSOLUTE NUMBER OF DAYS FROM IMAGINARY DATE
```

```
409 REM --         00/00/00 TO BEGINNING OF CURRENT PERIOD
410 X3=A4
420 PRINT "        END OF CURRENT PERIOD (MM,DD,YY)";
430 GOSUB 570
439 REM -- X4 = TOTAL NUMBER OF DAYS IN CURRENT PERIOD
440 X4=ABS(X3-A4)
450 PRINT "              SETTLEMENT DATE (MM,DD,YY)";
460 GOSUB 570
468 REM -- X3 = NUMBER OF DAYS FROM BEGINNING OF
469 REM --      CURRENT PERIOD TO SETTLEMENT DATE
470 X3=ABS(X3-A4)
480 X3=(X3/X4)+X1
490 PRINT
500 PRINT "ACCRUED INTEREST IS";I/N*X3;"% OF PAR."
510 PRINT
520 PRINT "WOULD YOU LIKE TO RE-RUN PROGRAM WITH NEW DATA (Y/N)?
530 Z$=INKEY$ : IF Z$="" THEN 530
540 IF Z$="Y" THEN 30
550 IF Z$="N" THEN 710
560 GOTO 520
570 INPUT M,D,Y
580 IF T=1 THEN 690
586 REM -- SUBROUTINE TO DETERMINE NUMBER OF DAYS BETWEEN
587 REM -- IMAGINARY DATE 00/00/00 AND MM/DD/YY USING 365/366
588 REM -- DAY YEAR.      REF. ACCOUNTS PAYABLE & ACCOUNTS
589 REM -- RECEIVABLE (WANG), P. 255
590 RESTORE
600 DATA 0,3,3,6,8,11,13,16,19,21,24,26
610 FOR I1=1 TO M
620 READ A4
630 NEXT I1
640 A4=A4+Y*365+INT(Y/4)+1+(M-1)*28+D
650 IF INT(Y/4)<>Y/4 THEN 680
660 IF M>2 THEN 680
670 A4=A4-1
680 RETURN
688 REM -- SUBROUTINE TO COMPUTE NUMBER OF DAYS FROM IMAGINARY
689 REM -- DATE 00/00/00 TO MM/DD/YY USING 360 DAY YEAR
690 A4=Y*360+M*30+D
700 RETURN
710 END
```

Reference

Stigum, Marcia. *The Money Market: Myth, Reality, and Practice.* Homewood, Ill.: Dow Jones-Irwin, 1978.
    Pages 538-47.

Continuous Interest Compounding

This program calculates the future value of an investment for which interest is compounded continuously. You must enter the interest rate, the number of years that interest will accrue, and the amount of the initial deposit. The total value is based on the following formula:

$$T = De^{IN}$$

where:

T = total value after N years
D = initial investment
I = interest rate
e = 2.718281828... (base of natural logarithms)

Example

Dan deposits $800.00 at 7½% interest, compounded continuously. How much will his account be worth in ten years?
Answer: $1,693.60

```
CONTINUOUS INTEREST COMPOUNDING

ENTER THE ANNUAL INTEREST RATE (%)
TO BE PAID ON THE ACCOUNT
? 7.5
ENTER THE NUMBER OF YEARS OR FRACTIONS
OF YEARS THAT INTEREST WILL ACCRUE
? 10
ENTER YOUR INITIAL DEPOSIT
? 800
WITH CONTINUOUS COMPOUNDING A DEPOSIT OF
$ 800   GROWS IN 10   YEARS AT 7.5 % TO
              $1,693.60

WOULD YOU LIKE TO RE-RUN PROGRAM WITH NEW DATA (Y/N)?
READY
```

Practice Problems

1. If George invests $5,000.00 at 9%, compounded continuously, how much will he have in 7 years and 3 months? (Enter 7 years 3 months as 7.25 years.)
Answer: $9,601.68

2. Dr. Williams invests $70.00 for his niece on the day she is born. How much will she get when she turns 21, at 6¼% compounded continuously?
Answer: $260.08

Program Listing

```
10 CLS : DEFDBL A-Z
20 PRINT "CONTINUOUS INTEREST COMPOUNDING"
30 PRINT
40 PRINT "ENTER THE ANNUAL INTEREST RATE (%)"
50 PRINT "TO BE PAID ON THE ACCOUNT"
60 INPUT I
70 IF I<=0 THEN 40
80 PRINT "ENTER THE NUMBER OF YEARS OR FRACTIONS"
90 PRINT "OF YEARS THAT INTEREST WILL ACCRUE"
100 INPUT N
110 IF N<=0 THEN 80
120 PRINT "ENTER YOUR INITIAL DEPOSIT"
130 INPUT D
140 IF D<=0 THEN 120
150 PRINT "WITH CONTINUOUS COMPOUNDING A DEPOSIT OF"
160 PRINT "$";D;" GROWS IN";N;" YEARS AT";I;"% TO"
170 PRINTUSING "$$####,####,####,####.##"; D*EXP(I/100*N)
180 PRINT
190 PRINT "WOULD YOU LIKE TO RE-RUN PROGRAM WITH NEW DATA (Y/N)?
200 Z$=INKEY$ : IF Z$="" THEN 200
210 IF Z$="Y" THEN 30
220 IF Z$<>"N" THEN 190
230 END
```

Rule of 78's Interest

This program computes the interest for each month of a loan in accordance with the rule of 78's. You enter the total interest which would have been earned had the loan continued to maturity, and the number of months in the original period of the loan. The program then prints out a table, with the number of each month, the interest earned during that month by the rule, the interest earned so far, and the balance of (unearned) interest remaining at the end of that month.

Example

A 24-month loan calls for total interest of $10,000.00. What is the interest for each month of the loan?
    Answer:

```
RULE OF 78'S INTEREST

ENTER TOTAL INTEREST (%) TO BE EARNED
TO MATURITY OF THE LOAN
? 10000
ENTER NO. OF MONTHS DURATION
OF THE LOAN TO MATURITY
? 24
```

MONTH OF LOAN	MONTH'S INTEREST	ACCUMULATED INTEREST	BALANCE OF INTEREST
1	$800.00	$800.00	$9,200.00
2	$766.67	$1,566.67	$8,433.33
3	$733.33	$2,300.00	$7,700.00
4	$700.00	$3,000.00	$7,000.00
5	$666.67	$3,666.67	$6,333.33
6	$633.33	$4,300.00	$5,700.00
7	$600.00	$4,900.00	$5,100.00
8	$566.67	$5,466.67	$4,533.33
9	$533.33	$6,000.00	$4,000.00
10	$500.00	$6,500.00	$3,500.00
11	$466.67	$6,966.67	$3,033.33
12	$433.33	$7,400.00	$2,600.00
13	$400.00	$7,800.00	$2,200.00
14	$366.67	$8,166.67	$1,833.33
15	$333.33	$8,500.00	$1,500.00
16	$300.00	$8,800.00	$1,200.00
17	$266.67	$9,066.67	$933.33
18	$233.33	$9,300.00	$700.00
19	$200.00	$9,500.00	$500.00
20	$166.67	$9,666.67	$333.33
21	$133.33	$9,800.00	$200.00
22	$100.00	$9,900.00	$100.00

```
23                  $66.67              $9,966.67              $33.33
24                  $33.33             $10,000.00               $0.00
PENNY BREAKAGE ADJUSTED IN LAST MONTH

WOULD YOU LIKE TO RE-RUN PROGRAM WITH NEW DATA (Y/N)?
READY
```

Practice Problems

1. Laurie took out a 36-month loan. Her total interest was $3,614.59. What was the balance of unearned interest if she terminated the loan after 2 years?
Answer: $423.33

2. Bob Johnson pays off a 3-year loan 2 years early. If the total interest would have been $180.00, how much interest did he actually pay?
Answer: $98.94

Program Listing

```
10 CLS
20 PRINT "RULE OF 78'S INTEREST"
30 PRINT
40 PU$="$$####,####,####.##"
50 DEFDBL A-Z : DEFINT M,T
60 PRINT "ENTER TOTAL INTEREST (%) TO BE EARNED"
70 PRINT "TO MATURITY OF THE LOAN"
80 INPUT I
90 PRINT "ENTER NO. OF MONTHS DURATION"
100 PRINT "OF THE LOAN TO MATURITY"
110 INPUT T
120 T1=T*(T+1)/2
130 PRINT "MONTH"TAB(14)"MONTH'S"TAB(30)"ACCUMULATED"TAB(50)
140 PRINT "BALANCE OF": PRINT "OF LOAN"TAB(13)"INTEREST";
150 PRINT TAB(32)"INTEREST"TAB(51)"INTEREST"
159 REM -- PRINT TABLE
160 FOR M=1 TO T-1
170 J=INT(((T-M+1)*I/T1)*100+.5)/100
180 A=A+J
190 B=I-A
200 PRINTUSING "###"; M; : PRINTUSING PU$; J; A; B
210 NEXT M
220 PRINTUSING "###"; T; : PRINTUSING PU$; B; A+B; 0
230 PRINT "PENNY BREAKAGE ADJUSTED IN LAST MONTH"
240 PRINT
250 PRINT "WOULD YOU LIKE TO RE-RUN PROGRAM WITH NEW DATA (Y/N)?
260 Z$=INKEY$ : IF Z$="" THEN 260
270 IF Z$="Y" THEN RUN
280 IF Z$<>"N" THEN 250
290 END
```

Present Value of a Tax Deduction

When evaluating an investment, the value of the tax savings is often a consideration. This program calculates the amount of any savings you might realize by deducting interest payments.

You must enter the tax rate, the interest rate on the debt, the term of the debt (in years), and the amount of interest to be paid during each year of the term.

Program Notes

If the level of debt will be constant throughout the term of the investment, you may want to change the program to calculate interest amounts as a percentage of a fixed dollar debt amount. Make these changes.

```
120 INPUT N
122 PRINT "ENTER THE AMOUNT OF DEBT ($)";
124 INPUT Z
130 P=0
  .
  .
  .
190 PRINT J;
200 PRINTUSING "$$###,######.##"; Z*K
210 P=P+(Z*T*K)/(1+K)[J]
220 NEXT J
```

Example

What is the present value of the tax savings on projected interest payments of $4,000, $3,500, $4,500, $4,000, and $5,000 over the next 5 years if the tax rate is 48% and the interest rate on that debt will be 19%?

Answer: If the 5 interest payments are deducted from taxable income, the present value of the taxes saved is $6,044.74.

```
PRESENT VALUE OF AN INTEREST TAX DEDUCTION

WHAT IS THE TAX RATE (%)? 48
ENTER INTEREST RATE (%)? 19
NUMBER OF PERIODS? 5
INTEREST AMOUNT ($) FOR PERIOD 1 ? 4000
                              2 ? 3500
                              3 ? 4500
                              4 ? 4000
                              5 ? 5000

PRESENT VALUE OF DEDUCTION =                    $6,044.74

WOULD YOU LIKE TO RE-RUN PROGRAM WITH NEW DATA (Y/N)?
READY
```

Practice Problems

1. If Nick buys a new truck for the shipping business he plans to start, the principal will be $6,250.00 and the interest rate 16%. Nick will make interest payments of $1,000.00, $900.00, and $800.00 during the 3 year term of the loan. If his new company will be in a 33% tax bracket, what is the present value of the taxes he will not have to pay when he deducts the interest payments?
Answer: The present value of the tax savings realized by deducting the interest payments is $674.34.

2. If the tax rate is 30% and the interest rate is 15%, what is the present value of taxes saved by deducting interest payments of $45.00, $40.00, $35.00, and $30.00 during the next 4 years?
Answer: The present value of the tax savings here is $32.86.

Program Listing

```
10 CLS
20 DEFDBL A-Z : DEFINT N,J
30 PRINT "PRESENT VALUE OF AN INTEREST TAX DEDUCTION"
40 PRINT
50 PRINT "WHAT IS THE TAX RATE (%)";
60 INPUT T
70 T=T/100
80 PRINT "ENTER INTEREST RATE (%)";
90 INPUT K
100 K=K/100
110 PRINT "NUMBER OF PERIODS";
120 INPUT N
130 P=0
140 FOR J=1 TO N
150 IF J>1 THEN 180
160 PRINT "INTEREST AMOUNT ($) FOR PERIOD";
170 GOTO 190
180 PRINT "                              ";
190 PRINT J;
200 INPUT Z
210 P=P+Z*T/(1+K)[J
220 NEXT J
230 PRINT
240 PRINT "PRESENT VALUE OF DEDUCTION = ";
250 PRINTUSING "$$####,####,####,####.##"; P
260 PRINT
270 PRINT "WOULD YOU LIKE TO RE-RUN PROGRAM WITH NEW DATA (Y/N)?
280 Z$=INKEY$ : IF Z$="" THEN 280
290 IF Z$="Y" THEN 40
300 IF Z$<>"N" THEN 270
310 END
```

Reference

Solomon and Pringle. *An Introduction to Financial Management.* Santa Monica, Calif.: Goodyear Publishing Co., 1977. Pages 376-78.

Future Value of an Investment (Uneven Cash Flow)

Often it is useful to project the future (or terminal) value of monies to be received from an investment. The accept/reject criterion stipulates you should reject any investment whose future value of all cash flows, including the initial investment, is less than zero. This program computes that value, based on the term (in years), the growth rate, and the cash flow amounts for each year. The growth rate should be the rate at which you have alternative opportunities to invest.

Example

Aunt Lonna wants to start a college fund for her nephew Brian. She plans to put $200.00 into savings this year, $350.00 next year, and $250.00 the following year. The interest rate is 6%. What will Brian's fund be worth at the end of the third year?
   Answer: Brian's fund will be worth $845.72.

```
FUTURE VALUE OF AN INVESTMENT

   NUMBER OF CASH FLOWS? 3
        GROWTH RATE (%)? 6

(ENTER INFLOWS AS POSITIVE, OUTFLOWS AS NEGATIVE)
AMOUNT OF CASH FLOW 1 ? 200
                    2 ? 350
                    3 ? 250

FUTURE VALUE AT END OF PERIOD 3 =                    $845.72

DO YOU WANT TO RE-RUN PROGRAM WITH NEW DATA? (Y/N)
READY
```

Practice Problems

1. What will the value of $25,000 be in 8 years if another $25,000 is invested in year three and $10,000 is withdrawn during the fifth year? The growth rate is 15%.
   Answer: $101,575.69

2. If the growth rate above was 18%, what would the future value be?
   Answer: $120,400.48

Program Listing

```
5 CLS
10 PRINT "FUTURE VALUE OF AN INVESTMENT"
20 DEFDBL A-Z : DEFINT N,J
30 PRINT
40 PRINT "  NUMBER OF CASH FLOWS";
50 INPUT N
```

```
60 PRINT "          GROWTH RATE (%)";
70 INPUT R
80 R=R/100
90 PRINT
100 T=0
110 PRINT "(ENTER INFLOWS AS POSITIVE, OUTFLOWS AS NEGATIVE)"
120 FOR J=1 TO N
130 IF J>1 THEN 160
140 PRINT "AMOUNT OF CASH FLOW";
150 GOTO 170
160 PRINT "                    ";
170 PRINT J;
180 INPUT C
190 REM ADD FUTURE VALUES OF EACH YEAR BASED ON RATE OF R
200 T=T+INT(C*(1+R)[(N-J)*100+.5)/100
210 NEXT J
220 PRINT
230 PRINT "FUTURE VALUE AT END OF PERIOD";N;"= ";
235 PRINTUSING "$$####,####,####,####.##"; T
240 REM RESTART OR END PROGRAM?
250 PRINT
260 PRINT "DO YOU WANT TO RE-RUN PROGRAM WITH NEW DATA? (Y/N)"
270 Z$=INKEY$ : IF Z$="" THEN 270
280 IF Z$="Y" THEN 30
290 IF Z$="N" THEN 300 ELSE 260
300 END
```

Reference

Solomon and Pringle. *An Introduction to Financial Management.* Santa Monica, Calif.: Goodyear
    Publishing, 1977.

Net Present Value of an Investment

Net Present Value (NPV) is defined as the present value of all cash flows associated with an investment, including the initial outlay. The NPV accept/reject criterion for an investment is: accept any investment whose NPV is greater than zero.

To use this program, you first enter the amount of the initial outlay, the term of the investment (in years), the required rate of return and the cash flow amounts for each year.

Program Notes

To obtain the present value of an investment, enter an initial investment of zero.

Example

Jack has an investment opportunity that requires an initial investment of $10,000 and offers cash returns of $3,000, $5,000, and $4,000 over the next 3 years. Jack wants at least a 15% return on his money. What is the NPV of this investment? Should Jack accept?

Answer: The NPV of this investment is −$980.52. Jack should not accept.

```
NET PRESENT VALUE

INVESTMENT? 10000
NUMBER OF YEARS? 3
REQUIRED RATE OF RETURN (%)? 15

ENTER CASH FLOW AMOUNTS EACH YEAR (ENTER OUTFLOWS AS NEGATIVE).

INFLOW FOR YEAR 1 ? 3000
              2 ? 5000
              3 ? 4000

NET PRESENT VALUE =                     -$980.52

DO YOU WANT TO RE-RUN PROGRAM WITH NEW DATA? (Y/N)

READY
```

Practice Problems

1. Doris holds a note for $1,000.00 which matures in 2 years, but she wants to invest that money now in new sound equipment. Her bank will buy the note at a 10% discount. What price is the bank offering? (Hint: This is a *present* value calculation.)

Answer: The bank will pay Doris $826.45 for the note.

2. What is the NPV of a $1,500 investment which offers returns of $800.00 year 1, $900.00 year 2, requires $1,000 more to be invested year 3, returns $900.00 year 4, and $800.00 year 5? Comparable 5 year investments currently offer a 15% return.

Answer: The NPV of this investment is $130.98, quite acceptable.

Program Listing

```
10 CLS
20 PRINT "NET PRESENT VALUE"
30 DEFDBL A-Z : DEFINT J,N
39 REM CHANGE SIZE OF ARRAY C() TO MAXIMUM NUMBER OF CASH FLOWS
40 DIM C(10)
50 PRINT
60 PRINT "INVESTMENT";
70 INPUT CO
80 CO=-CO
90 PRINT "NUMBER OF YEARS";
100 INPUT N
110 PRINT "REQUIRED RATE OF RETURN (%)";
120 INPUT R
130 R=R/100+1
140 F=0
150 PRINT
160 PRINT "ENTER CASH FLOW AMOUNTS EACH YEAR ";
170 PRINT "(ENTER OUTFLOWS AS NEGATIVE)."
180 PRINT
190 FOR J=1 TO N
200 IF J>1 THEN 230
210 PRINT "INFLOW FOR YEAR";
220 GOTO 240
230 PRINT "                    ";
240 PRINT J;
250 INPUT C(J)
260 NEXT J
270 T=CO
279 REM ADD PRESENT VALUES FOR EACH YEAR BASED ON RATE OF R
280 FOR J=1 TO N
290 T=T+C(J)/R[J
300 NEXT J
310 PRINT
320 PRINT "NET PRESENT VALUE = ";
330 PRINTUSING "$$####,####,####,####.##"; T
339 REM RESTART OR END PROGRAM?
340 PRINT
350 PRINT "DO YOU WANT TO RE-RUN PROGRAM WITH NEW DATA? (Y/N)"
360 Z$=INKEY$ : IF Z$="" THEN 360
370 IF Z$="Y" THEN 50
380 IF Z$<>"N" THEN 350
390 END
```

References

Rosen, Lawrence R. *Dow Jones-Irwin Guide to Interest.* Homewood, Ill.: Dow Jones-Irwin, Inc., 1974.

Solomon and Pringle. *An Introduction to Financial Management.* Santa Monica, Calif.: Goodyear Publishing, 1977. Pages 261-62.

Lease/Buy Decision

This program computes the present value of the cost to lease, and the present value of the cost to buy. Any difference between those amounts is the advantage of leasing or of buying. It is assumed that the asset would be financed over the same period of time that it would be leased.

To use the program, enter the price of the asset, the interest rate, the term in years, the salvage value at the end of that term, the tax rate, annual amount of loan payments, and the annual amount of lease payments. The program outputs the present value of the cost to buy, the present value of the cost to lease, and the difference between those amounts.

While this program may be instructive in pointing out decision factors you may have overlooked, it is not meant to replace your judgment. Capital planning requirements and lease/loan terms must ultimately guide your decision. In general, depreciation and salvage value reduce the cost of buying. However, if an asset is subject to rapid obsolescence, leasing may be the less expensive choice.

Program Notes

This program is actually a modified version of the Net Present Value of an Investment program. As such, you may find it instructive of modifications you may make to any of the programs in this book.

Example

Acme Landscaping has need for a small truck for everyday use. They are considering buying a truck for $6,000. Salvage value after 4 years is estimated to be $2,000. The bank will lend $6,000 at 16 percent interest to be repaid in 4 equal installments of $2,145. The lease will cost $2,000 per year. Taxes are 40%, and straight-line depreciation of $1,000 per year will be used. What is the present value of the cost to buy? What is the present value of the cost to lease? Should Acme lease or buy?

Answer: The present value of the loan is $3,011.90. The present value of the lease is $3,357.82. Acme should buy the truck.

```
LEASE/BUY DECISION

ENTER THE COST TO ACQUIRE ASSET (PRINCIPAL OF LOAN)? 6000
ENTER THE INTEREST RATE (%)? 16
ENTER THE TERM IN YEARS? 4
WHAT IS THE SALVAGE VALUE AT THE END OF 4 YEARS? 2000

WHAT IS THE TAX RATE (%)? 40
ENTER THE ANNUAL AMOUNT OF LOAN PAYMENTS? 2145
ENTER THE ANNUAL AMOUNT OF LEASE PAYMENTS? 2000

ENTER THE DEPRECIATION AMOUNT FOR EACH YEAR.

YEAR NUMBER 1 ? 1000
            2 ? 1000
            3 ? 1000
            4 ? 1000

PRESENT VALUE OF COST OF LOAN  =              $3,011.90
```

PRESENT VALUE OF COST OF LEASE = $3,357.82

ADVANTAGE OF BUYING = $345.92

WOULD YOU LIKE TO RE-RUN PROGRAM WITH NEW DATA? (Y/N)
READY

Practice Problems

1. In the above example, what if the lease is $1,200 per year?
Answer: Leasing would be the best choice. The present value of the lease would be $2,014.69. The leasing advantage would be $997.21.

2. Industrial Supply Company needs a computer for their in-house use. The model they want will cost $30,000, to be financed at 17% interest over five years. After five years ISC plans to sell the computer for $10,000 and buy a larger model. The tax rate is 48%, annual loan payments will be $9,375.00, and a five year lease on the equipment would cost $3,500.00 per year. Depreciation would be $6,000.00 the first year, $5,000 year 2, $4,000 year 3, $3,000 year 4, and $2,000 year 5. What is the advantage of leasing or buying?
Answer: ISC would realize an advantage of $7,362.25 if they lease the new computer.

Program Listing

```
10 CLS
20 PRINT "LEASE/BUY DECISION"
30 PU$="$$####,####,####,####.##"
40 DEFDBL A-Z : DEFINT Y,Z
50 PRINT
60 PRINT "ENTER THE COST TO ACQUIRE ASSET (PRINCIPAL OF LOAN)";
70 INPUT B1
80 PRINT "ENTER THE INTEREST RATE (%)";
90 INPUT I1
99 REM - CONVERT INTEREST RATE TO DECIMAL
100 I1=I1/100
110 PRINT "ENTER THE TERM IN YEARS";
120 INPUT Y1
130 PRINT "WHAT IS THE SALVAGE VALUE AT THE END OF";Y1;"YEARS";
140 INPUT S1
150 PRINT
160 PRINT "WHAT IS THE TAX RATE (%)";
170 INPUT R1
179 REM - CONVERT TAX RATE TO DECIMAL
180 R1=R1/100
190 PRINT "ENTER THE ANNUAL AMOUNT OF LOAN PAYMENTS";
200 INPUT A1
210 PRINT "ENTER THE ANNUAL AMOUNT OF LEASE PAYMENTS";
220 INPUT A2
229 REM - RESET TOTAL AMOUNTS TO ZERO
230 T1=0
240 L1=0
250 PRINT
260 PRINT "ENTER THE DEPRECIATION AMOUNT FOR EACH YEAR."
```

```
270 PRINT
279 REM - LOOP TO INPUT, CALCULATE & ACCUMULATE VALUES EACH YEAR
280 FOR Z=1 TO Y1
290 IF Z>1 THEN 320
300 PRINT "YEAR NUMBER";
310 GOTO 330
320 PRINT "              ";
330 PRINT Z;
340 INPUT D1
349 REM - CALCULATE INTEREST AMOUNT FOR EACH YEAR
350 BO=ABS(B1-INT(B1*(1+I1)*100+.5)/100)
359 REM - CONVERT D1 TO PRESENT VALUE OF COST OF OWNING EACH YR
360 D1=INT((A1-INT((D1+BO)*R1*100+.5)/100)/(1+I1)[Z*100+.5)/100
369 REM - SUBTRACT ANNUAL PAYMENT, ADD ANNUAL INT. TO PRINCIPAL
370 B1=B1-A1+BO
379 REM - SUM PRESENT VALUE AMOUNTS FOR EACH YEAR
380 T1=T1+D1
389 REM - COMPUTE PRESENT VALUE OF COST TO LEASE FOR EACH YEAR
390 L1=L1+INT((A2-(A2*R1))/(1+I1)[Z*100+.5)/100
400 NEXT Z
408 REM - SUBTRACT PRESENT VALUE AS SALVAGE VALUE FROM TOTAL
409 REM - COST TO OWN
410 T1=T1-INT(S1/(1+I1)[Y1*100+.5)/100
419 REM - OUTPUT RESULTS
420 PRINT
430 PRINT "PRESENT VALUE OF COST OF LOAN  =";
440 PRINTUSING PU$; T1
450 PRINT "PRESENT VALUE OF COST OF LEASE =";
460 PRINTUSING PU$; L1
470 PRINT
480 IF L1<T1 THEN 520
490 PRINT "ADVANTAGE OF BUYING =";
500 PRINTUSING PU$; L1-T1
510 GOTO 540
520 PRINT "ADVANTAGE OF LEASING =";
530 PRINTUSING PU$; T1-L1
540 PRINT
549 REM - RESTART OR END PROGRAM?
550 PRINT "WOULD YOU LIKE TO RE-RUN PROGRAM WITH NEW DATA? (Y/N)
560 Z$=INKEY$ : IF Z$="" THEN 560
570 IF Z$="Y" THEN 50
580 IF Z$<>"N" THEN 550
590 END
```

Reference

Chase and Aquilano. *Production and Operations Management.* Homewood, Ill.: Richard D. Irwin, Inc., 1977. Pages 138-40.

Syndicated Investment Analysis

This program evaluates tax savings and net cash flows from an investment by a syndicate, or group of investors, to a participating investor. The program considers the investor's tax bracket, as well as the proportion of the original investment, participation in cash income, taxable income/loss, and tax credits.

To use this program, enter the length of the analysis in years and the first year of syndication. Then, for each year, enter the cash income for the syndicate, followed by its taxable income. Enter the year (1,2, and so forth) and total investment for that year by the syndicate. Then, enter the year and amount of investment or other tax credits (entered as a negative number), or credit recapture (entered as a positive number). Next, enter allocation percentages for the investor: percentage of total investment, cash, income, and taxable income (or loss) and credits. The final entry is the investor's tax bracket, entered as a percentage.

The program then prints its analysis, which shows the investor his/her original investment, cash income, taxable income, tax saving (tax savings are negative; tax paid is positive), net end-of-year cash flow and cumulative net cash flows. You may repeat the analysis for different tax brackets when the program asks for a new tax bracket to consider. (All other investment factors remain as you last entered them.) Enter a tax bracket of 999 to respecify the percentage allocations. Enter an investment allocation percentage of 999 to end the program.

Program Notes

The program is set for 40 years of projections. You can change this amount by modifying lines 20 and 30 as follows:

```
50 N9 = I
60 DIM C(I),D(I),J(I),K(I),S(I),T(I),U(I),V(I)
```

Make sure that you replace the expression I with a constant equal to the maximum number of years.

Example

Consider this syndicated investment: An income property with a $35,000 down payment which will generate $4,500 cash over the first four years, $5,200 over the next four years, and $5,500 over the remaining five years. The investment earns a $3,500 investment tax credit in the first year. Taxable income will start at $3,800 and increase by $1,100 per year for the life of the investment.

The investor is in the 55% tax bracket, and is contributing 30% of the original cash outlay. Participation is 30% on cash income and taxable income. How will this investor run the program?

Answer: The printout below shows the investor's portion of cash income, tax savings, net and cumulative cash flow. At the end of the investment projection, cumulative cash to this investor is $4,432, and the investment is sheltered until the end of 1985, when a tax of $109 must be paid.

```
SYNDICATED INVESTMENT ANALYSIS

FOR HOW MANY YEARS DO YOU WANT
THIS PROJECTION (LIMIT: 40 )? 13

ENTER THE FIRST YEAR OF
SYNDICATION (E.G. 1981)? 1980
```

```
FOR ENTIRE SYNDICATE, ENTER CASH INCOME
FOR EACH YEAR OF PRODUCTION
YEAR 1 CASH INCOME=? 4500
YEAR 2 CASH INCOME=? 4500
YEAR 3 CASH INCOME=? 4500
YEAR 4 CASH INCOME=? 4500
YEAR 5 CASH INCOME=? 5200
YEAR 6 CASH INCOME=? 5200
YEAR 7 CASH INCOME=? 5200
YEAR 8 CASH INCOME=? 5200
YEAR 9 CASH INCOME=? 5500
YEAR 10 CASH INCOME=? 5500
YEAR 11 CASH INCOME=? 5500
YEAR 12 CASH INCOME=? 5500
YEAR 13 CASH INCOME=? 5500

FOR ENTIRE SYNDICATE, ENTER TAXABLE
INCOME FOR EACH YEAR OF PROJECTION
POSITIVE FOR INCOME NEGATIVE FOR LOSS
YEAR 1 TAXABLE=? -3800
YEAR 2 TAXABLE=? -2700
YEAR 3 TAXABLE=? -1600
YEAR 4 TAXABLE=? -500
YEAR 5 TAXABLE=? 600
YEAR 6 TAXABLE=? 1700
YEAR 7 TAXABLE=? 2800
YEAR 8 TAXABLE=? 3900
YEAR 9 TAXABLE=? 5000
YEAR 10 TAXABLE=? 6100
YEAR 11 TAXABLE=? 7200
YEAR 12 TAXABLE=? 8300
YEAR 13 TAXABLE=? 9400

ENTER YEAR OF VENTURE (1, 2, ETC.) AND
AMOUNT OF INVESTMENT BY ENTIRE GROUP
OF INVESTORS THAT YEAR.  AFTER LAST
YEAR, ENTER 9999,0
? 1,35000
? 9999,0

ENTER YEAR OF VENTURE (1, 2, ETC.) AND
AMOUNT OF INVESTMENT CREDIT OR OTHER
SIMILAR CREDIT FOR ENTIRE SYNDICATE
(AS NEGATIVE), AND CREDIT RECAPTURE
(AS POSITIVE) FIGURE.  AFTER LAST
ENTRY, ENTER 9999,0
? 1,-3500
? 9999,0

ENTER PERCENTAGE ALLOCATIONS (0-100%)
FOR THIS INVESTOR...

PCT. OF INVESTMENT (999=END)? 30
      PCT. OF CASH INCOME? 30
   PCT. OF TAXABLE INCOME
   (OR LOSS), AND CREDITS? 30
```

```
ENTER TAX BRACKET (999=CHANGE ALLOCATIONS)? 55
RESULTS FOR INVESTOR IN 55 % TAX BRACKET
```

YEAR	INVEST- MENT	CASH INCOME	TAX SAVINGS	NET CASH	CUMULATIVE CASH
1980	$10,500	$1,350	-$1,677	-$7,473	-$7,473
1981	$0	$1,350	-$445	$1,795	-$5,678
1982	$0	$1,350	-$264	$1,614	-$4,064
1983	$0	$1,350	-$82	$1,432	-$2,632
1984	$0	$1,560	$99	$1,461	-$1,171
1985	$0	$1,560	$281	$1,279	$108
1986	$0	$1,560	$462	$1,098	$1,206
1987	$0	$1,560	$644	$916	$2,122
1988	$0	$1,650	$825	$825	$2,947
1989	$0	$1,650	$1,007	$643	$3,590
1990	$0	$1,650	$1,188	$462	$4,052
1991	$0	$1,650	$1,370	$280	$4,332
1992	$0	$1,650	$1,551	$99	$4,431

```
THIS SCHEDULE DISREGARDS MINIMUM TAX,
DISALLOWANCE OF INVESTMENT INTEREST EXPENSE,
CODE SEC.183, ETC.




ENTER TAX BRACKET (999=CHANGE ALLOCATIONS)? 999

ENTER PERCENTAGE ALLOCATIONS (0-100%)
FOR THIS INVESTOR...
PCT. OF INVESTMENT (999=END)? 999
READY
```

Practice Problems

1. Alvin wants to start a musical career with his brothers Simon and Theodore. Alvin is in the 40% tax bracket. He will contribute 45% of the $30,000 needed to build a recording studio. He will participate 20% in the cash earnings, and 45% in the taxable earnings of the company. Alvin expects that the studio will generate $8,000 cash per year for the first two years. A further investment of $15,000 will come up in the third year for new equipment. The studio's taxable earnings will start at $4,200 increasing by $1,000 each year. Cash income for the recording studio will increase to $12,000 per year from year 3 to year 10 (the last year of projection).

What will Alvin's cumulative cash flow be from this investment? In what year will Alvin have to start paying taxes on his share of the investment? Assume that the studio will earn a 10% investment tax credit for the initial cash outlay as well as the $15,000 in the third year.

Answer: Alvin's cumulative cash flow will be $3,635 at the end of year 10. Assuming the first year is 1980, Alvin will have to start paying taxes on this investment in 1985 ($144).

2. Fred wants to start a helicopter tour service. He is in the 65% tax bracket, and will participate in all aspects of the syndicate at 51%. The initial investment for a four-passenger helicopter is $12,500. Fred plans on trading up to a six-passenger helicopter after three years. The group will receive a $6,500 tax credit in year 1. If they trade up in year 3, they will receive an $8,500 tax credit, and will have to invest

another $19,000. They will sell the four-passenger helicopter in year 4, losing $4,167 from credit recapture. Cash income will start at $40,000 per year, growing to $48,000 per year at the start of year 3, up until year 8 (the final year of projection). Taxable income starts at $9,000, growing by $2,000 every year.

What will the total cumulative cash flow be for the eight years of projection? How will the credit recapture affect him in year 4?

Answer: Total cumulative cash flow will be $182,440. Fred will have to pay $1,131 in taxes in year 4, due to the credit recapture.

Program Listing

```
10 CLS
20 PRINT "SYNDICATED INVESTMENT ANALYSIS"
30 PRINT
40 DEFDBL A-Z : DEFINT I,Y,N
48 REM N9=MAX YRS FOR PROJECTION
49 REM     AND MAX DIMENSION FOR LINE 60
50 N9=40
60 DIM C(40),J(40),T(40),U(40)
70 PRINT "FOR HOW MANY YEARS DO YOU WANT"
80 PRINT "THIS PROJECTION (LIMIT:";N9;")";
90 INPUT Y
100 IF Y>N9 THEN 70
110 PRINT
120 PRINT "ENTER THE FIRST YEAR OF"
130 PRINT "SYNDICATION (E.G. 1981)";
140 INPUT Y1
150 PRINT
160 PRINT "FOR ENTIRE SYNDICATE, ENTER CASH INCOME"
170 PRINT "FOR EACH YEAR OF PRODUCTION"
180 FOR I=1 TO Y
190 PRINT "YEAR";I;"CASH INCOME=";
200 INPUT C(I)
210 NEXT I
220 PRINT
230 PRINT "FOR ENTIRE SYNDICATE, ENTER TAXABLE"
240 PRINT "INCOME FOR EACH YEAR OF PROJECTION"
250 PRINT "POSITIVE FOR INCOME NEGATIVE FOR LOSS"
260 FOR I=1 TO Y
270 PRINT "YEAR";I;"TAXABLE=";
280 INPUT T(I)
290 NEXT I
300 PRINT
310 PRINT "ENTER YEAR OF VENTURE (1, 2, ETC.) AND"
320 PRINT "AMOUNT OF INVESTMENT BY ENTIRE GROUP"
330 PRINT "OF INVESTORS THAT YEAR.  AFTER LAST"
340 PRINT "YEAR, ENTER 9999,0"
350 INPUT I,X0
360 IF I=9999 THEN 390
370 J(I)=X0
380 GOTO 350
390 PRINT
400 PRINT "ENTER YEAR OF VENTURE (1, 2, ETC.) AND"
```

```
410 PRINT "AMOUNT OF INVESTMENT CREDIT OR OTHER"
420 PRINT "SIMILAR CREDIT FOR ENTIRE SYNDICATE"
430 PRINT "(AS NEGATIVE), AND CREDIT RECAPTURE"
440 PRINT "(AS POSITIVE) FIGURE.  AFTER LAST"
450 PRINT "ENTRY, ENTER 9999,0"
460 INPUT I,X0
470 IF I=9999 THEN 500
480 U(I)=X0
490 GOTO 460
500 PRINT
510 PRINT "ENTER PERCENTAGE ALLOCATIONS (0-100%)"
520 PRINT "FOR THIS INVESTOR..."
530 PRINT "PCT. OF INVESTMENT (999=END)";
540 INPUT P1
550 IF P1>998 THEN 2170
560 P1=P1/100
570 PRINT "     PCT. OF CASH INCOME";
580 INPUT P2
590 P2=P2/100
600 PRINT "   PCT. OF TAXABLE INCOME"
610 PRINT "    (OR LOSS), AND CREDITS";
620 INPUT P3
630 P3=P3/100
640 PRINT
650 PRINT "ENTER TAX BRACKET (999=CHANGE ALLOCATIONS)";
660 INPUT T1
670 IF T1>998 THEN 500
680 PRINT "RESULTS FOR INVESTOR IN";T1;"% TAX BRACKET"
690 T1=T1/100
700 PRINT
710 PRINT "YEAR"TAB(8)"INVEST-"TAB(22)"CASH"TAB(34)"TAX"TAB(46);
720 PRINT "NET"TAB(54)"CUMULATIVE";: PRINT TAB(9)"MENT"TAB(21)
730 PRINT "INCOME"TAB(32)"SAVINGS"TAB(46)"CASH"TAB(57)"CASH"
740 PRINT
750 S1=0
760 FOR I=1 TO Y
770 K=INT(P1*J(I)+.5)
780 D=INT(P2*C(I)+.5)
790 V=INT(P3*T(I)*T1+P3*U(I)+.5)
800 S=D-K-V
810 S1=S1+S
820 PU$="$$######,####"
830 PRINTUSING "####"; Y1+I-1; : PRINTUSING PU$;K;D;V;S;S1;
840 IF I/3<>INT(I/3) THEN 860
850 PRINT
860 NEXT I
2099 REM PRINT DISCLAIMER/BLANK LINES
2100 PRINT "THIS SCHEDULE DISREGARDS MINIMUM TAX,"
2110 PRINT "DISALLOWANCE OF INVESTMENT INTEREST EXPENSE,"
2120 PRINT "CODE SEC.183, ETC."
2130 PRINT
2140 PRINT
2150 PRINT
2160 GOTO 650
2170 END
```

Depreciation Switch

An accelerated depreciation method provides for greatest depreciation in the earlier years. At some point, switching to a straight-line depreciation will allow a larger amount to be depreciated in later years than could be done by continuing to use the accelerated method.

Calculations are made using a fixed cost of $1 million. The actual cost of the asset involved is unimportant. The million dollar cost serves only to separate close calculations. Enter the depreciation method to use for this asset, in percent (that is, 125, 150, 200, and so forth); the useful life of the asset, in years; and the number of months of depreciation the first year of the useful life (a full first year should be entered as 12 months).

Example

Champion Products acquired a plastic injection machine that has a useful life of five years. Six months of depreciation remains in this fiscal year, and Champion plans to use 200% declining balance depreciation. When should they switch from declining balance method to straight-line depreciation in order to maximize the amounts depreciated?

Answer: Champion should switch methods in the fifth year.

```
DEPRECIATION SWITCH

              ENTER METHOD, IN PERCENT (0=END)? 200
           ENTER USEFUL LIFE OF ASSET, IN YEARS? 5
ENTER NO. OF MONTHS DEPRECIATION LEFT IN FIRST YEAR? 6

                      YEAR OF SWITCH = 5


              ENTER METHOD, IN PERCENT (0=END)? 0
READY
```

Practice Problems

1. In the above example, what if 12 months of depreciation remains in the current fiscal year?
Answer: The switch should be effected in the fourth year.

2. Using 150% depreciation, when should an asset with an eight-year life be depreciated by the straight-line method, assuming a full year's depreciation remains in the first year?
Answer: The switch to straight-line should be made in the fourth year.

Program Listing

```
10 CLS
20 PRINT "DEPRECIATION SWITCH"
28 REM - USE MILLION DOLLAR COST TO
```

```
29 REM - SEPARATE CLOSE CALCULATIONS
30 C=1E6
39 REM - RESET ACCUMULATED DEPRECIATION TO ZERO
40 A=0
50 PRINT
60 PRINT "                            ENTER METHOD, IN PERCENT (0=END)";
70 INPUT T
80 IF T=0 THEN 280
90 T=T/100
100 PRINT "                     ENTER USEFUL LIFE OF ASSET, IN YEARS";
110 INPUT L
120 IF L>=3 THEN 150
130 PRINT "LIMIT 3 YEARS MINIMUM LIFE, PLEASE RE-ENTER."
140 GOTO 100
150 PRINT "ENTER NO. OF MONTHS DEPRECIATION LEFT IN FIRST YEAR";
160 INPUT M
170 Y=1
179 REM - CALCULATE DEPRECIATION ACCUMULATED IN THE FIRST YEAR
180 A=INT(M/12*T/L*C*100+.5)/100
190 Y=Y+1
199 REM - COMPUTE AMOUNT OF DEPRECIATION THIS YEAR
200 D=INT(T/L*(C-A)*100+.5)/100
208 REM - IF DEPRECIATION IS LESS THAN BOOK VALUE DIVIDED BY
209 REM - REMAINING LIFE, PRINT YEAR NUMBER
210 IF D<(C-A)/(L-Y+1+(12-M)/12) THEN 240
219 REM - IF NOT, INCREMENT ACCUMULATED DEPRECIATION
220 A=A+D
230 GOTO 190
240 PRINT
250 PRINT "                              YEAR OF SWITCH ="; Y
260 PRINT
270 GOTO 40
280 END
```

References

U.S. Internal Revenue Service Code, Section 167(b) and Section 167(e)(1).

U.S. Treasury Department, Internal Revenue Service. Regulations, Sections 1.167(b)-0, 1.167(b)-1, 1.167(b)-2, and 1.167(e)-1.

Apportionment By Ratios

This program divides a quantity into the proportion that each of a group of numbers bears to the sum of that group. You are first asked for the number of decimal places that you wish shown from whole numbers down to thirteen decimal places (if your computer is that accurate). You then enter the value to be apportioned, and the number of parts into which it is to be divided. You then enter each component of the group to be used as the basis for apportionment. The program prints out a table that shows each of these amounts, the percentage each is of the group total, and the corresponding apportioned amount. At the conclusion, it prints the totals of these three columns.

Example

Ten employees at Widgets, Inc., are receiving bonuses from a $30,000 pool. If each receives a share proportionate to his salary, how much does each one get?

Name	Salary
Abelson	$54,000
Boucher	$47,000
Charleston	$40,000
Dryden	$33,500
Evans	$29,750
Freisner	$26,000
Goodine	$24,500
Holloway	$21,000
Ishikawa	$17,500
Johnson	$15,000

Answer:

```
APPORTIONMENT BY RATIOS

ENTER THE NUMBER OF DECIMAL
PLACES OF ROUNDING YOU WANT:
0 FOR WHOLE NUMBERS, 1 FOR TENTHS, ETC.
UP TO THIRTEEN
? 2
ENTER TOTAL TO BE APPORTIONED
? 30000
ENTER NUMBER OF PORTIONS
? 10
ENTER AMOUNT 1
? 54000
ENTER AMOUNT 2
? 47000
ENTER AMOUNT 3
? 40000
ENTER AMOUNT 4
? 33500
ENTER AMOUNT 5
? 29750
```

```
ENTER AMOUNT 6
? 26000
ENTER AMOUNT 7
? 24500
ENTER AMOUNT 8
? 21000
ENTER AMOUNT 9
? 17500
ENTER AMOUNT 10
? 15000
                AMOUNT      PERCENT            APPORTIONED

                 54000      17.5182             5255.47
                 47000      15.2474             4574.21
                 40000      12.9765             3892.94
                 33500      10.8678             3260.34
                 29750       9.6513             2895.38
                 26000       8.4347             2530.41
                 24500       7.9481             2384.43
                 21000       6.8127             2043.80
                 17500       5.6772             1703.16
                 15000       4.8661             1459.86

TOTALS          308250     100.0000            30000.00

LAST ITEM ADJUSTED WHERE NECESSARY
TYPE 'R' TO RERUN OR 'E' TO END-
READY
```

Practice Problems

1. A mayor running for re-election wants to divide his campaign workers among the city's six districts based on the population of each district. He has 42 campaign workers, and the districts are populated as follows: District 1: 29,842; District 2: 17,420; District 3: 14,625; District 4: 24,314; District 5: 21,209; District 6: 18,956. How many workers should he place in each district?

Answer: District 1: 10; District 2: 6; District 3: 5; District 4: 8; District 5: 7; District 6: 6.

2. A winery has 120 bottles of wine that it wants to distribute among its employees. If the wine is divided in proportion to each employee's seniority, how much wine does each employee get?

Name	Years Employed
Jones	22
Romero	18
Lippitt	14
Doyle	8
Peterson	4
Covey	2
Miller	2
Bennett	1

Answer: Jones: 37 bottles; Romero: 30 bottles; Lippitt: 24 bottles; Doyle: 14 bottles; Peterson: 7 bottles; Covey: 3 bottles; Miller: 3 bottles; Bennett: 2 bottles.

Program Listing

```
10 CLS : DEFDBL A-Z : DEFINT D,I,N
20 PRINT "APPORTIONMENT BY RATIOS"
30 PRINT
40 DIM A(100)
50 PRINT "ENTER THE NUMBER OF DECIMAL"
60 PRINT "PLACES OF ROUNDING YOU WANT:"
70 PRINT "0 FOR WHOLE NUMBERS, 1 FOR TENTHS, ETC."
80 PRINT "UP TO THIRTEEN "
90 INPUT DP
100 IF DP<0 OR DP>13 THEN 50
110 PRINT "ENTER TOTAL TO BE APPORTIONED"
120 INPUT S2
130 PRINT "ENTER NUMBER OF PORTIONS"
140 INPUT N
149 REM ENTER RATIO AMOUNTS ONE BY ONE
150 FOR I=1 TO N
160 PRINT "ENTER AMOUNT";I
170 INPUT A(I)
180 S1=S1+A(I)
190 NEXT I
200 PRINTTAB(16)"AMOUNT"TAB(26)"PERCENT"TAB(42)"APPORTIONED"
210 PRINT
219 REM PRINT OUT TABLE
220 FOR I=1 TO N-1
230 P=INT(1E6*A(I)/S1+.5)/1E4
240 P1=P1+P
250 R=INT((S2*A(I)/S1)*10[(DP)+.5)/10[(DP)
260 S3=S3+R
270 PA$="#############" : PP$="###.####"
280 DP$="################.#############"
290 FX=LEN(STR$(FIX(S2)))-1
300 IF FX+DP<=16 THEN 340
310 DP=16-FX : PRINT "---  ONLY 16 DIGITS OF PRECISION ARE ";
320 PRINT "AVAILABLE  ---"
330 PRINT "   ROUNDING HAS BEEN LIMITED TO";DP;"DECIMAL PLACES"
340 IF DP=0 THEN LZ=16 ELSE LZ=17
350 DP$=MID$(DP$,DP+1,LZ)
360 PRINTTAB(9): PRINTUSING PA$; A(I);: PRINTTAB(25)
370 PRINTUSING PP$; P;: PRINTTAB(36): PRINTUSING DP$; R
380 NEXT I
390 PRINTTAB(9): PRINTUSING PA$; A(N);: PRINTTAB(25)
400 PRINTUSING PP$; 100-P1;: PRINTTAB(36): PRINTUSING DP$; S2-S3
410 PRINT
420 PRINT "TOTALS"TAB(9): PRINTUSING PA$; S1;
430 PRINTTAB(25)"100.0000"TAB(36): PRINTUSING DP$; S2
440 PRINT
450 PRINT "LAST ITEM ADJUSTED WHERE NECESSARY"
460 PRINT "TYPE 'R' TO RERUN OR 'E' TO END-";
470 Z$=INKEY$ : IF Z$="" THEN 470
480 IF Z$="R" THEN RUN ELSE IF Z$<>"E" THEN 460
490 END
```

Internal Rate of Return

Internal Rate of Return (IRR) is the rate at which the sum of all cash flows discount to the amount of the initial investment. This program finds the rate by using a half-interval search.

To use the program, enter the amount of the initial investment, then the term of the investment (in years), and the cash flow amount for each year. Enter outflows (funds you invest) as negative numbers. Enter an initial investment of zero to end the program.

IRR can also be used to compute the yield to maturity of a bond by entering the price of the bond as the initial investment, the number of years to maturity as the term, coupon amounts for each year they will be received as the cash flow amounts for those years (enter the total amount to be received in each year), and coupon amount(s) plus the maturity value of the bond in the last year (when the bond will mature). The IRR returned by the program is the yield to maturity of the bond.

Program Notes

The half-interval search at lines 249 to 400 will find rates of return between 0% and 99%. If this range is not wide enough to suit your needs, change the initial values of variable L at line 250 and H at line 260. These are the low and high search limits. Make sure that upon the first execution of line 280, the value of $(L+H)/2$ is not zero, as that will cause premature exit from the search algorithm.

Example

Bob T. has an opportunity to invest in a venture. An initial investment of $10,000 is needed, with cash returns of $4,000, $5,000, and $3,000 over the next three years. His required rate of return is 15%. Should Bob accept this investment?

Answer: No. The IRR of this investment is 10.1331%. The accept/reject criterion stipulates rejection of any investment whose IRR is less than the required rate of return.

```
INTERNAL RATE OF RETURN

ENTER AMOUNT OF THE INITIAL INVESTMENT (0 TO END)? 10000

                NUMBER OF CASH FLOW PERIODS ? 3

(ENTER INFLOWS AS POSITIVE, OUTFLOWS AS NEGATIVE AMOUNTS)
                        CASH FLOW FOR PERIOD 1 ? 4000
                                      2 ? 5000
                                      3 ? 3000


INTERNAL RATE OF RETURN = 10.1331 %


ENTER AMOUNT OF THE INITIAL INVESTMENT (0 TO END)? 0
READY
```

Practice Problem

A new bond issue offers a coupon rate of 8.25% and matures in seven years. What is the yield to maturity of a $10,000 bond if the price is $8,500?
    Answer: The yield to maturity is 11.4831%.

Program Listing

```
10 CLS
20 PRINT "INTERNAL RATE OF RETURN"
29 REM CHANGE SIZE OF ARRAY C() IF NECESSARY
30 DIM C(12)
40 PRINT
50 PRINT "ENTER AMOUNT OF THE INITIAL INVESTMENT (O TO END)";
60 INPUT I
69 REM END PROGRAM?
70 IF I=0 THEN 450
80 PRINT
90 PRINT "                         NUMBER OF CASH FLOW PERIODS ";
100 INPUT N
109 REM RESTART IF NUMBER OF CASH FLOW PERIODS IS INVALID
110 IF N<1 THEN 40
119 REM LOOP TO INPUT AND SUM CASH FLOW AMOUNT(S)
120 F=0
130 PRINT
140 PRINT "(ENTER INFLOWS AS POSITIVE, OUTFLOWS AS NEGATIVE ";
150 PRINT "AMOUNTS)"
160 FOR J=1 TO N
170 IF J>1 THEN 200
180 PRINT "                         CASH FLOW FOR PERIOD";
190 GOTO 210
200 PRINT "                                        ";
210 PRINT J;
220 INPUT C(J)
230 NEXT J
240 PRINT
249 REM INITIALIZE VALUES
250 L=0
260 H=1
270 R1=0
279 REM GUESS RATE = (HIGH RATE + LOW RATE) / 2
280 R=(L+H)/2
289 REM EXIT IF RATE REMAINS UNCHANGED
290 IF R=R1 THEN 410
299 REM SET LAST GUESS TO CURRENT GUESS
300 R1=R
309 REM ADD PRESENT VALUES FOR EACH YEAR BASED ON RATE OF R
310 T=0
320 FOR J=1 TO N
330 T=T+INT(C(J)/(R+1)[J*100+.5)/100
340 NEXT J
349 REM IF TOTAL PRESENT VALUES EQUAL INVESTMENT, EXIT
350 IF T=I THEN 410
```

```
359 REM SET HIGH OR LOW RATE TO CURRENT GUESS
360 IF I>T THEN 390
370 L=R
380 GOTO 280
390 H=R
400 GOTO 280
410 PRINT
420 PRINT "INTERNAL RATE OF RETURN =";R*100;"%"
430 PRINT
440 GOTO 40
450 END
```

References

Chase and Aquilano. *Production and Operations Management.* Homewood, Ill.: Richard D. Irwin, Inc., 1977. Pages 131-32.

Rosen, Lawrence R. *The Dow Jones-Irwin Guide to Interest.* Homewood, Ill.: Dow Jones-Irwin, 1974.

Solomon and Pringle. *An Introduction to Financial Management.* Santa Monica, Calif.: Goodyear Publishing, 1977. Pages 257-61.

Financial Management Rate of Return

Financial Management Rate of Return (FMRR) differs from Internal Rate of Return in several respects. For some investments, particularly real estate ventures, FMRR will provide a more realistic value than IRR will. FMRR assumes only cash flows after financing and taxes are considered, and it ignores the fact that other sources of funds may be available.

To use the program, you enter the term of the investment (in years), then a liquid investment rate. This is a rate at which funds can be invested in any amount, at a guaranteed after-tax rate, and withdrawn as needed (such as a savings account). You also enter a "safe" fixed investment rate. "Safe" means the return on the investment will be at least that high. This investment can be a real estate project or other fixed investment of comparable risk at after-tax rates above the liquid rate, such as certificates of deposit or Treasury bills. The fixed investment should have a minimum amount that can be invested. Enter this amount, too.

The program will indicate points where you will be expected to invest funds in the liquid and fixed investments, the actual initial investment you will need to make (the difference between that amount and the original initial investment must be invested at the fixed rate at the beginning of the first year), the actual total return on the investment, and the rate at which the actual total return discounts to the actual initial investment (the FMRR).

Example

Horatio plans to buy an apartment house. The terms require $10,000 down payment to be made now, and payments of $50,000 to be made next year and the following year. Cash flows indicate that at the end of years 3 and 5, Horatio can expect to receive $30,000 from his investment. He plans to remodel the building during year 4, at an estimated cost of $20,000. Finally, in year 6 he plans to sell the building for $250,000. The liquid investment rate available is 5%, and a minimum $10,000 fixed investment will earn at least 10%. What is the FMRR on Horatio's investment?

Answer: 19.348% (The IRR of this investment is 25.2%.)

```
'FINANCIAL MANAGEMENT' RATE OF RETURN

NUMBER OF YEARS? 6
LIQUID INVESTMENT INTEREST RATE? 5
'SAFE' FIXED INVESTMENT INTEREST RATE? 10
MINIMUM AMOUNT OF FIXED INVESTMENT? 10000

(ENTER INFLOWS AS POSITIVE, OUTFLOWS AS NEGATIVE.)

ENTER CASH FLOW AMOUNT FOR YEAR 0 ? -10000
                               1 ? -50000
                               2 ? -50000
                               3 ? 30000
                               4 ? -20000
                               5 ? 30000
                               6 ? 250000

LIQUID INVESTMENT OF      $19,048 TO BE MADE AT END OF YEAR 3

 FIXED INVESTMENT OF      $10,952 TO BE MADE AT END OF YEAR 3
```

```
   FIXED INVESTMENT OF          $30,000 TO BE MADE AT END OF YEAR 5

ACTUAL TOTAL INITIAL INVESTMENT =      $102,971
       TOTAL RETURN ON INVESTMENT =    $297,577

'FINANCIAL MANAGEMENT' RATE OF RETURN = 19.3476 %

WOULD YOU LIKE TO RE-RUN PROGRAM USING NEW DATA (Y/N)
READY
```

Practice Problems

1. What is the FMRR on a six-year project if the liquid rate is 7.25%, the fixed rate is 15% (with a minimum investment of $10,000), and the initial investment is $100,000? Cash flows will be $30,000 inflow year 1, $45,000 outflow year 2, and $50,000 inflows during each of the remaining four years of the term.
Answer: The FMRR is 11.7828%.

2. On a four-year investment, requiring $10,000 initially and cash flows of $-$2,500, $5,000, $-$2,500, and $25,000 during the term, what is the FMRR? The liquid rate is 8.5%, and a minimum $1,000 fixed investment will return at least 13%.
Answer: The FMRR is 23.3032%.

Program Listing

```
10 CLS
20 PRINT "'FINANCIAL MANAGEMENT' RATE OF RETURN"
30 PU$="$$####,#####"
39 REM -- CHANGE DIMENSION OF ARRAY C() TO MAX. NUMBER OF YEARS
40 DIM C(20)
50 PRINT
60 PRINT "NUMBER OF YEARS";
70 INPUT N
80 PRINT "LIQUID INVESTMENT INTEREST RATE";
90 INPUT R1
100 R1=R1/100+1
110 PRINT "'SAFE' FIXED INVESTMENT INTEREST RATE";
120 INPUT R2
130 R2=R2/100+1
140 PRINT "MINIMUM AMOUNT OF FIXED INVESTMENT";
150 INPUT M
160 PRINT
170 PRINT "(ENTER INFLOWS AS POSITIVE, OUTFLOWS AS NEGATIVE.)"
180 PRINT
190 PRINT "ENTER CASH FLOW AMOUNT FOR YEAR 0 ";
200 INPUT C0
210 FOR J=1 TO N
220 PRINT "                                  ";J;
230 INPUT C(J)
240 NEXT J
250 PRINT
256 REM REMOVE ALL FUTURE OUTFLOWS BY UTILIZING
```

```
257 REM PRIOR INFLOWS WHERE POSSIBLE
258 REM
259 REM FIRST, FIND OUTFLOWS
260 FOR J=1 TO N-1
269 REM SKIP OVER INFLOWS AND ZERO AMOUNTS
270 IF C(J)>=0 THEN 420
279 REM OUTFLOW FOUND
280 A=C(J)
289 REM NOW FIND PRIOR INFLOW(S)
290 K=0
300 K=K+1
310 IF K=J THEN 420
320 IF C(J-K)<=0 THEN 300
328 REM INFLOW FOUND, REMOVE AMOUNT NEEDED
329 REM TO ZERO OUTFLOW IF POSSIBLE
330 C(J-K)=C(J-K)+INT(A/R1[K)
340 IF C(J-K)>=0 THEN 390
349 REM IF NOT ENOUGH MONEY AVAILABLE, CORRECT TO ZERO INFLOW
350 A=A+INT(ABS(C(J-K))*R1[K)
360 C(J-K)=0
370 C(J)=A
380 GOTO 400
390 C(J)=0
400 PRINT "LIQUID INVESTMENT OF ";: PRINTUSING PU$; ABS(A/R1[K);
410 PRINT " TO BE MADE AT END OF YEAR";J-K
420 NEXT J
430 PRINT
438 REM DISCOUNT REMAINING OUTFLOWS TO
439 REM   PRESENT AT LIQUID INTEREST RATE
440 FOR J=1 TO N-1
450 IF C(J)>=0 THEN 480
460 CO=CO+C(J)/R1[J
470 C(J)=0
480 NEXT J
490 CO=INT(ABS(CO)+.5)
498 REM COMPOUND FORWARD ALL REMAINING INFLOWS GREATER
499 REM THAN THE MINIMUM FIXED INVESTMENT AMOUNT
500 FOR J=1 TO N-1
510 IF C(J)<M THEN 550
520 C(N)=C(N)+C(J)*R2[(N-J)
530 PRINT " FIXED INVESTMENT OF ";:PRINTUSING PU$; C(J);
540 PRINT " TO BE MADE AT END OF YEAR";J
550 NEXT J
560 PRINT
570 C(N)=INT(ABS(C(N))+.5)
580 PRINT "ACTUAL TOTAL INITIAL INVESTMENT = ";
590 PRINTUSING PU$; CO
600 PRINT "       TOTAL RETURN ON INVESTMENT = ";
610 PRINTUSING PU$; C(N)
620 L=0
630 H=1
640 R0=0
650 R=(H+L)/2
659 REM EXIT IF RATE REMAINS UNCHANGED
660 IF R=R0 THEN 750
```

```
669 REM SET LAST GUESS TO CURRENT GUESS
670 RO=R
678 REM CALCULATE PRESENT VALUE OF FUTURE
679 REM   VALUE BASED ON RATE OF R
680 T=INT(C(N)/((R+1)[N))
689 REM IF PRESENT VALUE EQUALS INVESTMENT, EXIT
690 IF T=CO THEN 750
700 IF T>CO THEN 730
709 REM SET HIGH OR LOW GUESS TO CURRENT GUESS
710 H=R
720 GOTO 650
721 REM INITIALIZE LOW AND HIGH GUESSES, SET LAST GUESS TO ZERO
730 L=R
740 GOTO 650
750 PRINT
760 PRINT "'FINANCIAL MANAGEMENT' RATE OF RETURN =";R*100;"%"
769 REM RESTART OR END PROGRAM?
770 PRINT
780 PRINT "DO YOU WANT TO RERUN THIS PROGRAM WITH NEW DATA (Y/N)
790 Z$=INKEY$ : IF Z$="" THEN 790
800 IF Z$="Y" THEN 50
810 IF Z$<>"N" THEN 780
820 END
```

References

Determination and Usage of FM Rate of Return. Detroit: Realtron Corporation, 1973.

Messner, Schreiber, and Lyon. *Marketing Investment Real Estate Finance Taxation Techniques.* Chicago: Realtors National Marketing Institute of the National Association of Realtors, 1975.

Financial Statement Ratio Analysis

This program calculates 22 ratios of interest to an investor, based on data you enter from a firm's financial statements. They indicate a firm's profitability, liquidity, activity, and capital structure. You should only compare the ratios of a firm with others in the same industry, or against an industry average.

To use the program, enter the name of the firm which you are analyzing, the date of financial statement and selected dollar amounts from it. You also need to enter the number of common shares outstanding, market price per share and dividends paid per share.

Example

Jim would like to invest in an issue of common stock from a manufacturer of computer equipment. Its financial statements are shown below. Wimpytron has 7,000 shares of common stock outstanding at a market price of $17.50 per share. Dividends of $1.25 per share were paid to stockholders of record from July 1979 through June 1980.

WIMPYTRON, Inc.
Balance Sheet as of July 1, 1980
(figures in thousands of dollars)

ASSETS			LIABILITIES AND EQUITY		
Cash	$ 50		Accounts Payable	$ 75	
Accounts Receivable	100		Notes Payable	155	
Marketable Securities	20		Total Current Liabilities		$230
Inventory	200				
Total Current Assets		$370	Long-Term Debt		190
			STOCKHOLDERS' EQUITY		
Plant and Equipment	500		Common Stock	40	
Less: Depreciation	30		Retained Earnings	380	
Total Fixed Assets		470			420
TOTAL ASSETS		$840	TOTAL LIABILITIES AND EQUITY		$840

WIMPYTRON, Inc.
Income Statement as of July 1, 1980
(figures in thousands of dollars)

Net Sales		$985
Cost of Goods Sold		
Beginning Inventory	$380	
Purchases	200	
Less: Ending Inventory	200	
Total Cost of Goods Sold		380
Gross Margin		$605
Selling Expenses	150	
General & Administrative Expenses	220	
Interest Expense	70	
Total Expenses		440
Income Before Taxes		155
Income Taxes		78
Net Earnings After Taxes		$ 73

How would you run the program to analyze this firm?

FINANCIAL STATEMENT RATIO ANALYSIS

     NAME OF FIRM? WIMPYTRON INC.
    MONTH/DAY/YEAR? JULY 1 1980
    ------INCOME STATEMENT------
    ENTER AMOUNTS FOR:
                           NET SALES? 985000
                   BEGINNING INVENTORY? 380000
                     ENDING INVENTORY? 200000
                   COST OF GOODS SOLD? 380000
                      INTEREST EXPENSE? 70000
                       PRE-TAX INCOME? 155000
                          INCOME TAXES? 78000
    --------BALANCE SHEET--------
    ENTER AMOUNTS FOR:

                               CASH? 50000
                 ACCOUNTS RECEIVABLE? 100000
        NOTES & MARKETABLE SECURITIES? 20000
                        TOTAL ASSETS? 840000
                   CURRENT LIABILITIES? 230000
                 STOCKHOLDERS' EQUITY? 420000

    ALSO ENTER:
            COMMON SHARES OUTSTANDING? 7000
               MARKET PRICE PER SHARE? 17.5
                  DIVIDENDS PER SHARE? 1.25

    ------EVALUATION OF WHIMPYTRON INC. BY RATIO ANALYSIS------
                   PERIOD ENDING: JULY 1 1980

                     -----PROFITABILITY-----
                  RETURN ON ASSETS 9.2 %
                  RETURN ON EQUITY 18.3 %
         RETURN ON INVESTED CAPITAL 12.6 %
                 EARNINGS PER SHARE $ 11
                    OPERATING RATIO .843 :1

                     -----LIQUIDITY-----
              NET WORKING CAPITAL $ 140000
          ACID TEST (QUICK) RATIO .739 :1
                    CURRENT RATIO 1.609 :1

                     -----ACTIVITY-----
                   SALES PER DAY $ 2698.63
           DAYS SALES OUTSTANDING 37.056 DAYS
               INVENTORY TURNOVER 1.31 TIMES

                     -----INDEBTEDNESS-----
         CREDITORS' INTEREST IN FIRM 50 %
               TIMES INTEREST EARNED 4.329
                      DEBT TO EQUITY 1 :1
         LONG TERM DEBT TO NET WORTH .452 :1
           LONG TERM DEBT TO CAPITAL .311 :1

```
              -----EQUITY-----
   STOCKHOLDERS' INTEREST IN FIRM 50 %
                 PAYOUT RATIO .114 :1
                EARNINGS YIELD 62.9 %
              BOOK VALUE/SHARE $ 60
          PRICE/EARNINGS RATIO 1.591 :1
                DIVIDEND YIELD 7.1 %


DO YOU WANT ANOTHER ANALYSIS (Y/N)
READY
```

Practice Problems

1. If the stockholders' equity is changed to $390,000, the long debt will become $230,000. What ratios will change, and what will their new values be?

Answer: Return on equity, 19.7%; creditors' interest, 53.6%; debt to equity, 1.154:1; long-term debt to net worth, 0.564:1; long-term debt to capital, 0.361:1; stockholders' interest, 46.4%; book value, $55.714.

2. If you interchange the amounts for accounts receivable and cash, what ratios will change and what will their new values be?

Answer: Days sales outstanding changes to 18.528 days. All other ratios remain unchanged.

Program Listing

```
10 CLS
20 PRINT "FINANCIAL STATEMENT RATIO ANALYSIS"
30 DIM D(20)
37 REM
   REM  D(1)  = NET SALES
   REM  D(2)  = BEGINNING INVENTORY
   REM  D(3)  = ENDING INVENTORY
   REM  D(4)  = COST OF GOODS SOLD
   REM  D(5)  = INTEREST EXPENSE
38 REM  D(6)  = PRETAX INCOME
   REM  D(7)  = TAXES
   REM  D(8)  = CASH
   REM  D(9)  = ACCOUNTS RECEIVABLE
   REM  D(10) = NOTES RECEIVABLE
   REM  D(11) = TOTAL ASSETS
39 REM  D(12) = CURRENT LIABILITIES
   REM  D(13) = EQUITY
   REM  D(14) = SHARES OUTSTANDING
   REM  D(15) = MARKET PRICE PER SHARE
   REM  D(16) = DIVIDENDS PAID
   REM
40 DATA "NET SALES","BEGINNING INVENTORY","ENDING INVENTORY"
50 DATA "COST OF GOODS SOLD","INTEREST EXPENSE"
60 DATA "PRE-TAX INCOME","INCOME TAXES","CASH"
70 DATA "ACCOUNTS RECEIVABLE","NOTES & MARKETABLE SECURITIES"
80 DATA "TOTAL ASSETS","CURRENT LIABILITIES"
90 DATA "STOCKHOLDERS' EQUITY","COMMON SHARES OUTSTANDING"
```

```
100 DATA "MARKET PRICE PER SHARE","DIVIDENDS PER SHARE"
110 PRINT
120 PRINT "   NAME OF FIRM";
130 INPUT N$
140 PRINT " MONTH/DAY/YEAR";
150 INPUT D$
159 REM ENTER INCOME STATEMENT ACCOUNTS
160 RESTORE
170 PRINT "------INCOME STATEMENT------"
180 PRINT "ENTER AMOUNTS FOR:"
190 FOR I=1 TO 7
200 GOSUB 1400
210 NEXT I
219 REM ENTER BALANCE SHEET AMOUNTS
220 PRINT "--------BALANCE SHEET--------"
230 PRINT "ENTER AMOUNTS FOR:"
240 FOR I=8 TO 13
250 GOSUB 1400
260 NEXT I
270 PRINT
280 PRINT "ALSO ENTER:"
290 FOR I=14 TO 16
300 GOSUB 1400
310 NEXT I
320 PRINT
330 PRINT "-----EVALUATION OF ";N$;" BY RATIO ANALYSIS-----"
340 PRINT ,"PERIOD ENDING: ";D$
350 PRINT
360 PRINT ,"-----PROFITABILITY-----"
370 T$="RETURN ON ASSETS"
380 X1=2
390 X0=(D(6)-D(7))/D(11)
400 GOSUB 1440
410 T$="RETURN ON EQUITY"
420 X0=(D(6)-D(7))/D(13)
430 GOSUB 1440
440 T$="RETURN ON INVESTED CAPITAL"
450 X1=2
460 X0=(D(6)-D(7))/(D(11)-D(12))
470 GOSUB 1440
480 T$="EARNINGS PER SHARE"
490 X1=3
500 X0=(D(6)-D(7))/D(14)
510 GOSUB 1440
520 T$="OPERATING RATIO"
530 X1=1
540 X0=(D(1)-D(6))/D(1)
550 GOSUB 1440
560 PRINT
570 PRINT ,"-----LIQUIDITY-----"
580 T$="NET WORKING CAPITAL"
590 X1=3
599 REM CALCULATE CURRENT ASSETS
600 C1=D(8)+D(9)+D(10)+D(3)
609 REM CALCULATE LONG-TERM DEBT
```

```
610 L0=D(11)-D(12)-D(13)
620 X0=C1-D(12)
630 GOSUB 1440
640 T$="ACID TEST (QUICK) RATIO"
650 X1=1
660 X0=(C1-D(3))/D(12)
670 GOSUB 1440
680 T$="CURRENT RATIO"
690 X0=C1/D(12)
700 GOSUB 1440
710 PRINT
720 PRINT ,"-----ACTIVITY-----"
730 T$="SALES PER DAY"
740 X1=3
750 X0=D(1)/365
760 GOSUB 1440
770 T$="DAYS SALES OUTSTANDING"
780 X1=0
790 X0=D(9)/(D(1)/365)
800 GOSUB 1440
810 PRINT "DAYS"
819 REM IF NO INVENTORY DATA, SKIP PRINTING
820 IF D(2)+D(3)=0 THEN 870
830 T$="INVENTORY TURNOVER"
840 X0=D(4)/((D(2)+D(3))/2)
850 GOSUB 1440
860 PRINT "TIMES"
870 PRINT
880 PRINT ,"-----INDEBTEDNESS-----"
890 T$="CREDITORS' INTEREST IN FIRM"
900 X1=2
910 X0=(D(11)-D(13))/D(11)
920 GOSUB 1440
930 T$="TIMES INTEREST EARNED"
940 X1=0
950 X0=(D(6)+D(7)+D(5))/D(5)
960 GOSUB 1440
970 PRINT
980 T$="DEBT TO EQUITY"
990 X1=1
1000 X0=(D(11)-D(13))/D(13)
1010 GOSUB 1440
1020 T$="LONG TERM DEBT TO NET WORTH"
1030 X0=L0/D(13)
1040 GOSUB 1440
1050 T$="LONG TERM DEBT TO CAPITAL"
1060 X0=L0/(L0+D(13))
1070 GOSUB 1440
1080 PRINT
1090 PRINT ,"-----EQUITY-----"
1100 T$="STOCKHOLDERS' INTEREST IN FIRM"
1110 X1=2
1120 X0=(D(13))/D(11)
1130 GOSUB 1440
1140 T$="PAYOUT RATIO"
```

```
1150 X1=1
1160 X0=D(16)/((D(6)-D(7))/D(14))
1170 GOSUB 1440
1180 T$="EARNINGS YIELD"
1190 X1=2
1200 X0=((D(6)-D(7))/D(14))/D(15)
1210 GOSUB 1440
1220 T$="BOOK VALUE/SHARE"
1230 X1=3
1240 X0=D(13)/D(14)
1250 GOSUB 1440
1260 T$="PRICE/EARNINGS RATIO"
1270 X1=1
1280 X0=D(15)/((D(6)-D(7))/D(14))
1290 GOSUB 1440
1300 T$="DIVIDEND YIELD"
1310 X1=2
1320 X0=D(16)/D(15)
1330 GOSUB 1440
1340 PRINT
1350 PRINT "DO YOU WANT ANOTHER ANALYSIS (Y/N)"
1360 T$=INKEY$ : IF T$="" THEN 1360
1370 IF T$="Y" THEN 110
1380 IF T$<>"N" THEN 1350
1390 GOTO 1570
1399 REM DATA ENTRY ROUTINE
1400 READ T$
1410 PRINT TAB(31-LEN(T$));T$;
1420 INPUT D(I)
1430 RETURN
1439 REM SUBROUTINE TO PRINT RATIOS & TURNOVER DATA
1440 PRINT TAB(31-LEN(T$));T$;
1450 X0=INT(X0*1000+.5)/1000
1459 REM RATIO FORMAT IF X1=1
1460 IF X1=1 THEN 1510
1469 REM RATE FORMAT IF X1=2
1470 IF X1=2 THEN 1530
1479 REM DOLLAR FORMAT IF IF X1=3
1480 IF X1=3 THEN 1550
1489 REM DEFAULT TO NO FORMAT IF X1=0
1490 PRINT X0;
1500 RETURN
1510 PRINT X0;":1"
1520 RETURN
1530 PRINT X0*100;"%"
1540 RETURN
1550 PRINT " $";X0
1560 RETURN
1570 END
```

References

Slavin, Albert, and Reynolds, Isaac. *Basic Accounting* (3rd ed.). Hinsdale, Ill.: Dryden Press, 1975.

Solomon, Ezra. *An Introduction to Financial Management,* Santa Monica: Goodyear Publishing Company, 1977.

Profit Sharing Contributions

This program calculates the profit sharing contributions for up to 250 employees. Some profit sharing plans are not "integrated," that is, the contribution made for each employee is exactly proportionate to his salary. If his compensation is 5% of the total compensation of all participants, then he is allotted 5% of the total contribution for that year, and so on.

Integrated profit sharing plans are less straightforward. In this case, a salary level no higher than the current social security wage base ($22,900 in 1979, $25,900 in 1980) is chosen as the integration level. Each employee whose salary exceeds the integration level receives a percentage (not more than 7%) of the amount by which his earnings exceed the integration level. The remainder of the total contribution is distributed proportionate to salary. If the integrated portion of the total contribution exceeds the total, it is reduced proportionately. If this happens, those whose salary is less than the integration level receive nothing.

This program handles both integrated and non-integrated plans of up to 250 participants. You first enter the name and salary of each employee/participant. After you enter the last employee's name and salary, enter anything for the name, and −1 for the salary when the program requests them. The program then prints out the total of the salaries, and the usual 15% limit on contributions. You then enter the amount of the contribution as a decimal fraction of the total compensation. You are asked if the plan is integrated and, if so, what the integration level and percentage are.

The program then prints a table showing each employee's name, salary, and the amount of his allocation, divided into integrated and non-integrated portions. The program prints the totals for all employees, and then allows you to go back to change some or all of the data.

Example

The following employees are all participants in a profit sharing plan:

Name	Salary
Connell	$150,000
Johnson	22,900
Smith	15,000
Jones	12,000
Brown	10,000

Assuming a 15% company contribution, what allocation would be made to each employee in a non-integrated plan?
Answer:

```
PROFIT SHARING CONTRIBUTIONS

ENTER EACH EMPLOYEE'S NAME AND SALARY
ENTER -1 AS THE SALARY TO END ENTRY
? CONNELL,150000
? JOHNSON,22900
? SMITH,15000
? JONES,12000
? BROWN,10000
? A,-1
TOTAL COMPENSATION=    $209,900.00
    15% LIMITATION=     $31,485.00
```

```
P/S % CONTRIBUTION AS A DECIMAL=
? .15
IS PLAN INTEGRATED? (Y/N)
? N
```

NAME	SALARY	INTEGRATED PORTION	NON-INTEG. PORTION	TOTAL
CONNELL	$150,000.00	$0.00	$22,500.00	$22,500.00
JOHNSON	$22,900.00	$0.00	$3,435.00	$3,435.00
SMITH	$15,000.00	$0.00	$2,250.00	$2,250.00
JONES	$12,000.00	$0.00	$1,800.00	$1,800.00
BROWN	$10,000.00	$0.00	$1,500.00	$1,500.00
TOTALS	$209,900.00	$0.00	$31,485.00	$31,485.00

```
WANT DIFFERENT SALARIES? (Y/N)
? N
DIFFERENT CONTRIBUTION? (Y/N)
? N
CHANGE WHETHER INTEGRATED? (Y/N)
? N
DIFFERENT INTEGRATION LEVEL? (Y/N)
? N
DIFFERENT INTEGRATION %? (Y/N)
? N
READY
```

Practice Problems

1. For the same group of employees, what would be the allocations in a plan integrated at 3% over $15,000?
    Answer: Connell: $23,486.40; Johnson: $3,204.29; Smith: $1,943.64; Jones: $1,554.91; Brown: $1,295.76.

2. If the plan is integrated at 7% over $22,900, what are the allocations for these same employees?
    Answer: Connell: $25,038.97; Johnson: $2,464.34; Smith: $1,614.20; Jones: $1,291.36; Brown: $1,076.13.

Program Listing

```
10 CLS : CLEAR 666
20 PRINT "PROFIT SHARING CONTRIBUTIONS"
30 PRINT
40 DIM A$(250),B(250),C(250),D(250)
50 DEFDBL A-Z : DEFINT I,J
60 PU$="$$###,###.##"
70 PT$="$$####,####.##"
80 PRINT "ENTER EACH EMPLOYEE'S NAME AND SALARY"
90 PRINT "ENTER -1 AS THE SALARY TO END ENTRY"
100 K=0
110 J=1
120 INPUT A$(J),B(J)
```

```
130 IF B(J)=-1 THEN 170
140 K=K+B(J)
150 J=J+1
160 GOTO 120
170 J=J-1
180 PRINT "TOTAL COMPENSATION=";:PRINTUSING PT$; K
190 PRINT "     15% LIMITATION=";:PRINTUSING PT$; .15*K
200 PRINT "P/S % CONTRIBUTION AS A DECIMAL="
210 INPUT M
220 IF M>=1 THEN 200
230 IF M<=0 THEN 200
240 PRINT "IS PLAN INTEGRATED? (Y/N)"
250 INPUT Y$
260 IF Y$="N" THEN 600
270 IF Y$<>"Y" THEN 240
280 PRINT "INTEGRATION LEVEL="
290 INPUT L
300 PRINT "INTEGRATION % AS A DECIMAL="
310 INPUT P
320 S=0
330 H=0
339 REM CALCULATE INTEGRATED PORTION FOR EACH EMPLOYEE
340 FOR I=1 TO J
350 IF B(I)>L THEN 380
360 C(I)=0
370 GOTO 410
380 C(I)=INT(P*(B(I)-L)*100+.5)/100
390 S=S+1
400 H=H+C(I)
410 NEXT I
420 IF H<M*K THEN 640
430 IF H>M*K THEN 480
440 FOR I=1 TO J
450 D(I)=0
460 NEXT I
470 GOTO 680
480 R=0
490 T=0
499 REM REDUCE INTEGRATED AMOUNT TO TOTAL CONTRIBUTION
500 FOR I=1 TO J
510 IF C(I)=0 THEN 580
520 T=T+1
530 IF T=S THEN 570
540 C(I)=INT(C(I)*M*K/H*100+.5)/100
550 R=R+C(I)
560 GOTO 580
570 C(I)=M*K-R
580 NEXT I
590 GOTO 680
600 H=0
610 FOR I=1 TO J
620 C(I)=0
630 NEXT I
640 G=M-H/K
649 REM CALCULATE NON-INTEGRATED PORTION
```

```
650 FOR I=1 TO J
660 D(I)=INT(B(I)*G*100+.5)/100
670 NEXT I
680 Q=0
690 X=0
700 PRINT,"                    INTEGRATED   NON-INTEG."
710 PRINT "   NAME"TAB(20)"SALARY"TAB(31)"PORTION";
720 PRINT TAB(43)"PORTION"TAB(57)"TOTAL"
729 REM PRINT OUT RESULTS
730 FOR I=1 TO J
740 X=X+C(I)+D(I)
750 Q=Q+D(I)
760 PRINTUSING "%               %";A$(I);
770 PRINTUSING PU$; B(I);C(I);D(I);C(I)+D(I)
780 NEXT I
790 PRINT
800 PRINT "TOTALS        ";:PRINTUSING PT$; K;
810 IF H>M*K THEN 840
820 PRINTUSING PU$; H;
830 GOTO 850
840 PRINTUSING PU$; M*K;
850 PRINTUSING PU$; Q; X
860 PRINT
870 PRINT "WANT DIFFERENT SALARIES? (Y/N)"
880 INPUT Z$
890 IF Z$="Y" THEN 80
900 PRINT "DIFFERENT CONTRIBUTION? (Y/N)"
910 INPUT Z$
920 IF Z$="Y" THEN 200
930 PRINT "CHANGE WHETHER INTEGRATED? (Y/N)"
940 INPUT Z$
950 IF Z$="Y" THEN 240
960 PRINT "DIFFERENT INTEGRATION LEVEL? (Y/N)"
970 INPUT Z$
980 IF Z$="Y" THEN 280
990 PRINT "DIFFERENT INTEGRATION %? (Y/N)"
1000 INPUT Z$
1010 IF Z$="Y" THEN 300
1020 END
```

Reference

U.S. Internal Revenue Service Code, Sections 401-04.

Checkbook Reconciliation

This program can remove a considerable burden from you each time you reconcile your checking account. Since the computer performs all of the addition and subtraction, the chance for errors to occur is greatly reduced.

You must enter the ending balance from your statement, then each deposit or credit made since the statement date. After you have entered all outstanding deposits and credits, enter zero. This signals the program to continue to the next section, entry of outstanding checks. Enter check and other debit amounts as you did for deposits, and enter zero when all outstanding checks and debits have been entered.

You should enter only positive dollar amounts for each response. The exception is that you may enter negative amounts for your previous balance and your checkbook balance.

If your account won't balance, check all of your entries to make sure they are complete and correct. Do your check register entries match the amounts on the cancelled checks? Have you entered all checks, deposits, and automatic debits and credits? If you can't find any mistakes, call your bank.

Example

Janet's checking account statement does not show the $600.00 paycheck she deposited yesterday. She also wrote two checks that aren't shown either, one for $87.32, and one for $250.00. If the ending balance from the statement is $348.55, Janet's check register shows a balance of $614.54, and service charges on the statement are $3.31, what is her adjusted account balance? Is Janet's account balanced?

Answer: Janet's adjusted balance is $611.23. Her account is balanced.

```
CHECKBOOK RECONCILIATION

WHAT IS THE ENDING BALANCE FROM THE STATEMENT? 348.55

ENTER THE AMOUNT OF EACH DEPOSIT NOT SHOWN ON THE STATEMENT
(ENTER ZERO WHEN ALL OUTSTANDING DEPOSITS ARE ENTERED)
? 600
? 0

ENTER THE AMOUNT OF EACH CHECK NOT SHOWN ON THE STATEMENT
(ENTER ZERO WHEN ALL OUTSTANDING CHECKS ARE ENTERED)
? 87.32
? 250
? 0

        ACCOUNT BALANCE =                $611.23

ENTER YOUR CHECKBOOK BALANCE? 614.54
ENTER THE AMOUNT OF SERVICE CHARGES? 3.31

ADJUSTED ACCOUNT BALANCE =               $611.23

WOULD YOU LIKE TO RE-RUN THIS PROGRAM WITH NEW DATA (Y/N)
READY
```

Practice Problems

1. Ending balance is $352.13. Not shown on the statement are three deposits of $100.00 each, and six checks: $159.21, $25.00, $14.75, $29.54, $45.67, and $22.50. What is the account balance? The checkbook balance is $358.97. Service charges on this statement are $3.51. What is the adjusted account balance? Does the account balance?

Answer: The account balance is $355.46. The adjusted account balance is $355.46. Yes, the account does balance.

2. Ending balance is −$17.39. One deposit of $250.00 is outstanding, as are three checks ($50.00, $25.00, and $12.98). A pre-authorized withdrawal of $35.00 also has occurred, but is not shown on this statement. What is the account balance? If the checkbook balance is $118.99, and service charges are $9.36, what is the adjusted account balance? Is the account balanced?

Answer: The account balance is $109.63. The adjusted account balance is $109.63. Yes, the account is balanced.

Program Listing

```
10 CLS
20 PRINT "CHECKBOOK RECONCILIATION"
30 PU$="$$####,####,####,####.##"
40 PRINT
50 PRINT "WHAT IS THE ENDING BALANCE FROM THE STATEMENT";
60 INPUT E
69 REM - SPECIAL TEST FOR VALID INPUT (NEGATIVE NUMBER ALLOWED)
70 Q=E : GOSUB 1000
79 REM - INVALID AMOUNT. DISPLAY ERROR MESSAGE, LOOP TO RE-ENTER
80 IF Q$="N" THEN GOSUB 610 : GOTO 50
90 PRINT
100 PRINT "ENTER THE AMOUNT OF EACH DEPOSIT";
110 PRINT " NOT SHOWN ON THE STATEMENT"
120 PRINT "(ENTER ZERO WHEN ALL OUTSTANDING";
130 PRINT " DEPOSITS ARE ENTERED)"
140 D=0
150 INPUT A
159 REM - ALL DEPOSITS ENTERED?
160 IF A=0 THEN 220
167 REM - NO, TEST FOR VALID ENTRY
168 REM - POSITIVE ENTRY ELSE PRINT STANDARD ERROR MESSAGE AND
169 REM - LOOP TO RE-ENTER
170 IF A<0 THEN GOSUB 650 : GOTO 150
180 Q=A : GOSUB 1000
189 REM - INVALID, PRINT STANDARD ERROR, LOOP TO RE-ENTER
190 IF Q$="N" THEN GOSUB 650 : GOTO 150
200 D=D+A
210 GOTO 150
220 PRINT
230 PRINT "ENTER THE AMOUNT OF EACH CHECK";
240 PRINT " NOT SHOWN ON THE STATEMENT"
250 PRINT "(ENTER ZERO WHEN ALL OUTSTANDING CHECKS ARE ENTERED)"
260 C=0
270 INPUT A
279 REM - ALL OUTSTANDING CHECKS ENTERED?
280 IF A=0 THEN 340
```

```
288 REM - NO, TEST FOR VALID ENTRY
289 REM - POSITIVE ENTRY ELSE PRINT STANDARD ERROR MESSAGE AND
        LOOP TO RE-ENTER
290 IF A<0 THEN GOSUB 650 : GOTO 270
300 Q=A : GOSUB 1000
309 REM - INVALID, PRINT STANDARD ERROR, LOOP TO RE-ENTER
310 IF Q$="N" THEN GOSUB 650 : GOTO 270
320 C=C+A
330 GOTO 270
340 PRINT
350 PRINT TAB(9)"ACCOUNT BALANCE = ";: PRINTUSING PU$; E+D-C
360 PRINT
370 PRINT "ENTER YOUR CHECKBOOK BALANCE";
380 INPUT B
390 PRINT "ENTER THE AMOUNT OF SERVICE CHARGES";
400 INPUT S
408 REM - NO, TEST FOR VALID ENTRY
409 REM - POSITIVE ENTRY ELSE PRINT STANDARD ERROR MESSAGE AND
        LOOP TO RE-ENTER
410 IF S<0 THEN GOSUB 650 : GOTO 400
420 Q=A : GOSUB 1000
429 REM - INVALID, PRINT STANDARD ERROR, LOOP TO RE-ENTER
430 IF Q$="N" THEN GOSUB 650 : GOTO 400
440 PRINT
450 PRINT "ADJUSTED ACCOUNT BALANCE = ";: PRINTUSING PU$; B-S
460 IF INT(E+D-C)=INT(B-S) THEN 540
470 PRINT
480 PRINT "YOUR ACCOUNT IS OUT OF BALANCE."
490 PRINT "MAKE SURE YOU HAVE INCLUDED ALL TRANSACTIONS AGAINST"
500 PRINT "THIS ACCOUNT, INCLUDING AUTOMATIC DEPOSITS AND"
510 PRINT "INTEREST PAYMENTS, AS WELL AS";
520 PRINT " PRE-AUTHORIZED WITHDRAWALS"
530 PRINT
539 REM - END PROGRAM OR RE-START?
540 PRINT
550 PRINT "WOULD YOU LIKE TO RE-RUN THIS";
560 PRINT " PROGRAM WITH NEW DATA (Y/N)"
570 Z$=INKEY$ : IF Z$="" THEN 570
580 IF Z$="Y" THEN 40
590 IF Z$="N" THEN 690
600 GOTO 550
610 PRINT
620 PRINT "ERROR: ENTER A VALID DOLLAR AMOUNT ONLY."
630 PRINT
640 RETURN
650 PRINT
660 PRINT "ERROR: ENTER A POSITIVE VALID DOLLAR AMOUNT ONLY."
670 PRINT
680 RETURN
999 REM - ROUTINE TO CHECK VALID ENTRY
1000 Q$=STR$(Q) : FOR K=1 TO LEN(Q$)
1010 IF MID$(Q$, K, 1)<>"." THEN 1040
1020 IF LEN(Q$)>K+2 THEN Q$="N"
1040 NEXT K
1050 RETURN
1060 END
```

Home Budgeting

This program sets up a cash budget for personal use, allowing for a variety of expenses which can occur at many different times. Once you enter the income and expense information requested by the program, day-by-day details of income and expenses print as they occur. The program also allows you to use credit cards as a means of paying expenses when the cash you have is insufficient to meet your obligations. Or, if you wish, you can delay them until the next time they come up.

To use the program, enter the date where the budget will begin. The program then guides you through a series of entries, starting with net income(s), followed by secured loans, credit cards, and, finally, normal living expenses. If your budget does not include items requested by the program, just enter zero for those items. The program will then skip to the next budget item.

Whenever you have a budget item to enter, you will have to enter its periodic amount, how often it occurs, and when it will occur next. The exceptions to this are secured loans and credit cards, which ask for more information. The periodic amount is the amount you regularly receive as income, or pay as an expense. When you enter how often the budget item occurs, it must be an integer from 1 to 99, inclusive. This number tells the program how many times per year the item occurs (1=yearly, 2=semi-annually, 4=quarterly, 6=bimonthly, 12=monthly, 24=semimonthly, 26=biweekly, and 52=weekly).

If the next date for the budget item happens to be the same as the budget start date, enter zero. Otherwise, enter the next date as one number (for example, 91580=Sept. 15, 1980). You can enter a date, months or even years after the budget start date if you like. When the program performs its cash flow analysis, it will "activate" future income or expenses when it reaches the date you specify.

With secured loans, you have to enter the remaining balance of the loan as well as the periodic amount, frequency, and next date. When you enter credit card information, you will input the annual percentage rate for the card, the remaining balance, and its authorized credit limit. The program automatically calculates the number and amount of remaining payments for each credit card, and displays them. If you want to change the payment that the program calculates, just specify a new periodic payment of a higher or lower amount. Note: the program will calculate an even stream of payments to make budgeting more predictable. When the remaining balance of the credit card goes below the calculated payment amount during the cash flow analysis, only the remaining balance is paid.

Once you have entered all of the budget items, the program will ask how much cash you have on hand. Enter this amount, and the program will begin its cash flow analysis. At the end of each month's detail, total cash inflows and outflows print. At this point, you can choose to go to the next month's analysis or stop the program.

Because you will be entering a significant amount of data in order to run this program, you should know how to correct data entry errors. You can only correct errors that you make on the current budget item (that is, you cannot backtrack to the fifth item when you are on the tenth).

On a current budget item, you can move as far back as the periodic amount entry by entering −1. For example, you notice that you have entered the wrong periodic amount for salary 1, and the program now wants you to enter the next date for this item. Rather than entering the next date for salary 1, enter −1. The computer will accept this entry and then ask you to enter the periodic amount for salary 1 again.

Program Notes

Home budgeting/cash flow allows for a maximum of 3 incomes, 3 loans, 5 credit cards and 25 expense items. At present, the program will allocate cash to loans first, then credit cards, and finally other expenses. The expenses are arranged in descending order of importance, that is, if a loan, charge card and restaurant expense all appear on the same day, the program will allocate cash to the loan first and to the restaurant expense last.

Changing this program to allow for more budget items is a three-step process. First, change line 30, substituting the terms A, B, C, and D in parentheses with actual numbers. These items are explained below.

$$30\ \text{DIM}\ D(12),\ I_0(A,2),\ C_0(B,3),\ C_1(C,5),\ C_1\$(C),\ E_0(D,2)$$

A = Maximum number of incomes
B = Maximum number of secured loans
C = Maximum number of charge cards
D = Maximum number of expense items

The second step is to put descriptions of the extra budget items in the DATA statements at the beginning of the program. You can add any extra loans by placing DATA statements between lines 40 and 50, which contain descriptions of the loans. Note: you do not need to change DATA statements to allow for more incomes or more credit cards. To add more expenses, add DATA statements anywhere from lines 50 through 120.

The third and last step is to change FOR/NEXT loops in the program. If you change the number of secured loans, be sure to also change lines 450 and 940 of the program. Currently they are set for three iterations. Change the number 3 in these two statements to the new number of secured loans. If you have added or eliminated expense items, you will need to change lines 640 and 1210. Change the number 25 in these two statements to the new number of expense items.

Example

```
HOME BUDGETING/CASHFLOW MODEL


        DATE TO START ANALYSIS FROM:
        ENTER MONTH-DAY-YEAR (MMDDYY)? 90180
```
Start analysis on Sept. 1, 1980.

```
-------NET SALARY 1 ------
        PERIODIC AMOUNT FOR INCOME? 512
            HOW MANY TIMES PER YEAR? 26
        ENTER MONTH-DAY-YEAR (MMDDYY)? 90580
-------NET SALARY 2 ------
        PERIODIC AMOUNT FOR INCOME? 100
            HOW MANY TIMES PER YEAR? 4
        ENTER MONTH-DAY-YEAR (MMDDYY)? 100180
-------NET SALARY 3 ------
        PERIODIC AMOUNT FOR INCOME? 0
```
First net income is $512.00, paid bi-weekly. The next paycheck will be on Sept. 5, 1980.

Finish entering income data.

```
    PERIODIC AMOUNT FOR MORTGAGE? 0


    PERIODIC AMOUNT FOR CAR LOAN? 80
        HOW MANY TIMES PER YEAR? 12
    ENTER MONTH-DAY-YEAR (MMDDYY)?-1
                CURRENT BALANCE?-1
    PERIODIC AMOUNT FOR CAR LOAN?-1
```
Car loan payment was incorrect. −1 entry used to back up to the incorrect entry.

```
    PERIODIC AMOUNT FOR CAR LOAN? 95
        HOW MANY TIMES PER YEAR? 12
    ENTER MONTH-DAY-YEAR (MMDDYY)? 91580
                CURRENT BALANCE? 1290


    PERIODIC AMOUNT FOR OTHER LOAN? 0
```

```
NAME OF CREDIT CARD 1 (ENTER TO END)? VISA
               ANNUAL INTEREST RATE? 18
                     CURRENT BALANCE? 525
                        CREDIT LIMIT? 1000
 12 PAYMENTS OF            $52.50  NEEDED TO PAY DEBT
               CHANGE AMOUNT (Y/N)? Y
         ENTER DESIRED PAYMENT AMOUNT? 35
 18 PAYMENTS OF            $35.00  NEEDED TO PAY DEBT
               CHANGE AMOUNT (Y/N)? N
ENTER NEXT VISA BILLING DATE:
        ENTER MONTH-DAY-YEAR (MMDDYY)? 92080
NAME OF CREDIT CARD 2 (ENTER TO END)? MASTERCARD
               ANNUAL INTEREST RATE? 18
                     CURRENT BALANCE? 230
                        CREDIT LIMIT? 500
 12 PAYMENTS OF            $23.00  NEEDED TO PAY DEBT
               CHANGE AMOUNT (Y/N)? N
ENTER NEXT MASTERCARD BILLING DATE:
        ENTER MONTH-DAY-YEAR (MMDDYY)? 92480
NAME OF CREDIT CARD 3 (ENTER TO END)?

      PERIODIC AMOUNT FOR PROPERTY TAX? 0

            PERIODIC AMOUNT FOR RENT? 300
               HOW MANY TIMES PER YEAR? 12
        ENTER MONTH-DAY-YEAR (MMDDYY)? 90180

      PERIODIC AMOUNT FOR LIFE INSURANCE? 12.5
               HOW MANY TIMES PER YEAR? 12
        ENTER MONTH-DAY-YEAR (MMDDYY)? 92480

   PERIODIC AMOUNT FOR HOUSE INSURANCE? 0

      PERIODIC AMOUNT FOR CAR INSURANCE? 125
               HOW MANY TIMES PER YEAR? 4
        ENTER MONTH-DAY-YEAR (MMDDYY)? 102180

            PERIODIC AMOUNT FOR TELEPHONE? 35
               HOW MANY TIMES PER YEAR? 12
        ENTER MONTH-DAY-YEAR (MMDDYY)? 90880

      PERIODIC AMOUNT FOR GAS & ELECTRIC? 17
               HOW MANY TIMES PER YEAR? 12
        ENTER MONTH-DAY-YEAR (MMDDYY)? 91880

            PERIODIC AMOUNT FOR WATER? 0

   PERIODIC AMOUNT FOR TRASH PICKUP? 0

         PERIODIC AMOUNT FOR GROCERIES? 25
               HOW MANY TIMES PER YEAR? 52
        ENTER MONTH-DAY-YEAR (MMDDYY)? 90580

         PERIODIC AMOUNT FOR CLOTHING? 40
               HOW MANY TIMES PER YEAR? 4
```

Enter credit card 1.
Note: calculation of payments allows for interest over 12 payments.

Payment was changed to a lower amount.

Finish entering credit card data.

Quarterly expense.

Weekly expense.

```
        ENTER MONTH-DAY-YEAR (MMDDYY)? 110180

        PERIODIC AMOUNT FOR PHYSICIAN? 30
                HOW MANY TIMES PER YEAR? 4
        ENTER MONTH-DAY-YEAR (MMDDYY)? 120180

          PERIODIC AMOUNT FOR DENTIST? 0

           PERIODIC AMOUNT FOR DRUGS? 0

          PERIODIC AMOUNT FOR TUITION? 0

       PERIODIC AMOUNT FOR CHILD CARE? 0

          PERIODIC AMOUNT FOR GAS/OIL? 15
                HOW MANY TIMES PER YEAR? 52
        ENTER MONTH-DAY-YEAR (MMDDYY)? 90680
```

```
        PERIODIC AMOUNT FOR AUTO REPAIR? 40
                HOW MANY TIMES PER YEAR? 3
        ENTER MONTH-DAY-YEAR (MMDDYY)? 10181
```
Expense occurs every 4 months.

```
        PERIODIC AMOUNT FOR COMMUTING? 0

      PERIODIC AMOUNT FOR MEDICAL PLAN? 0

       PERIODIC AMOUNT FOR HOME REPAIR? 0
```

```
       PERIODIC AMOUNT FOR RESTAURANTS? 15
                HOW MANY TIMES PER YEAR? 52
        ENTER MONTH-DAY-YEAR (MMDDYY)? 0
```
Next date for this item is the same
as the budget start date.

```
    PERIODIC AMOUNT FOR MOVIES/CONCERTS? 10
                HOW MANY TIMES PER YEAR? 26
        ENTER MONTH-DAY-YEAR (MMDDYY)? 0

      PERIODIC AMOUNT FOR SUBSCRIPTIONS? 0

      PERIODIC AMOUNT FOR MISCELLANEOUS? 18
                HOW MANY TIMES PER YEAR? 52
```
```
        ENTER MONTH-DAY-YEAR (MMDDYY)? 91580
                    ENTER CASH ON HAND? 400
```
Cash available at start of analysis.

```
CASH FLOWS FOR  9 / 80
OPENING CASH BALANCE                        $400.00
  1       RENT                                              -$300.00
  1       RESTAURANTS                                       -$15.00
  1       MOVIES/CONCERTS                                   -$10.00
FRI 5     INCOME 1                  $512.00
FRI 5     GROCERIES                                         -$25.00
SAT 6     GAS/OIL                                           -$15.00
MON 8     TELEPHONE                                         -$35.00
MON 8     RESTAURANTS                                       -$15.00
FRI 12    GROCERIES                                         -$25.00
SAT 13    GAS/OIL                                           -$15.00
```

```
MON 15    CAR LOAN PAYMENT                                  -$95.00
MON 15    RESTAURANTS                                       -$15.00
MON 15    MOVIES/CONCERTS                                   -$10.00
MON 15    MISCELLANEOUS                                     -$18.00
THU 18    GAS & ELECTRIC                                    -$17.00
FRI 19    INCOME 1                   $512.00
FRI 19    GROCERIES                                         -$25.00
SAT 20    VISA                                              -$35.00
SAT 20    GAS/OIL                                           -$15.00
MON 22    RESTAURANTS                                       -$15.00
MON 22    MISCELLANEOUS                                     -$18.00
WED 24    MASTERCARD                                        -$23.00
WED 24    LIFE INSURANCE                                    -$12.50
FRI 26    GROCERIES                                         -$25.00
SAT 27    GAS/OIL                                           -$15.00
MON 29    RESTAURANTS                                       -$15.00
MON 29    MOVIES/CONCERTS                                   -$10.00
MON 29    MISCELLANEOUS                                     -$18.00
              CASH IN:     $1,024.00  CASH OUT:        $836.50
```

Total monthly cash income and expenses.

```
DO YOU WANT TO SEE THE NEXT MONTH (Y/N)? Y
CASH FLOWS FOR  10 / 80
OPENING CASH BALANCE                        $587.50
WED 1     INCOME 2                   $100.00
WED 1     RENT                                             -$300.00
THU 2     INCOME 1                   $512.00
THU 2     GROCERIES                                         -$25.00
FRI 3     GAS/OIL                                           -$15.00
SUN 5     RESTAURANTS                                       -$15.00
SUN 5     MISCELLANEOUS                                     -$18.00
WED 8     TELEPHONE                                         -$35.00
THU 9     GROCERIES                                         -$25.00
FRI 10    GAS/OIL                                           -$15.00
SUN 12    RESTAURANTS                                       -$15.00
SUN 12    MOVIES/CONCERTS                                   -$10.00
SUN 12    MISCELLANEOUS                                     -$18.00
WED 15    CAR LOAN PAYMENT                                  -$95.00
THU 16    INCOME 1                   $512.00
THU 16    GROCERIES                                         -$25.00
FRI 17    GAS/OIL                                           -$15.00
SAT 18    GAS & ELECTRIC                                    -$17.00
SUN 19    RESTAURANTS                                       -$15.00
SUN 19    MISCELLANEOUS                                     -$18.00
MON 20    VISA                                              -$35.00
TUE 21    CAR INSURANCE                                    -$125.00
THU 23    GROCERIES                                         -$25.00
FRI 24    MASTERCARD                                        -$23.00
FRI 24    LIFE INSURANCE                                    -$12.50
FRI 24    GAS/OIL                                           -$15.00
SUN 26    RESTAURANTS                                       -$15.00
SUN 26    MOVIES/CONCERTS                                   -$10.00
SUN 26    MISCELLANEOUS                                     -$18.00
THU 30    INCOME 1                   $512.00
THU 30    GROCERIES                                         -$25.00
FRI 31    GAS/OIL                                           -$15.00
              CASH IN:     $1,636.00  CASH OUT:        $994.50
```

```
DO YOU WANT TO SEE THE NEXT MONTH (Y/N)? Y
CASH FLOWS FOR  11 / 80
OPENING CASH BALANCE                          $1,229.00
SAT 1      RENT                                              -$300.00
SAT 1      CLOTHING                                           -$40.00
SUN 2      RESTAURANTS                                        -$15.00
SUN 2      MISCELLANEOUS                                      -$18.00
THU 6      GROCERIES                                          -$25.00
FRI 7      GAS/OIL                                            -$15.00
SAT 8      TELEPHONE                                          -$35.00
SUN 9      RESTAURANTS                                        -$15.00
SUN 9      MOVIES/CONCERTS                                    -$10.00
SUN 9      MISCELLANEOUS                                      -$18.00
THU 13     INCOME 1                     $512.00
THU 13     GROCERIES                                          -$25.00
FRI 14     GAS/OIL                                            -$15.00
SAT 15     CAR LOAN PAYMENT                                   -$95.00
SUN 16     RESTAURANTS                                        -$15.00
SUN 16     MISCELLANEOUS                                      -$18.00
TUE 18     GAS & ELECTRIC                                     -$17.00
THU 20     VISA                                               -$35.00
THU 20     GROCERIES                                          -$25.00
FRI 21     GAS/OIL                                            -$15.00
SUN 23     RESTAURANTS                                        -$15.00
SUN 23     MOVIES/CONCERTS                                    -$10.00
SUN 23     MISCELLANEOUS                                      -$18.00
MON 24     MASTERCARD                                         -$23.00
MON 24     LIFE INSURANCE                                     -$12.50
THU 27     INCOME 1                     $512.00
THU 27     GROCERIES                                          -$25.00
FRI 28     GAS/OIL                                            -$15.00
SUN 30     RESTAURANTS                                        -$15.00
SUN 30     MISCELLANEOUS                                      -$18.00
                   CASH IN:    $1,024.00  CASH OUT:      $902.50

DO YOU WANT TO SEE THE NEXT MONTH (Y/N)? Y
CASH FLOWS FOR  12 / 80
OPENING CASH BALANCE                          $1,350.50
MON 1      RENT                                              -$300.00
MON 1      PHYSICIAN                                          -$30.00
THU 4      GROCERIES                                          -$25.00
FRI 5      GAS/OIL                                            -$15.00
SUN 7      RESTAURANTS                                        -$15.00
SUN 7      MOVIES/CONCERTS                                    -$10.00
SUN 7      MISCELLANEOUS                                      -$18.00
MON 8      TELEPHONE                                          -$35.00
THU 11     INCOME 1                     $512.00
THU 11     GROCERIES                                          -$25.00
FRI 12     GAS/OIL                                            -$15.00
SUN 14     RESTAURANTS                                        -$15.00
SUN 14     MISCELLANEOUS                                      -$18.00
MON 15     CAR LOAN PAYMENT                                   -$95.00
THU 18     GAS & ELECTRIC                                     -$17.00
THU 18     GROCERIES                                          -$25.00
FRI 19     GAS/OIL                                            -$15.00
```

```
SAT 20    VISA                                         -$35.00
SUN 21    RESTAURANTS                                  -$15.00
SUN 21    MOVIES/CONCERTS                              -$10.00
SUN 21    MISCELLANEOUS                                -$18.00
WED 24    MASTERCARD                                   -$23.00
WED 24    LIFE INSURANCE                               -$12.50
THU 25    INCOME 1                 $512.00
THU 25    GROCERIES                                    -$25.00
FRI 26    GAS/OIL                                      -$15.00
SUN 28    RESTAURANTS                                  -$15.00
SUN 28    MISCELLANEOUS                                -$18.00
              CASH IN:    $1,024.00  CASH OUT:     $859.50


DO YOU WANT TO SEE THE NEXT MONTH (Y/N)? Y
CASH FLOWS FOR  1 / 81
OPENING CASH BALANCE                      $1,515.00
THU 1     INCOME 2                 $100.00
THU 1     RENT                                         -$300.00
THU 1     GROCERIES                                    -$25.00
THU 1     AUTO REPAIR                                  -$40.00
FRI 2     GAS/OIL                                      -$15.00
SUN 4     RESTAURANTS                                  -$15.00
SUN 4     MOVIES/CONCERTS                              -$10.00
SUN 4     MISCELLANEOUS                                -$18.00
THU 8     INCOME 1                 $512.00
THU 8     TELEPHONE                                    -$35.00
THU 8     GROCERIES                                    -$25.00
FRI 9     GAS/OIL                                      -$15.00
SUN 11    RESTAURANTS                                  -$15.00
SUN 11    MISCELLANEOUS                                -$18.00
THU 15    CAR LOAN PAYMENT                             -$95.00
THU 15    GROCERIES                                    -$25.00
FRI 16    GAS/OIL                                      -$15.00
SUN 18    GAS & ELECTRIC                               -$17.00
SUN 18    RESTAURANTS                                  -$15.00
SUN 18    MOVIES/CONCERTS                              -$10.00
SUN 18    MISCELLANEOUS                                -$18.00
TUE 20    VISA                                         -$35.00
WED 21    CAR INSURANCE                                -$125.00
THU 22    INCOME 1                 $512.00
THU 22    GROCERIES                                    -$25.00
FRI 23    GAS/OIL                                      -$15.00
SAT 24    MASTERCARD                                   -$23.00
SAT 24    LIFE INSURANCE                               -$12.50
SUN 25    RESTAURANTS                                  -$15.00
SUN 25    MISCELLANEOUS                                -$18.00
THU 29    GROCERIES                                    -$25.00
FRI 30    GAS/OIL                                      -$15.00
              CASH IN:    $1,124.00  CASH OUT:   $1,034.50


DO YOU WANT TO SEE THE NEXT MONTH (Y/N)? Y
CASH FLOWS FOR  2 / 81
OPENING CASH BALANCE                      $1,604.50
SUN 1     RENT                                         -$300.00
SUN 1     CLOTHING                                     -$40.00
```

```
SUN  1     RESTAURANTS                                      -$15.00
SUN  1     MOVIES/CONCERTS                                  -$10.00
SUN  1     MISCELLANEOUS                                    -$18.00
THU  5     INCOME 1                      $512.00
THU  5     GROCERIES                                        -$25.00
FRI  6     GAS/OIL                                          -$15.00
SUN  8     TELEPHONE                                        -$35.00
SUN  8     RESTAURANTS                                      -$15.00
SUN  8     MISCELLANEOUS                                    -$18.00
THU 12     GROCERIES                                        -$25.00
FRI 13     GAS/OIL                                          -$15.00
SUN 15     CAR LOAN PAYMENT                                 -$95.00
SUN 15     RESTAURANTS                                      -$15.00
SUN 15     MOVIES/CONCERTS                                  -$10.00
SUN 15     MISCELLANEOUS                                    -$18.00
WED 18     GAS & ELECTRIC                                   -$17.00
THU 19     INCOME 1                      $512.00
THU 19     GROCERIES                                        -$25.00
FRI 20     VISA                                             -$35.00
FRI 20     GAS/OIL                                          -$15.00
SUN 22     RESTAURANTS                                      -$15.00
SUN 22     MISCELLANEOUS                                    -$18.00
TUE 24     MASTERCARD                                       -$23.00
TUE 24     LIFE INSURANCE                                   -$12.50
THU 26     GROCERIES                                        -$25.00
FRI 27     GAS/OIL                                          -$15.00
              CASH IN:     $1,024.00  CASH OUT:     $869.50


DO YOU WANT TO SEE THE NEXT MONTH (Y/N)? Y
CASH FLOWS FOR  3 / 81
OPENING CASH BALANCE                     $1,759.00
SUN  1     RENT                                            -$300.00
SUN  1     PHYSICIAN                                        -$30.00
SUN  1     RESTAURANTS                                      -$15.00
SUN  1     MOVIES/CONCERTS                                  -$10.00
SUN  1     MISCELLANEOUS                                    -$18.00
THU  5     INCOME 1                      $512.00
THU 5      GROCERIES                                        -$25.00
FRI  6     GAS/OIL                                          -$15.00
SUN  8     TELEPHONE                                        -$35.00
SUN  8     RESTAURANTS                                      -$15.00
SUN  8     MISCELLANEOUS                                    -$18.00
THU 12     GROCERIES                                        -$25.00
FRI 13     GAS/OIL                                          -$15.00
SUN 15     CAR LOAN PAYMENT                                 -$95.00
SUN 15     RESTAURANTS                                      -$15.00
SUN 15     MOVIES/CONCERTS                                  -$10.00
SUN 15     MISCELLANEOUS                                    -$18.00
WED 18     GAS & ELECTRIC                                   -$17.00
THU 19     INCOME 1                      $512.00
THU 19     GROCERIES                                        -$25.00
FRI 20     VISA                                             -$35.00
FRI 20     GAS/OIL                                          -$15.00
SUN 22     RESTAURANTS                                      -$15.00
SUN 22     MISCELLANEOUS                                    -$18.00
```

```
TUE  24      MASTERCARD                                              -$23.00
TUE  24      LIFE INSURANCE                                          -$12.50
THU  26      GROCERIES                                               -$25.00
FRI  27      GAS/OIL                                                 -$15.00
SUN  29      RESTAURANTS                                             -$15.00
SUN  29      MOVIES/CONCERTS                                         -$10.00
SUN  29      MISCELLANEOUS                                           -$18.00
                         CASH IN:     $1,024.00    CASH OUT:        $902.50


DO YOU WANT TO SEE THE NEXT MONTH (Y/N)? Y
CASH FLOWS FOR   4 / 81
OPENING CASH BALANCE                           $1,880.50
WED  1       INCOME 2              $100.00
WED  1       RENT                                                   -$300.00
THU  2       INCOME 1              $512.00
THU  2       GROCERIES                                               -$25.00
FRI  3       GAS/OIL                                                 -$15.00
SUN  5       RESTAURANTS                                             -$15.00
SUN  5       MISCELLANEOUS                                           -$18.00
WED  8       TELEPHONE                                               -$35.00
THU  9       GROCERIES                                               -$25.00
FRI  10      GAS/OIL                                                 -$15.00
SUN  12      RESTAURANTS                                             -$15.00
SUN  12      MOVIES/CONCERTS                                         -$10.00
SUN  12      MISCELLANEOUS                                           -$18.00
WED  15      CAR LOAN PAYMENT                                        -$95.00
THU  16      INCOME 1              $512.00
THU  16      GROCERIES                                               -$25.00
FRI  17      GAS/OIL                                                 -$15.00
SAT  18      GAS & ELECTRIC                                          -$17.00
SUN  19      RESTAURANTS                                             -$15.00
SUN  19      MISCELLANEOUS                                           -$18.00
MON  20      VISA                                                    -$35.00
TUE  21      CAR INSURANCE                                          -$125.00
THU  23      GROCERIES                                               -$25.00
FRI  24      MASTERCARD                                              -$23.00
FRI  24      LIFE INSURANCE                                          -$12.50
FRI  24      GAS/OIL                                                 -$15.00
SUN  26      RESTAURANTS                                             -$15.00
SUN  26      MOVIES/CONCERTS                                         -$10.00
SUN  26      MISCELLANEOUS                                           -$18.00
THU  30      INCOME 1              $512.00
THU  30      GROCERIES                                               -$25.00
                         CASH IN:     $1,636.00    CASH OUT:        $979.50


DO YOU WANT TO SEE THE NEXT MONTH (Y/N)? N
READY
```

Program Listing

```
10 CLS : PU$="$$####,###.##"
19 REM HOME BUDGETING/CASHFLOW ANALYSIS (CONVERTED 9/17/81)
20 DEFDBL A-Z : DEFINT J,K
30 DIM D(12),IO(3,2),CO(4,3),C1(5,5),C1$(5),EO(25,2)
```

```
34 REM D()    --DAY OFFSET FACTORS
35 REM IO()   --SALARIED INCOME
36 REM C1()   --CREDIT INSTRUMENTS
37 REM EO()   --EXPENSES
38 REM C1$() --DESCRIPTIONS OF CREDIT CARDS
39 REM CO()   --FIXED TERM LOANS
40 DATA "MORTGAGE","CAR LOAN","OTHER LOAN"
49 REM EXPENSES
50 DATA "PROPERTY TAX","RENT"
60 DATA "LIFE INSURANCE","HOUSE INSURANCE","CAR INSURANCE"
70 DATA "TELEPHONE","GAS & ELECTRIC","WATER","TRASH PICKUP"
80 DATA "GROCERIES","CLOTHING","PHYSICIAN","DENTIST"
90 DATA "DRUGS","TUITION","CHILD CARE","GAS/OIL"
100 DATA "AUTO REPAIR","COMMUTING","MEDICAL PLAN"
110 DATA "HOME REPAIR","RESTAURANTS","MOVIES/CONCERTS"
120 DATA "SUBSCRIPTIONS","MISCELLANEOUS"
130 D(1)=31
140 D(2)=28
150 D(3)=31
160 D(4)=30
170 D(5)=31
180 D(6)=30
190 D(7)=31
200 D(8)=31
210 D(9)=31
220 D(10)=31
230 D(11)=30
240 D(12)=31
250 D$="SATSUNMONTUEWEDTHUFRI"
260 PRINT "HOME BUDGETING/CASHFLOW MODEL"
270 PRINT
280 PRINT "          DATE TO START ANALYSIS FROM:"
290 GOSUB 2810
300 D1=D2
310 Y1=Y
320 M1=M
330 D4=Y*10000+M*100+D2
340 PRINT
349 REM ENTER INCOMES--AMOUNTS AND FREQUENCY
350 I2=0
360 X$="INCOME"
370 PRINT "------NET SALARY";I2+1;"------"
380 GOSUB 2230
390 IF A2(1)=0 THEN 440
400 I2=I2+1
410 IO(I2,1)=A2(1)
420 IO(I2,2)=A2(2)
430 GOTO 370
440 PRINT
449 REM ENTER SECURED LOANS
450 FOR I%=1 TO 3
460 READ X$
470 PRINT
480 GOSUB 2230
490 IF A2(1)=0 THEN 560
```

```
500 IF A2(1)<0 THEN 470
510 CO(I%,1)=A2(1)
520 CO(I%,2)=A2(2)
530 PRINT "                     CURRENT BALANCE";
540 INPUT CO(I%,3)
550 IF CO(I%,3)<1 THEN 480
560 NEXT I%
568 REM ENTER CREDIT CARDS AND DESCRIPTIONS
569 REM MONTHLY PAYMENTS ARE ASSUMED
570 PRINT
580 K=1
590 GOSUB 1890
600 IF C1$(K)<=" " THEN 630
610 K=K+1
620 GOTO 590
630 C4=K-1
639 REM ENTER EXPENSES
640 FOR K=1 TO 25
650 PRINT
660 READ X$
670 GOSUB 2230
680 EO(K,1)=A2(1)
690 EO(K,2)=A2(2)
700 NEXT K
709 REM INPUT PRESENT CASH RESERVES
710 PRINT "                   ENTER CASH ON HAND";
720 INPUT BO
729 REM BEGIN ANALYSIS
730 PRINT
740 PRINT "CASH FLOWS FOR ";M1;"/";Y1
750 PRINT "OPENING CASH BALANCE ";TAB(37): PRINTUSING PU$; BO
760 E1=0
770 I1=0
780 FOR K1=D1 TO D(M1)
790 RESTORE
800 FOR J=1 TO I2
809 REM CHECK FOR INCOME
810 IF INT(IO(J,2))>D4 THEN 930
820 BO=BO+IO(J,1)
830 I1=I1+IO(J,1)
840 M=M1
850 D2=D1
860 Y=Y1
870 D3=INT((IO(J,2)-INT(IO(J,2)))*100+.5)
880 A2(1)=D3/100
890 GOSUB 2360
900 IO(J,2)=A2(1)+Y*10000+M*100+D2
910 PRINT A$;D1;TAB(9)"INCOME";J;TAB(26)
920 PRINTUSING PU$; IO(J,1)
930 NEXT J
939 REM CALCULATE OUTFLOWS FOR FIXED-TERM LOANS
940 FOR J=1 TO 3
950 READ X$
960 IF CO(J,3)=0 THEN 1070
970 IF INT(CO(J,2))>D4 THEN 1070
```

```
980 IF CO(J,3)>CO(J,1) THEN 1000
990 CO(J,1)=CO(J,3)
1000 A2(1)=CO(J,1)
1010 A2(2)=CO(J,2)
1020 GOSUB 1560
1030 CO(J,2)=(CO(J,2)-INT(CO(J,2)))+Y*10000+M*100+D2
1040 PRINT A$;D1;TAB(9)X$;" PAYMENT";TAB(50)
1050 PRINTUSING PU$; -1*A2(1)
1060 CO(J,3)=CO(J,3)-A2(1)
1070 NEXT J
1079 REM CALCULATE OUTFLOWS FOR CHARGE CARDS
1080 FOR J=1 TO C4
1090 IF C1(J,5)>D4 THEN 1200
1100 IF C1(J,2)=0 THEN 1200
1110 IF C1(J,2)>C1(J,4) THEN 1130
1120 C1(J,4)=C1(J,2)
1130 A2(1)=C1(J,4)
1140 A2(2)=C1(J,5)+.12
1150 X$=C1$(J)
1160 GOSUB 1560
1170 PRINT A$;D1;TAB(9)C1$(J);TAB(50): PRINTUSING PU$; -1*A2(1)
1180 C1(J,2)=C1(J,2)-A2(1)
1190 C1(J,5)=Y*10000+M*100+D2
1200 NEXT J
1209 REM CALCULATE OUTFLOWS FOR EXPENSES
1210 FOR J=1 TO 25
1220 READ X$
1230 IF EO(J,1)=0 THEN 1300
1240 IF INT(EO(J,2))>D4 THEN 1300
1250 A2(1)=EO(J,1)
1260 A2(2)=EO(J,2)
1270 GOSUB 1560
1280 PRINT A$;D1;TAB(9)X$;TAB(50): PRINTUSING PU$; -1*A2(1)
1290 EO(J,2)=(EO(J,2)-INT(EO(J,2)))+Y*10000+M*100+D2
1300 NEXT J
1310 D1=D1+1
1320 D4=Y1*10000+M1*100+D1
1330 M=M1
1340 D2=D1
1350 Y=Y1
1360 GOSUB 2720
1370 NEXT K1
1380 D3=1
1390 D2=D(M1)
1400 M=M1
1410 Y=Y1
1420 GOSUB 2590
1430 D1=1
1440 M1=M
1450 Y1=Y
1460 GOSUB 2720
1470 D4=Y1*10000+M1*100+D1
1480 PRINT TAB(18)"CASH IN:";: PRINTUSING PU$; I1;
1490 PRINT TAB(41)"CASH OUT:";: PRINTUSING PU$; E1
1500 PRINT
```

```
1510 PRINT "DO YOU WANT TO SEE THE NEXT MONTH (Y/N)";
1520 INPUT X0$
1530 IF X0$="Y" THEN 740
1540 IF X0$="N" THEN END
1550 GOTO 1510
1559 REM APPLY EXPENSES
1560 X0$=""
1570 IF B0-A2(1)>=0 THEN 1790
1580 PRINT "CASH NEEDED FOR: ";X$;: PRINTUSING PU$; A2(1);
1590 PRINT "  ON HAND: ";: PRINTUSING PU$; B0
1600 PRINT "ENTER D=DELAY EXPENSE; C=USE CREDIT CARD";
1610 INPUT X0$
1620 IF X0$="D" THEN 1810
1630 IF X0$<>"C" THEN 1600
1640 IF C4=1 THEN X0=1 : GOTO 1690
1650 PRINT "CREDIT CARD NUMBER (1 -";C4;"OR ZERO)";
1660 INPUT X0
1670 IF X0<1 THEN 1600
1680 IF X0>C4 THEN 1650
1690 IF C1(X0,2)+A2(1)<=C1(X0,3) THEN 1730
1700 PRINT "AVAILABLE ";C1$(X0);" CREDIT:";
1710 PRINTUSING PU$; C1(X0,3)-C1(X0,2)
1720 GOTO 1650
1730 C1(X0,2)=C1(X0,2)+A2(1)
1740 K=X0
1750 X0$="1"
1760 GOSUB 2020
1770 X0$=""
1780 GOTO1800
1790 B0=B0-A2(1)
1800 E1=E1+A2(1)
1810 D3=INT((A2(2)-INT(A2(2)))*100+.5)
1820 Y=INT(A2(2)/10000)
1830 M=INT((A2(2)-Y*10000)/100)
1840 D2=INT((A2(2)-(Y*10000+M*100)))
1849 REM CALCULATE NEXT DATE
1850 GOSUB 2360
1860 IF X0$<>"D" THEN 1880
1870 PRINT "EXPENSE IS DELAYED UNTIL";M;"/";D2;"/";Y
1880 RETURN
1889 REM ROUTINE TO ENTER CREDIT & CHARGE CARD DATA
1890 PRINT "NAME OF CREDIT CARD";K;"(ENTER TO END)";
1900 INPUT C1$(K)
1910 IF C1$(K)<=" " THEN 2220
1920 PRINT "                 ANNUAL INTEREST RATE";
1930 INPUT C1(K,1)
1940 IF C1(K,1)<0 THEN 1890
1950 PRINT "                 CURRENT BALANCE";
1960 INPUT C1(K,2)
1970 IF C1(K,2)<0 THEN 1920
1980 PRINT "                 CREDIT LIMIT";
1990 INPUT C1(K,3)
2000 IF C1(K,3)<0 THEN 1950
2010 IF C1(K,1)=0 THEN 2160
2020 C1(K,4)=INT(.1*C1(K,2)*100+.5)/100
```

```
2030 IP=C1(K,1)/100
2040 P1=C1(K,2)
2050 A1=C1(K,4)
2060 IF P1<=0 THEN 2160
2070 GOSUB 3010
2080 PRINT A1;"PAYMENTS OF ";: PRINTUSING PU$; C1(K,4);
2090 PRINT "  NEEDED TO PAY DEBT"
2100 PRINT "                    CHANGE AMOUNT (Y/N)";
2110 INPUT X1$
2120 IF X1$<>"Y" THEN 2160
2130 PRINT "         ENTER DESIRED PAYMENT AMOUNT";
2140 INPUT C1(K,4)
2150 GOTO 2040
2160 IF X0$="1" THEN 2220
2170 PRINT "ENTER NEXT ";C1$(K);" BILLING DATE:"
2180 A2(2)=0
2190 GOSUB 2320
2200 IF X1=-1 THEN 1980
2210 C1(K,5)=A2(2)
2220 RETURN
2228 REM ROUTINE TO CALCULATE EXPENSE FREQUENCIES
2229 REM A2() ARRAY CONTAINS RESULTS
2230 PRINT TAB(16-LEN(X$))"PERIODIC AMOUNT FOR ";X$;
2240 INPUT A2(1)
2250 IF A2(1)<=0 THEN 2350
2260 PRINT "                HOW MANY TIMES PER YEAR";
2270 INPUT A2(2)
2280 IF A2(2)<=0 THEN 2230
2290 IF A2(2)<100 THEN 2320
2300 PRINT "FREQUENCY CANNOT EXCEED 99 DAYS"
2310 GOTO 2260
2320 GOSUB 2810
2330 IF X1=-1 THEN 2350
2340 A2(2)=A2(2)/100+Y*10000+M*100+D2
2350 RETURN
2359 REM FIND NEXT MONTHLY, BIMONTHLY OR QUARTERLY OCCURRENCE
2360 IF 24/D3<>INT(24/D3) THEN 2580
2370 IF D3=24 THEN 2450
2380 FOR K=1 TO 12/D3
2390 M=M+1
2400 IF M<=12 THEN 2430
2410 M=1
2420 Y=Y+1
2430 NEXT K
2440 RETURN
2449 REM CALCULATE NEXT SEMIMONTHLY OCCURENCE
2450 IF D2<>D(M) THEN 2490
2460 IF D2<>1 THEN 2490
2470 D2=15
2480 GOTO 2530
2490 IF D2>D(M) THEN 2520
2500 D2=D2+15
2510 RETURN
2520 D2=D2-15
2530 M=M+1
2540 IF M<=12 THEN 2570
```

```
2550 Y=Y+1
2560 M=1
2570 RETURN
2580 D3=INT(365.25/D3)
2589 REM CALCULATE A DAY D3 DAYS FROM M/D2/Y
2590 IF D2+D3<=D(M) THEN 2700
2600 D3=D3-(D(M)-D2)
2610 D2=0
2620 M=M+1
2630 IF M<=12 THEN 2590
2640 Y=Y+1
2650 M=1
2660 D(2)=28
2670 IF Y/4<>INT(Y/4) THEN 2690
2680 D(2)=29
2690 GOTO 2590
2700 D2=D2+D3
2710 RETURN
2719 REM SUBROUTINE TO CALCULATE DAY OF WEEK
2720 IF Y>1900 THEN 2740
2730 Y=Y+1900
2740 IF M>2 THEN 2770
2750 M=M+12
2760 Y=Y-1
2770 N=D2+2*M+INT(.6*(M+1))+Y+INT(Y/4)-INT(Y/100)+INT(Y/400)+2
2780 N=INT((N/7-INT(N/7))*7+.5)
2790 A$=MID$(D$, (N*3)+1, 3)
2800 RETURN
2808 REM ROUTINE TO ENTER DATE
2809 REM DATE IS PASSED BACK IN M, D2, AND Y;
2810 D(2)=28
2820 PRINT "          ENTER MONTH-DAY-YEAR (MMDDYY)";
2830 INPUT X1
2840 IF X1=0 THEN 2960
2850 IF X1=-1 THEN 2990
2860 M=INT(X1/1E4)
2870 IF M>12 THEN 2820
2880 IF M<1 THEN 2820
2890 Y=INT((X1/100-INT(X1/100))*100+.5)
2900 IF Y/4 <> INT(Y/4) THEN 2920
2910 D(2)=29
2920 D2=INT((X1-(M*1E4+Y))/100)
2930 IF D2<1 THEN 2820
2940 IF D2>D(M) THEN 2820
2950 GOTO 2990
2960 M=M1
2970 D2=D1
2980 Y=Y1
2990 RETURN
2997 REM SUBROUTINE TO DETERMINE TERM OF LOAN
2998 REM IP=INTEREST RATE, P1=PRINCIPAL, A1=PAYMENT AMOUNT
2999 REM REFERENCE: SOME COMMON BASIC PROBLEMS 3RD. ED., P.38
3010 A1=-(LOG(1-(P1*IP)/(12*A1))/(LOG(1+(IP/12)*12)))
3020 A1=INT(A1*12+.5)
3030 RETURN
9999 END
```

Critical Path Method (CPM)

This program calculates the time needed to complete a set of interrelated activities.

Before using the program, set up a CPM diagram and a precedence table. As you establish the network, make sure you include "dummy" activities in the diagram. These activities have no duration, but they may be necessary to indicate precedence of some activities over others in the network.

One feature of this program allows you to revise the network by changing activity durations and costs. In this way, you can observe changes in the critical path. Depending on the degree to which you revise the network, the path may shift by adding or eliminating activities.

Program Notes

This program currently allows 100 activities. If you want to change this, modify line 10 of the program as follows:

10 DIM A(I, 2), S(I), F(I), E(I, 2)

Replace the expression I with your maximum (for example, 15, 20, and so forth).

Negative slack time can exist for an activity. However, the program does not factor this into start times, end times or the critical path length.

Example

Washoe Valves is having its statewide sale-a-thon, a contest in which the company's three salespersons travel up Indiana, covering accounts in their territories and making as many sales as possible. At the end of their sale-a-thon, all three salespeople go to Chicago for a recap meeting.

Nance Graham, the sales manager, wants to know when each salesperson should start the trip, how much time each will spend driving and selling, and when to expect each salesperson to arrive in Chicago. Her precedence chart contains daily reimbursements to help calculate travel advances.

Activity	Nodal Sequence	Time (hours)	Cost (dollars)
1. Gary drives to Terre Haute	1-2	2	30
2. Nance drives to Indianapolis	1-3	3	40
3. Lana drives to Muncie	1-4	3.5	49
4. Sell in Terre Haute	2-5	36	125
5. Sell in Indianapolis	3-6	48	320
6. Sell in Muncie	4-7	48	125
7. Gary drives to Lafayetee	5-8	3	40
8. Nance drives to Chicago	6-11	5	35
9. Lana drives to Ft. Wayne, drops off valves	7-10	2	30
10. Sell in Lafayette	8-9	16	90
11. Lana drives to Chicago	9-11	4	52
12. Gary drives to Chicago	10-11	2	30

How does Nance run this program?

Answer: The minimum time needed to complete the sale-a-thon is 61 hours (the critical path length), and it will cost $966 in travel advances.

CRITICAL PATH METHOD

HOW MANY ACTIVITIES IN THIS NETWORK? 12

ENTER START, END NODES FOR ACTIVITY 1 ? 1,2
          ENTER DURATION AND COST? 2,30

ENTER START, END NODES FOR ACTIVITY 2 ? 1,3
          ENTER DURATION AND COST? 3,40

ENTER START, END NODES FOR ACTIVITY 3 ? 1,4
          ENTER DURATION AND COST? 3.5,49

ENTER START, END NODES FOR ACTIVITY 4 ? 2,5
          ENTER DURATION AND COST? 36,125

ENTER START, END NODES FOR ACTIVITY 5 ? 3,6
          ENTER DURATION AND COST? 48,320

ENTER START, END NODES FOR ACTIVITY 6 ? 4,7
          ENTER DURATION AND COST? 48,125

ENTER START, END NODES FOR ACTIVITY 7 ? 5,8
          ENTER DURATION AND COST? 3,40

ENTER START, END NODES FOR ACTIVITY 8 ? 6,11
          ENTER DURATION AND COST? 5,35

ENTER START, END NODES FOR ACTIVITY 9 ? 7,10
          ENTER DURATION AND COST? 2,30

ENTER START, END NODES FOR ACTIVITY 10 ? 8,9
          ENTER DURATION AND COST? 16,90

ENTER START, END NODES FOR ACTIVITY 11 ? 9,11
          ENTER DURATION AND COST? 4,52

ENTER START, END NODES FOR ACTIVITY 12 ? 10,11
          ENTER DURATION AND COST? 2,30

START NODE	END NODE	EARLY START	LATE FINISH	DURATION	SLACK	COST
1	2	0	2	2	CRITICAL	30
1	3	0	8	3	5	40
1	4	0	9	3.5	5.5	49
2	5	2	38	36	CRITICAL	125
3	6	3	56	48	5	320
4	7	3.5	57	48	5.5	125
5	8	38	41	3	CRITICAL	40
6	11	51	61	5	5	35
7	10	51.5	59	2	5.5	30
8	9	41	57	16	CRITICAL	90
9	11	57	61	4	CRITICAL	52
10	11	53.5	61	2	5.5	30

```
THE CRITICAL PATH LENGTH IS  61
TOTAL COST OF THIS NETWORK = 966

DO YOU WANT TO CHANGE ANY
ACTIVITY DURATIONS (Y/N)
READY
```

Practice Problems

1. Suppose Gary only spends 30 hours in Terre Haute. Will the critical path be different? Who will be able to wait before leaving, and for how long?
Answer: The critical path reduces to 56 hours. Gary can now wait one hour before leaving on his trip, and Lana can wait half an hour.

2. Nance may take her plane, rather than drive. The flying time to Indianapolis is half an hour, and the time to Chicago is 45 minutes. She will have to pay a landing fee of $5 at Indianapolis, and $20 at Chicago, in addition to the costs shown above.
With this information, how long can she wait before leaving? What will the total cost be?
Answer: In the original network, Nance could wait five hours. She can now wait 11.75 hours before leaving. The total network cost is $991.

Program Listing

```
4 REM CRITICAL PATH METHOD (CPM)
5 REM   'A' ARRAY = START AND END NODES FOR EACH ACTIVITY
6 REM   'S' ARRAY = EARLY START TIMES FOR EACH ACTIVITY
7 REM   'F' ARRAY = LATE FINISH TIMES FOR EACH ACTIVITY
8 REM   'E' ARRAY = DURATIONS AND COSTS FOR NORMAL ACTIVITIES
9 REM   'C' ARRAY = DURATIONS AND COSTS OF CRASH ACTIVITIES
10 DIM A(100,2),S(100),F(100),E(100,2),C(100,2)
20 CLS
30 PRINT "CRITICAL PATH METHOD"
40 PRINT
50 PRINT "HOW MANY ACTIVITIES IN THIS NETWORK";
60 INPUT N
70 FOR I=1 TO N
80 PRINT
90 PRINT "ENTER START, END NODES FOR ACTIVITY";I;
100 INPUT A(I,1),A(I,2)
110 IF A(I,2) <= A(I,1) THEN 130
120 IF A(I,2)<N THEN 190
130 PRINT " START NODE MUST BE NUMBERED LOWER"
140 PRINT "   THAN END NODE, AND END NODE MUST"
150 PRINT "BE LESS THAN THE NUMBER OF ACTIVITIES."
160 PRINT "      *** TRY ENTRY AGAIN ***"
170 PRINT
180 GOTO 80
190 PRINT "                    ENTER DURATION AND COST";
200 INPUT E(I,1),E(I,2)
210 S(I)=0
220 F(I)=0
230 NEXT I
239 REM LOOP TO FIND EARLY START TIMES FOR NETWORK
```

```
240 FOR I=1 TO N
250 IF S(A(I,2))>=S(A(I,1))+E(I,1) THEN 270
260 S(A(I,2))=S(A(I,1))+E(I,1)
270 NEXT I
280 F(A(N,2))=S(A(N,2))
289 REM LOOP TO CALCULATE LATE FINISH TIMES FOR NETWORK
290 FOR I=N TO 1 STEP -1
300 IF F(A(I,1))=0 THEN 330
310 IF F(A(I,1))>F(A(I,2))-E(I,1) THEN 330
320 GOTO 340
330 F(A(I,1))=F(A(I,2))-E(I,1)
340 NEXT I
350 C1=0
360 L=0
370 PRINT
379 REM CALCULATE SLACK TIME IN S1
380 PRINT "START    END      EARLY    LATE"
390 PRINT "NODE      NODE     START   FINISH";
400 PRINT TAB(31) "DURATION     SLACK    COST"
410 FOR I=1 TO N
420 PRINT A(I,1);TAB(9);A(I,2);TAB(17);S(A(I,1));TAB(24);
430 PRINT F(A(I,2));TAB(32);E(I,1);TAB(42);
440 S1=F(A(I,2))-S(A(I,1))-E(I,1)
450 IF S1>0 THEN 500
460 IF L>=F(A(I,2)) THEN 510
470 PRINT "CRITICAL";
480 L=L+E(I,1)
490 GOTO 510
500 PRINT S1;
510 PRINT TAB(51);E(I,2)
520 C1=C1+E(I,2)
530 NEXT I
540 PRINT
550 PRINT "THE CRITICAL PATH LENGTH IS ";L
560 PRINT "TOTAL COST OF THIS NETWORK =";C1
570 PRINT
580 PRINT "DO YOU WANT TO CHANGE ANY"
590 PRINT "ACTIVITY DURATIONS (Y/N)"
600 A$=INKEY$ : IF A$="" THEN 600
610 IF A$="N" THEN 780
620 IF A$="Y" THEN 570
630 PRINT
640 PRINT "WHICH ACTIVITY";
650 INPUT I
660 IF I<1 THEN 630
670 IF I>N THEN 630
680 PRINT "CURRENT DURATION IS";E(I,1);",COST=";E(I,2)
690 PRINT "ENTER NEW DURATION AND COST";
700 INPUT E(I,1),E(I,2)
710 PRINT "---RECALCULATING NETWORK---"
720 PRINT
730 FOR I=1 TO N
740 S(I)=0
750 F(I)=0
760 NEXT I
```

```
770 GOTO 240
780 END
```

Reference

Brown, Kenneth S., and ReVelle, Jack B. *Quantitative Methods for Managerial Decisions.* Reading, Mass.: Addison-Wesley, 1979.

Program Evaluation and Review Technique (PERT)

This program calculates the minimum time needed to complete a complex project under uncertain conditions, and calculates the probability of the project's completion by a target time that you enter and can modify.

The program also calculates late start, early finish, and late finish times for each activity, as well as the slack time and standard deviation of expected activity times.

Before using the program, you must first organize the project, using PERT's graphing technique or a precedence table. To use the program, you must enter the number of activities in this project, including dummy activities. For each activity, you need to enter its start and end nodes, followed by the optimistic, most likely and pessimistic duration estimates.

When you enter each activity, you must be sure each start node you enter is greater than the previous end node; if not, the program will ask you to re-enter the start and end nodes.

Program Notes

This program is set for a maximum of 100 activities. If you want to change this, modify line 10 of the program as follows:

10 DIM A(I,2), S(I), F(I), E(I,2)

Replace the expression I with your maximum.

Negative slack time can exist for an activity; however, the program does not factor this into start times, end times, or the critical path length.

Example

Harriet just bought a Victorian house, advertised as a fixer-upper. She asked her contractor to provide her with three time estimates for each task involved in the remodeling. Her PERT chart and precedence table look like this:

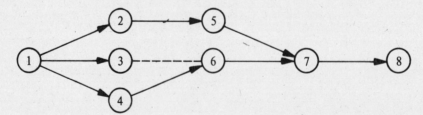

(Time given in days)

Activity	Start Node	End Node	Optimistic Time	Most Likely Time	Pessimistic Time
1. Scrape exterior	1	2	1	2	4
2. Remove wallpaper	1	3	2	3	5
3. Replace cabinetry	1	4	3	4	7
4. Paint exterior	2	5	2	3	6
5. (dummy activity)	3	6	0	0	0
6. Lay kitchen floor	4	6	1	2	2.5
7. Paint exterior trim	5	7	1.5	2	4
8. Paint interior walls	6	7	2	3	3
9. Refinish wood floors	7	8	2	4	5

How will she run the program? What is the minimum time needed to complete the project? What is the probability of completing it one day sooner than expected?

Answer: The minimum time to complete the project is 12.916 days. The probability of completing the remodeling in 11.916 days is approximately 12.95%.

```
PROGRAM EVALUATION
AND REVIEW TECHNIQUE

  ENTER THE NUMBER OF
ACTIVITIES IN THIS NETWORK? 9

-----ACTIVITY 1 -----
ENTER START NODE, END NODE? 1 , 2
ENTER THREE TIME ESTIMATES
FOR THIS ACTIVITY (A,M,B)? 1 , 2 , 4

-----ACTIVITY 2 -----
ENTER START NODE, END NODE? 1 , 3
ENTER THREE TIME ESTIMATES
FOR THIS ACTIVITY (A,M,B)? 2 , 3 , 5

-----ACTIVITY 3 -----
ENTER START NODE, END NODE? 1 , 4
ENTER THREE TIME ESTIMATES
FOR THIS ACTIVITY (A,M,B)? 3 , 4 , 7

-----ACTIVITY 4 -----
ENTER START NODE, END NODE? 2 , 5
ENTER THREE TIME ESTIMATES
FOR THIS ACTIVITY (A,M,B)? 2 , 3 , 6

-----ACTIVITY 5 -----
ENTER START NODE, END NODE? 3 , 6
ENTER THREE TIME ESTIMATES
FOR THIS ACTIVITY (A,M,B)? 0 , 0 , 0

-----ACTIVITY 6 -----
ENTER START NODE, END NODE? 4 , 6
ENTER THREE TIME ESTIMATES
FOR THIS ACTIVITY (A,M,B)? 1 , 2 , 2.5

-----ACTIVITY 7 -----
ENTER START NODE, END NODE? 5 , 7
ENTER THREE TIME ESTIMATES
FOR THIS ACTIVITY (A,M,B)? 1.5 , 2 , 4

-----ACTIVITY 8 -----
ENTER START NODE, END NODE? 6 , 7
ENTER THREE TIME ESTIMATES
FOR THIS ACTIVITY (A,M,B)? 2 , 3 , 3

-----ACTIVITY 9 -----
ENTER START NODE, END NODE? 7 , 8
ENTER THREE TIME ESTIMATES
FOR THIS ACTIVITY (A,M,B)? 2 , 4 , 5
-----------------------------------------------------
```

```
ACTIVITY 1 (NODE 1 TO NODE 2 )
IS A NON-CRITICAL EVENT.
EXPECTED DURATION: 2.167    STD. DEVIATION: .5
EARLY START: 0              LATE START: 1.333
EARLY FINISH: 2.167         LATE FINISH: 3.5
SLACK TIME: 1.333
-------------------------------------------------


ACTIVITY 2 (NODE 1 TO NODE 3 )
IS A NON-CRITICAL EVENT.
EXPECTED DURATION: 3.167    STD. DEVIATION: .5
EARLY START: 0              LATE START: 3.083
EARLY FINISH: 3.167         LATE FINISH: 6.25
SLACK TIME: 3.083
-------------------------------------------------


ACTIVITY 3 (NODE 1 TO NODE 4 )
IS A CRITICAL EVENT.
EXPECTED DURATION: 4.333    STD. DEVIATION: .666333
 START NO LATER THAN: 0
MUST BE COMPLETED BY: 4.333
-------------------------------------------------


ACTIVITY 4 (NODE 2 TO NODE 5 )
IS A NON-CRITICAL EVENT.
EXPECTED DURATION: 3.333    STD. DEVIATION: .666333
EARLY START: 2.167         LATE START: 3.5
EARLY FINISH: 5.5          LATE FINISH: 6.833
SLACK TIME: 1.333
-------------------------------------------------


ACTIVITY 5 (NODE 3 TO NODE 6 )
IS A NON-CRITICAL EVENT.
EXPECTED DURATION: 0    STD. DEVIATION: 0
EARLY START: 3.167         LATE START: 6.25
EARLY FINISH: 3.167        LATE FINISH: 6.25
SLACK TIME: 3.083
-------------------------------------------------


ACTIVITY 6 (NODE 4 TO NODE 6 )
IS A CRITICAL EVENT.
EXPECTED DURATION: 1.917    STD. DEVIATION: .250998
 START NO LATER THAN: 4.333
MUST BE COMPLETED BY: 6.25
-------------------------------------------------


ACTIVITY 7 (NODE 5 TO NODE 7 )
IS A NON-CRITICAL EVENT.
EXPECTED DURATION: 2.25    STD. DEVIATION: .417133
EARLY START: 5.5          LATE START: 6.833
EARLY FINISH: 7.75        LATE FINISH: 9.083
SLACK TIME: 1.333
-------------------------------------------------
```

```
ACTIVITY 8 (NODE 6 TO NODE 7 )
IS A CRITICAL EVENT.
EXPECTED DURATION: 2.833   STD. DEVIATION: .167332
 START NO LATER THAN: 6.25
MUST BE COMPLETED BY: 9.083
------------------------------------------------

ACTIVITY 9 (NODE 7 TO NODE 8 )
IS A CRITICAL EVENT.
EXPECTED DURATION: 3.833   STD. DEVIATION: .5
 START NO LATER THAN: 9.083
MUST BE COMPLETED BY: 12.916

THE CRITICAL PATH LENGTH IS  12.916
PLUS OR MINUS .886002
ENTER DESIRED COMPLETION TIME (0 TO END) 11.916
PROBABILITY OF COMPLETION WITH
DURATION OF 11.916 IS .12951

ENTER DESIRED COMPLETION TIME (0 TO END) 0
READY
```

Practice Problems

1. A project is charted on the precedence table below:

Activity	Optimistic Time	Most Likely Time	Pessimistic Time
1-2	5	1	2
2-3	1	2	3
2-4	1	3	5
3-5	3	4	5
4-5	2	3	4
4-6	3	5	7
5-7	4	5	6
6-7	6	7	8
7-8	2	4	6
7-9	5	6	8
8-10	1	2	3
9-10	3	5	7

What is the critical path length? What is the probability of completing it within 30 weeks?
Answer: Critical path length is 27.25 weeks. The probability of completing the project within 30 weeks is 0.981009.

2. Here is another precedence table:

(Time Given in Days)

Activity	Optimistic Time	Most Likely Time	Pessimistic Time
1-2	1	4	7
1-3	1	6	11
2-4	3	5	13
3-4	2	7	12
3-5	2	5	8
4-5	6	8	16
4-6	2	5	14
5-7	3	4	5
6-7	1	2	3

What are the slack times for the non-critical activities in this network? How many days will the project take if we want to be at least 90% sure of completing it on time?

Answer: Slack times: activity 1, 3 days; activity 3, 3 days; activity 5, 11 days; activity 7, 5 days; activity 9, 5 days. The project will take 29.725 days at the 90% confidence level.

Program Listing

```
5 REM PROGRAM EVALUATION AND REVIEW TECHNIQUE (PERT)
6 REM 'A' ARRAY = START AND END NODES FOR EACH ACTIVITY
7 REM 'S' ARRAY = EARLY START TIMES FOR EACH ACTIVITY
8 REM 'F' ARRAY = LATE FINISH TIMES FOR EACH ACTIVITY
9 REM 'E' ARRAY = EXPECTED DURATIONS AND VARIANCES OF ACTIVITIES
10 DIM A(100,2),S(100),F(100),E(100,2)
20 CLS
30 PRINT "  PROGRAM EVALUATION"
40 PRINT " AND REVIEW TECHNIQUE"
50 PRINT
60 PRINT "   ENTER THE NUMBER OF"
70 PRINT "ACTIVITIES IN THIS NETWORK";
80 INPUT N
90 PRINT
100 FOR I=1 TO N
110 PRINT
120 PRINT "-----ACTIVITY";I;"-----"
130 PRINT "ENTER START NODE, END NODE";
140 INPUT A(I,1),A(I,2)
150 IF A(I,1)>=A(I,2) THEN 170
160 IF A(I,2)<N THEN 230
170 PRINT " START NODE MUST BE NUMBERED LOWER"
180 PRINT "   THAN END NODE, AND END NODE MUST"
190 PRINT "BE LESS THAN THE NUMBER OF ACTIVITIES."
200 PRINT "     *** TRY ENTRY AGAIN ***"
210 PRINT
220 GOTO 110
230 PRINT "ENTER THREE TIME ESTIMATES"
240 PRINT "FOR THIS ACTIVITY (A,M,B)";
250 INPUT A1,M,B
259 REM E(I,1) IS THE EXPECTED DURATION
260 E(I,1)=INT((A1+M*4+B)/6*1E3+.5)/1E3
269 REM E(I,2) IS THE ACTIVITY VARIANCE
270 E(I,2)=INT(((B-A1)/6)[2*1E3+.5)/1E3
280 S(I)=0
290 F(I)=0
300 NEXT I
309 REM LOOP TO FIND EARLY START TIMES FOR NETWORK
310 FOR I=1 TO N
320 IF S(A(I,2))>=S(A(I,1))+E(I,1) THEN 340
330 S(A(I,2))=S(A(I,1))+E(I,1)
339 REM LOOP TO CALCULATE LATE FINISH TIMES FOR NETWORK
340 NEXT I
350 F(A(N,2))=S(A(N,2))
360 FOR I=N TO 1 STEP -1
370 IF F(A(I,1))=0 THEN 400
```

```
380 IF F(A(I,1))>F(A(I,2))-E(I,1) THEN 400
390 GOTO 410
400 F(A(I,1))=F(A(I,2))-E(I,1)
410 NEXT I
420 V=0
430 C=0
440 L=0
450 FOR I=1 TO N
459 REM CALCULATE SLACK TIME IN S1
460 S1=INT((F(A(I,2))-S(A(I,1))-E(I,1))*1E3+.5)/1E3
470 PRINT "------------------------------------------------"
480 PRINT
490 PRINT "ACTIVITY";I;"(NODE";A(I,1);"TO NODE";A(I,2);")"
500 PRINT "IS A ";
510 IF S1<=0 THEN 530
520 PRINT "NON-";
530 PRINT "CRITICAL EVENT."
540 PRINT "EXPECTED DURATION:";E(I,1);"  STD. DEVIATION:";
550 PRINT SQR(E(I,2))
560 IF S1>0 THEN 630
570 PRINT " START NO LATER THAN:";S(A(I,1))
580 PRINT "MUST BE COMPLETED BY:";F(A(I,2))
589 REM ACCUMULATE PATH LENGTH IN L, VARIANCE IN V
590 IF L>=F(A(I,2)) THEN 610
600 L=F(A(I,2))
610 V=V+E(I,2)
620 GOTO 680
630 PRINT "EARLY START:";S(A(I,1));TAB(25);"LATE START:";
640 PRINT F(A(I,2))-E(I,1)
650 PRINT "EARLY FINISH:";S(A(I,1))+E(I,1);TAB(24);
660 PRINT "LATE FINISH:";F(A(I,2))
670 PRINT "SLACK TIME:";S1
680 NEXT I
690 PRINT
700 PRINT "THE CRITICAL PATH LENGTH IS ";L
710 P=SQR(V)
720 PRINT "PLUS OR MINUS";P
730 PRINT "ENTER DESIRED COMPLETION TIME (0 TO END)";
740 INPUT D
750 IF D<=0 THEN 870
759 REM CALCULATE Z-SCORE FOR DESIRED DURATION
760 Y=(D-L)/P
768 REM CALCULATE CUMULATIVE AREA UNDER NORMAL DISTRIBUTION
769 REM REFERENCE: SOME COMMON BASIC PROBLEMS, 3RD. ED. P.128
770 R=EXP(-(Y[2)/2)/2.5066282746
780 Z=Y
790 Y=1/(1+.33267*ABS(Y))
800 T=1-R*(.4361836*Y-.1201676*Y[2+.937298*Y[3)
810 IF Z>=0 THEN 830
820 T=1-T
830 PRINT "PROBABILITY OF COMPLETION WITH"
840 PRINT "DURATION OF";D;"IS";T
850 PRINT
860 GOTO 730
870 END
```

References

Brown, Kenneth S., and ReVelle, Jack B. *Quantitative Methods for Managerial Decisions.* Reading, Mass.: Addison-Wesley, 1979.

MacCrimmon, K.R., and Ryavec, C.A. *An Analytical Study of the PERT Assumptions.* Santa Monica, Calif.: RAND Corporation, Memo RM-3408-PR, 1962.

Moore, Franklin G., and Hendrick, Thomas E. *Production/Operations Management* (3rd ed.). Homewood, Ill.: Richard D. Irwin, 1977.

Transportation Algorithm

This program allows you to allocate a resource from multiple sources of supply to multiple destinations in the most cost-efficient way. The resource can be anything: manufactured goods, personnel, and so forth. Linear programming can be used to solve this type of problem. But here you do not need to convert costs into an objective function, nor do you need to express data as coefficients in a series of linear equations.

To use this program, you will need to know how many sources of supply are available, as well as the supply capacity for each source. The number of demand destinations, as well as their exact demand for the resource, are also needed. Finally, you need to know the cost of transporting the resource from each source to each destination. The program will ask you for all of this information when you run it, so be sure to have it organized before entering it into the computer.

If available supply does not equal prevailing demand, the program automatically assigns the difference to a dummy source (supply less than demand) or dummy destination (supply greater than demand). Each assignment of the resource, its transportation cost per unit and its total assignment cost, print out at the end of the program. If dummy variables exist in a given problem, these assignments are printed out for your information.

Program Notes

This program allows for 10 sources and 10 destinations. If you want to change this to another maximum, modify lines 20 and 30 as follows:

        20 DIM S(I,2), D(J,2), S1(I + J,2), C(I,J), A(I,J), Y(X,2), M(3)
        30 DIM R1(I), K1(J)

Replace the expression I with the maximum number of sources, and replace J with the maximum number of destinations. Replace X with the maximum number of sources plus the maximum number of destinations minus 1.

You may want to change the program to receive data through DATA statements, rather than INPUT statements. If so, modify the program as shown in the "Option" section.

Example

Smiling Jack owns an organic crop dusting operation. He has three planes that have capacities for 65, 150, and 80 gallons of insecticide each. Tomorrow, four farms need dusting. Jack calculates that, based on the sizes of the fields, they will need 100, 45, 90, and 60 gallons for the fields, respectively. Since each plane has a different capacity, and since the fields are in four different counties, Jack estimates the costs as follows for each gallon of insecticide:

For plane 1 to field 1, 0.05; to field 2, 0.12; to field 3, 0.08; to field 4, 0.11. For plane 2 to field 1, 0.04; to field 2, 0.03; to field 3, 0.06; to field 4, 0.04. For plane 3 to field 1, 0.09; to field 2, 0.14; to field 3, 0.13; to field 4, 0.18.

How does Jack enter this information, what are the assignments for tomorrow, and what is the total transportation cost?

Answer: The optimal assignments are: Plane 1 to field 1, where it will spray 20 gallons, and on to field 3 where it will spray 45 gallons. Plane 2 goes to field 2 first, spraying 45 gallons, then proceeds to field 3, where it uses 45 gallons of insecticide. Finally, Plane 2 goes on to field 4, where it uses the last 60 gallons of spray. Plane 3 goes to field 1 to complete the job which Plane 1 did partially. The total cost, based on those entered, is estimated at $18.25.

```
TRANSPORTATION ALGORITHM

      NUMBER OF SOURCES? 3
NUMBER OF DESTINATIONS? 4
CAPACITY FOR SOURCE 1 ? 65
CAPACITY FOR SOURCE 2 ? 150
CAPACITY FOR SOURCE 3 ? 80
DEMAND FROM DESTINATION 1 ? 100
DEMAND FROM DESTINATION 2 ? 45
DEMAND FROM DESTINATION 3 ? 90
DEMAND FROM DESTINATION 4 ? 60
ENTER TRANSPORTATION COSTS:
FROM SOURCE 1 TO DESTINATION 1 ? .05
FROM SOURCE 1 TO DESTINATION 2 ? .12
FROM SOURCE 1 TO DESTINATION 3 ? .08
FROM SOURCE 1 TO DESTINATION 4 ? .11
FROM SOURCE 2 TO DESTINATION 1 ? .04
FROM SOURCE 2 TO DESTINATION 2 ? .03
FROM SOURCE 2 TO DESTINATION 3 ? .06
FROM SOURCE 2 TO DESTINATION 4 ? .04
FROM SOURCE 3 TO DESTINATION 1 ? .09
FROM SOURCE 3 TO DESTINATION 2 ? .14
FROM SOURCE 3 TO DESTINATION 3 ? .13
FROM SOURCE 3 TO DESTINATION 4 ? .18


SOURCE        DESTINATION      # OF UNITS     COST        TOTAL COST
  1                1               20         $0.05          $1.00
SOURCE        DESTINATION      # OF UNITS     COST        TOTAL COST
  1                3               45         $0.08          $3.60
SOURCE        DESTINATION      # OF UNITS     COST        TOTAL COST
  2                2               45         $0.03          $1.35
SOURCE        DESTINATION      # OF UNITS     COST        TOTAL COST
  2                3               45         $0.06          $2.70
SOURCE        DESTINATION      # OF UNITS     COST        TOTAL COST
  2                4               60         $0.04          $2.40
SOURCE        DESTINATION      # OF UNITS     COST        TOTAL COST
  3                1               80         $0.09          $7.20

TOTAL COST OF SOLUTION:        $18.25

DO YOU WANT TO RE-RUN THIS PROGRAM WITH NEW DATA (Y/N) ?
READY
```

Practice Problems

1. The Skinheads Motorcycle Enthusiasts Society has three chapters in the state, and three imminent social engagements with competing clubs. Based on intelligence reports, the Skinheads know that they will encounter 75, 19, and 22 people respectively. Their three chapters have 35, 20, and 61 members. The mileage from Chapter 1 to location 1 is 35 miles; to location 2, 80 miles, and to location 3, 60 miles.

From Chapter 2 to location 1, the distance is 90 miles; to location 2, 40 miles, and to location 3, 55 miles. From Chapter 3 to location 1, the distance is 50 miles; to location 2, 28 miles; and to location 3, 65 miles.

How should people be assigned? How far, in miles, will everyone in the club have traveled to reach the destinations?

Answer: 35 persons from Chapter 1 to location 1; 20 people from chapter 2 to location 3; 40 people from Chapter 3 to location 1; 19 people from Chapter 3 to location 2, and 2 from Chapter 3 to location 3. The total miles traveled (assuming one person per bike): 4,987.

2. Given the following table, what is the optimal transportation mix? How much does it cost?

Project	Weekly Demand	Plant	Weekly Capacity
A	170	J	130
B	250	K	200
C	100	L	190

Costs:

From	To A	To B	To C
J	$2	$5	$5
K	9	13	9
L	2	4	6

Answer: 70 units from Plant J to Project Site A; 60 units from Plant J to Project B; 100 units from Plant K to Project A; 100 units from Plant K to Project C; and 190 units from Plant L to Project B. Total cost is $3,000.

Program Listing

```
10 CLS
20 DIM S(10,2),D(10,2),S1(20,2),C(10,10),A(10,10),Y(19,2),M(3)
30 DIM R1(10),K1(10)
40 PRINT "TRANSPORTATION ALGORITHM"
50 PRINT
60 PRINT "     NUMBER OF SOURCES";
70 INPUT S2
80 IF S2<1 THEN 60
90 PRINT "NUMBER OF DESTINATIONS";
100 INPUT D1
110 IF D1<1 THEN 90
119 REM ENTER SUPPLY CAPACITY FOR EACH SOURCE
120 T1=0
130 FOR R=1 TO S2
140 PRINT "CAPACITY FOR SOURCE";R;
150 INPUT S(R,1)
160 S(R,2)=S(R,1)
170 T1=T1+S(R,1)
180 NEXT R
190 T2=0
199 REM ENTER DEMAND FROM EACH DESTINATION
200 FOR R=1 TO D1
210 PRINT "DEMAND FROM DESTINATION";R;
220 INPUT D(R,1)
230 D(R,2)=D(R,1)
240 T2=T2+D(R,1)
250 NEXT R
```

```
259 REM LOOP TO ENTER TRANSPORTATION COSTS
260 PRINT "ENTER TRANSPORTATION COSTS:"
270 FOR R=1 TO S2
279 REM INITIALIZE ELEMENTS OF S1() ARRAY
280 S1(R,1)=0
290 S1(R,2)=0
300 FOR K=1 TO D1
310 PRINT "FROM SOURCE";R;"TO DESTINATION";K;
320 INPUT C(R,K)
330 IF C(R,K)<0 THEN 310
340 NEXT K
350 NEXT R
359 REM THE MATRIX HAS BEEN ENTERED--START FIRST SOLUTION PHASE
360 S0=0
370 D0=0
380 IF T1>=T2 THEN 430
389 REM SUPPLY MUST EQUAL DEMAND; SET UP DUMMY ROWS AND COLUMNS
390 S(S2+1,1)=T2-T1
400 S(S2+1,2)=T2-T1
410 S0=1
420 GOTO 470
430 IF T2=T1 THEN 470
440 D(D1+1,1)=T1-T2
450 D(D1+1,2)=T1-T2
460 D0=1
470 D2=0
480 T3=0
489 REM START SOLUTION WITH NORTHWEST CORNER RULE
490 FOR R=1 TO S2+S0
499 REM IF SUPPLY AT ROW R EXHAUSTED, MOVE TO NEXT SOURCE
500 IF S(R,2)=0 THEN 670
509 REM ALLOCATE SUPPLY TO DEMAND
510 FOR K=1 TO D1+D0
519 REM IF DESTINATION K FILLED, INCREMENT COLUMN INDEX
520 IF D(K,2)=0 THEN 660
530 IF S(R,2)=0 THEN 660
540 IF S(R,2)<D(K,2) THEN 590
549 REM SET UP STONE SQUARE IF DEMAND <= SUPPLY
550 A(R,K)=D(K,2)
560 S(R,2)=S(R,2)-D(K,2)
570 D(K,2)=0
580 GOTO 620
589 REM SET UP STONE SQUARE IF DEMAND > SUPPLY
590 A(R,K)=S(R,2)
600 D(K,2)=D(K,2)-S(R,2)
610 S(R,2)=0
620 D2=D2+1
630 T3=T3+(A(R,K)*C(R,K))
640 S1(D2,1)=R
650 S1(D2,2)=K
660 NEXT K
670 NEXT R
679 REM CHECK SOLUTION FOR FIRST-STAGE DEGENERACY
680 IF D2=S2+S0+D1+D0-1 THEN 1000
689 REM SOLVE DEGENERATE SOLUTION
```

```
690 R=0
700 K=0
710 I=0
720 I=I+1
730 IF A(S1(I,1),S1(I,2))=D(S1(I,2),1) THEN 750
740 IF A(S1(I,1),S1(I,2))<>S(S1(I,1),1) THEN 780
750 R=S1(I,1)+1
760 K=S1(I,2)
770 GOTO 890
780 IF I<D2+D0 THEN 720
789 REM IF R & K ARE ZERO, THE MATRIX IS NOT DEGENERATE
790 IF R+K=0 THEN 1000
800 IF S1(I-1,2)=K THEN 830
810 K=S1(I-1,2)
820 GOTO 870
830 IF K=D2+D0 THEN 860
840 K=K+1
850 GOTO 870
860 K=K-1
869 REM INSERT A NEW STONE SQUARE IN THE SOLUTION
870 IF K>S1(I,2) THEN 890
880 I=I-1
890 FOR J=D2+1 TO I+1 STEP -1
900 S1(J,1)=S1(J-1,1)
910 S1(J,2)=S1(J-1,2)
920 M0=J
930 NEXT J
940 S1(M0,1)=R
950 S1(M0,2)=K
960 Y(I,1)=0
970 Y(I,2)=0
980 D2=D2+1
990 GOTO 680
999 REM CALCULATE RIM VALUES
1000 FOR I=1 TO D1+D0
1010 K1(I)=-9E4
1020 NEXT I
1030 FOR I=1 TO S2+S0
1040 R1(I)=-9E4
1050 NEXT I
1060 R1(S1(1,1))=0
1070 K1(S1(1,2))=C(S1(1,1),S1(1,2))
1080 R=1
1090 K=1
1100 I=1
1110 I=I+1
1120 IF K1(S1(I,2))<>-9E4 THEN 1160
1130 IF R1(S1(I,1))=-9E4 THEN 1190
1140 K1(S1(I,2))=C(S1(I,1),S1(I,2))-R1(S1(I,1))
1150 K=K+1
1160 IF R1(S1(I,1))<>-9E4 THEN 1190
1170 R1(S1(I,1))=C(S1(I,1),S1(I,2))-K1(S1(I,2))
1180 R=R+1
1190 IF I<D2 THEN 1110
1200 IF K<D1+D0 THEN 1100
```

```
1210 IF R<S2+S0 THEN 1100
1220 I=1
1230 M(1)=0
1239 REM FIND AN ELEMENT WITH THE LOWEST INDEX
1240 FOR R=1 TO S2+S0
1250 FOR K=1 TO D1+D0
1260 IF R<>S1(I,1) THEN 1300
1270 IF K<>S1(I,2) THEN 1300
1280 I=I+1
1290 GOTO 1340
1300 IF M(1)<C(R,K)-R1(R)-K1(K) THEN 1340
1310 M(1)=C(R,K)-R1(R)-K1(K)
1320 M(2)=R
1330 M(3)=K
1340 NEXT K
1350 NEXT R
1360 IF M(1)>=0 THEN 2440
1369 REM FIND A CLOSED PATH FROM SQUARE AT ROW R, COLUMN K
1370 Y(1,1)=M(2)
1380 Y(1,2)=M(3)
1390 Q=1
1400 IF M(2)=S2+S0 THEN 1740
1408 REM M0=CURRENT ROW TO SEARCH ON
1409 REM M1=START COLUMN TO SEARCH ON
1410 M0=Y(Q,1)
1420 M1=1
1429 REM START ROW SEARCH
1430 I=0
1440 I=I+1
1450 IF S1(I,1)>M0 THEN 1490
1460 IF S1(I,1)<M0 THEN 1480
1470 IF S1(I,2)>=M1 THEN 1530
1480 IF I<D2 THEN 1440
1490 IF Q<>1 THEN 1520
1500 PRINT "MATRIX IS DEGENERATE"
1510 GOTO 2100
1519 REM AT THIS POINT, NO ROW NEIGHBORS EXIST
1520 GOTO 1620
1529 REM MAKE SURE V(I) IS NOT ALREADY ON THE CLOSED PATH
1530 X0=0
1540 FOR J=1 TO Q
1550 IF S1(I,1)<>Y(J,1) THEN 1580
1560 IF S1(I,2)<>Y(J,2) THEN 1580
1570 X0=1
1580 NEXT J
1590 IF X0=0 THEN 1680
1600 M1=S1(I,1)+1
1610 IF M1<=D1+D0 THEN 1480
1619 REM ROW SEARCH FAILED; SET NEXT COORDINATES FOR COL. SEARCH
1620 P=Y(Q,2)
1630 P1=Y(Q,1)+1
1640 Y(Q,1)=0
1650 Y(Q,2)=0
1660 Q=Q-1
1670 GOTO 1760
```

```
1680 Q=Q+1
1690 Y(Q,1)=S1(I,1)
1700 Y(Q,2)=S1(I,2)
1710 IF Q<=2 THEN 1730
1719 REM IF PATH CLOSES ON A ROW SEARCH, EXIT SEARCH ROUTINE
1720 IF Y(Q,2)=M(3) THEN 2050
1730 M1=Y(Q,2)+1
1738 REM COLUMN SEARCH AREA
1739 REM P=COL. NUMBER TO SEARCH ON; P1=STARTING ROW FOR SEARCH
1740 P=Y(Q,2)
1750 P1=1
1760 K=0
1770 K=K+1
1780 IF S1(K,1)<P1 THEN 1800
1790 IF S1(K,2)=P THEN 1870
1800 IF K<D2 THEN 1770
1809 REM COLUMN SEARCH FAILS; SET NEW COORDINATES FOR ROW SEARCH
1810 M0=Y(Q,1)
1820 M1=Y(Q,2)+1
1830 Y(Q,1)=0
1840 Y(Q,2)=0
1850 Q=Q-1
1860 GOTO 1430
1870 X0=0
1879 REM LOOKUP ROUTINE: CHECK FOR ALREADY USED STONE SQUARE
1880 FOR J=1 TO Q
1890 IF S1(K,1)<>Y(J,1) THEN 1920
1900 IF S1(K,2)<>Y(J,2) THEN 1920
1910 X0=1
1920 NEXT J
1930 IF X0=0 THEN 1970
1940 P1=S1(K,1)+1
1950 IF P1<=S2+S0 THEN 1800
1960 GOTO 1810
1968 REM A UNIQUE STONE SQUARE WAS FOUND---
1969 REM  ADD IT TO THE CLOSED PATH ARRAY
1970 Q=Q+1
1980 Y(Q,1)=S1(K,1)
1990 Y(Q,2)=S1(K,2)
1999 REM IF PATH CLOSES ON COLUMN SEARCH, EXIT SEARCH ROUTINE
2000 IF Y(Q,1)=M(2) THEN 2050
2010 P1=Y(Q,1)+1
2020 M0=Y(Q,1)
2030 M1=Y(Q,2)+1
2040 GOTO 1430
2049 REM FIND LOWEST ALLOCATION STONED SQUARE ON CLOSED PATH
2050 X0=A(Y(2,1),Y(2,2))
2060 FOR K=4 TO Q STEP 2
2070 IF X0<=A(Y(K,1),Y(K,2)) THEN 2090
2080 X0=A(Y(K,1),Y(K,2))
2090 NEXT K
2098 REM ALTERNATELY ADD & SUBTRACT X0 FROM
2099 REM  CLOSED PATH ALLOCATIONS
2100 P=0
2110 FOR K=1 TO Q
```

```
2120 IF K/2=INT(K/2) THEN 2150
2130 A(Y(K,1),Y(K,2))=A(Y(K,1),Y(K,2))+X0
2140 GOTO 2300
2150 A(Y(K,1),Y(K,2))=A(Y(K,1),Y(K,2))-X0
2160 IF A(Y(K,1),Y(K,2))>0 THEN 2300
2169 REM DELETE ANY SQUARES WITH A ZERO ALLOCATION
2170 I=0
2180 P=P+1
2188 REM IF P>1, MATRIX WILL BE DEGENERATE IF
2189 REM  SQUARE IS DELETED; SKIP IT
2190 IF P>1 THEN 2300
2200 I=I+1
2210 IF S1(I,1)<>Y(K,1) THEN 2200
2220 IF S1(I,2)<>Y(K,2) THEN 2200
2230 FOR J=I TO D2
2240 S1(J,1)=S1(J+1,1)
2250 S1(J,2)=S1(J+1,2)
2260 NEXT J
2270 S1(D2,1)=0
2280 S1(D2,2)=0
2290 D2=D2-1
2300 NEXT K
2309 REM INSERT NEW STONE SQUARE FROM 1ST ELEMENT OF Y()
2310 I=0
2320 I=I+1
2330 IF Y(1,1)>S1(I,1) THEN 2320
2340 IF Y(1,1)<S1(I,1) THEN 2360
2350 IF Y(1,2)>S1(I,2) THEN 2320
2360 FOR J=D2 TO I STEP -1
2370 S1(J+1,1)=S1(J,1)
2380 S1(J+1,2)=S1(J,2)
2390 NEXT J
2400 S1(I,1)=Y(1,1)
2410 S1(I,2)=Y(1,2)
2420 D2=D2+1
2429 REM END OF RE-ALLOCATION; REITERATE MODI CHECK
2430 GOTO 1000
2439 REM DISPLAY RESULTS AND COST OF SOLUTION
2440 PRINT
2450 IF D0+S0=0 THEN 2530
2460 PRINT "*** UNBALANCED SOLUTION ***"
2470 IF D0=0 THEN 2500
2480 PRINT "EXCESS SUPPLY ("; D(D1+D0,1);
2490 PRINT ") ASSIGNED TO DESTINATION"; D1+D0
2500 IF S0=0 THEN 2530
2510 PRINT "EXCESS DEMAND ("; S(S2+S0,1);
2520 PRINT ") ASSIGNED TO SOURCE"; S2+S0
2530 X0=0
2540 FOR I=1 TO D2
2550 PRINT "SOURCE      DESTINATION      # OF UNITS      COST";
2560 PRINT TAB(53) "TOTAL COST"
2570 PU$="######" : PV$="$$######.##"
2580 PRINTUSING PU$; S1(I,1) ;: PRINTTAB(12)
2590 PRINTUSING PU$; S1(I,2) ;: PRINTTAB(27)
2600 PRINTUSING PU$; A(S1(I,1),S1(I,2)) ;: PRINTTAB(35)
```

```
2610 PRINTUSING PV$; C(S1(I,1),S1(I,2));
2620 J=C(S1(I,1),S1(I,2))*A(S1(I,1),S1(I,2))
2630 IF J>0 THEN 2660
2640 PRINT TAB(57) "DUMMY"
2650 GOTO 2680
2660 X0=X0+J
2670 PRINT TAB(52) : PRINTUSING PV$; J
2680 NEXT I
2690 PRINT
2700 PRINT "TOTAL COST OF SOLUTION:";: PRINTUSING PV$; X0
2710 PRINT
2720 PRINT "DO YOU WANT TO RE-RUN THIS ";
2730 PRINT "PROGRAM WITH NEW DATA (Y/N) ?";
2740 X0$=INKEY$ : IF X0$="" THEN 2740
2750 IF X0$="Y" THEN 50
2760 IF X0$<>"N" THEN 2710
2770 END
```

Option

If you want to avoid using INPUT statements for data entry, you can change the program to read input from DATA statements. This is especially useful if you intend to enter a large transportation problem, or if you want to run the program repeatedly with slightly different data without re-entering the supply, demand, and cost figures. Modify the statements below to allow for this feature.

Also, delete lines 2720 through 2770.

```
140 PRINT "CAPACITY FOR SOURCE";R;
141 REM THIS DATA SHOWN TO SOLVE PROBLEM #1. PUT YOUR SUPPLY
          DATA HERE.
142 DATA 65,150,80
150 READ S(R,1)
155 PRINT S(R,1)
160 S(R,2)=S(R,1)
170 T1=T1+S(R,1)
180 NEXT R
190 T2=0
199 REM READ DATA LIST OF DEMAND FROM EACH DESTINATION
200 FOR R=1 TO D1
210 PRINT "DEMAND FROM DESTINATION";R;
211 REM PUT DEMAND DATA HERE.
212 DATA 100,45,90,60
220 READ D(R,1)
225 PRINT D(R,1)
230 D(R,2)=D(R,1)
240 T2=T2+D(R,1)
250 NEXT R
259 REM LOOP TO READ TRANSPORTATION COSTS
260 PRINT "ENTER TRANSPORTATION COSTS:"
270 FOR R=1 TO S2
279 REM INITIALIZE ELEMENTS OF S1() ARRAY
280 S1(R,1)=0
290 S1(R,2)=0
```

```
300 FOR K=1 TO D1
310 PRINT "FROM SOURCE";R;"TO DESTINATION";K;
311 REM PUT TRANSPORTATION COST DATA HERE.
312 DATA .05,.12,.08,.11,.04,.03,.06,.04,.09,.14,.13,.18
320 READ C(R,K)
330 PRINT C(R,K)
340 NEXT K
350 NEXT R
359 REM THE MATRIX HAS BEEN ENTERED--START FIRST SOLUTION PHASE
```

References

Chase, Richard B., and Aquilano, Nicholas J. *Production and Operations Management.* Homewood, Ill.: Richard D. Irwin, Inc., 1977.

Levin, Richard I., and Kirkpatrick, Charles A. *Quantitative Approaches to Management* (3rd ed.). New York: McGraw-Hill, 1975.

Swedish Machine (Queuing Theory)

This is the classic problem where you have X repairmen servicing Y machines. The machines are statistically identical; their times-to-failure follow the exponential law, characterized by the mean time-to-failure. The repairmen are also statistically identical; their repair completion times follow the exponential law and are characterized by its expected value. All elements are mutually independent.

This program is especially useful in that it can provide a cash flow analysis that can help project the feasibility of a particular machines-to-repairmen ratio, given the repairmen's wages, machine revenue, and overhead costs.

To use the program, enter the number of machines, the mean time-to-failure for a machine, the number of repairmen, and the mean time to repair a machine. You may use any time unit base you wish, as long as you use the same time units throughout the program. A variety of system characteristics are output. If you choose to obtain a cash flow analysis, you must also enter the cost for one repairman per unit of time, the cost of possessing a machine (overhead) per unit of time, and the amount of revenue produced by a machine per unit of time. You may use any monetary unit you wish (pennies, dollars, thousands of dollars, pesos, whatever).

Example

Ace Laundromat has a total of 50 machines operating throughout the city. The machines have a mean time-to-failure of 300 hours, and there are currently three repairmen. Each repairman requires 24 hours to repair a machine. At any time, how many machines can be expected to be operating? How many machines are being repaired? How many are waiting to be repaired? What is the mean down time per machine? How many repairmen are idle? Repairmen cost $5.25 per hour (including fringe benefits, and so forth). Cost of possessing a machine is the overhead involved, such as lease or purchase payments, insurance payments, pro-rated administrative expenses, depreciation expense, and so forth. In this example the cost of possessing a machine is $36.00 per month, or $0.05 per hour. What cash flow do the machines generate if they each produce revenues of $0.50 per hour?

Answer: 37 machines can be expected to be operational at any time, 3 are being repaired, and 10 are waiting to be repaired. The mean down time per machine is about 105 hours. The 50 machines will produce an average revenue of $0.268833 per hour.

```
SWEDISH MACHINE

INPUT THE NUMBER OF MACHINES (COUNT MUST EXCEED ONE)? 50
INPUT MEAN TIME-TO-FAILURE FOR A MACHINE? 300
INPUT NUMBER OF REPAIRMEN? 3
INPUT MEAN REPAIR TIME PER MACHINE FOR A REPAIRMAN? 24


THE SYSTEM IS SAID TO BE 'IN STATE J' IF J MACHINES
ARE IN A FAILED CONDITION. THE STATIONARY PROBABILITY
DISTRIBUTION OVER THE POSSIBLE STATES, 0 THRU 50 ,
AND OTHER CHARACTERISTICS OF INTEREST, FOLLOW.
```

STATE	PROBABILITY	NO. MACHINES OPERATING	NO. MACHINES WAITING	NO. REPAIRMEN IDLE
0	.0019631	50	0	3
1	.0078525	49	0	2

2	.0153909	48	0	1
3	.0197003	47	0	0
4	.0246910	46	1	0
5	.0302877	45	2	0
6	.0363452	44	3	0
7	.0426450	43	4	0
8	.0488996	42	5	0
9	.0547676	41	6	0
10	.0598792	40	7	0
11	.0638712	39	8	0
12	.0664260	38	9	0
13	.0673117	37	10	0
14	.0664142	36	11	0
15	.0637577	35	12	0
16	.0595071	34	13	0
17	.0539531	33	14	0
18	.0474788	32	15	0
19	.0405152	31	16	0
20	.0334926	30	17	0
21	.0267941	29	18	0
22	.0207207	28	19	0
23	.0154715	27	20	0
24	.0111395	26	21	0
25	.0077234	25	22	0
26	.0051489	24	23	0
27	.0032953	23	24	0
28	.0020211	22	25	0
29	.0011857	21	26	0
30	.0006640	20	27	0
31	.0003541	19	28	0
32	.0001794	18	29	0
33	.0000861	17	30	0
34	.0000390	16	31	0
35	.0000167	15	32	0
36	.0000067	14	33	0
37	.0000025	13	34	0
38	.0000009	12	35	0
39	.0000003	11	36	0
40	.0000001	10	37	0
41	.0000000	9	38	0
42	.0000000	8	39	0
43	.0000000	7	40	0
44	.0000000	6	41	0
45	.0000000	5	42	0
46	.0000000	4	43	0
47	.0000000	3	44	0
48	.0000000	2	45	0
49	.0000000	1	46	0
50	.0000000	0	47	0

TO CONTINUE, PRESS 'ENTER'?

```
          SYSTEM CHARACTERISTICS
          -----------------------
NO. OF MACHINES = 50
```

```
MEAN TIME-TO-FAILURE PER MACHINE = 300 TIME UNITS
NO. OF REPAIRMEN = 3
MEAN REPAIR-TIME PER REPAIRMAN = 24 TIME UNITS
NUMBER OF MACHINES PER REPAIRMAN = 16.6667

PROB.   (SERVICE SYSTEM IS EMPTY) = .0019631
PROB.   (NO MACHINES ARE WAITING FOR SERVICE) = .0449067

EXP. NO. OF MACHINES OPERATING = 37.0377
EXP. NO. OF INACTIVE MACHINES = 12.9623
EXP. NO. OF MACH. IN WAITING LINE = 9.9993
EXP. NO. OF MACH. IN A NON-EMPTY 'WAITING LINE' = 10.4694
MEAN DOWN-TIME PER MACHINE = 104.993 TIME UNITS
MEAN WAITING TIME PER MACHINE = 80.9929 TIME UNITS
EXP. NO. OF REPAIRMEN IDLE = .0369852

TO CONTINUE, PRESS 'ENTER'?
'COEFFICIENT OF LOSS' FOR MACHINES = FRACTION OF TIME
  A MACHINE IS 'DOWN' AS A CONSEQUENCE OF THE SYSTEM
  CHARACTERISTICS = .199986

'COEFFICIENT OF LOSS' FOR REPAIRMEN = FRACTION OF TIME A
  REPAIRMAN IS IDLE AS A CONSEQUENCE OF THE SYSTEM
  CHARACTERISTICS = .0123284

TYPE  1  FOR CASH FLOW ANALYSIS
      2  TO HALT
? 1
THIS ANALYSIS ASSUMES THAT REPAIRMEN ARE PAID 'A' MONETARY
UNITS PER UNIT TIME, THAT THE FIXED COST OF POSSESSING
EACH MACHINE IS 'B' MONETARY UNITS PER UNIT TIME, AND THAT
A MACHINE, WHEN OPERATING, IS CAPABLE OF PRODUCING 'C'
UNITS OF REVENUE PER UNIT TIME.

INPUT THE REPAIRMEN-COST PER UNIT TIME, 'A'? 5.25

INPUT THE FIXED COST PER UNIT TIME, 'B', OF PROCESSING
A MACHINE? .05

INPUT THE AMOUNT OF REVENUE A WORKING MACHINE PRODUCES,
PER UNIT OF (OPERATING) TIME? .5

THE AVERAGE CASH FLOW GENERATED BY THE COMBINATION OF 50
MACHINE(S) MAINTAINED BY 3 REPAIRMEN IS .268833 MONETARY
UNITS, PER UNIT TIME.
READY
```

Practice Problem

In the above example, suppose Ace invested $65.00 per machine to retrofit them with heavy duty motors, raising their mean times-to-failure to 305 hours. What cash flow will the machines produce? How much time must pass before Ace has recovered their $3,250.00 investment?

   Answer: If retrofit, the machines will produce an average revenue of $0.528526 per hour. The investment will be recovered within 17 months.

Program Listing

```
10 CLS
20 PRINT "SWEDISH MACHINE"
29 REM -- CHANGE DIMENSION OF Q() TO MAX. NUMBER OF MACHINES + 1
30 DIM Q(100)
40 PRINT
50 PRINT "INPUT THE NUMBER OF MACHINES (COUNT MUST EXCEED ONE)";
60 INPUT N
70 PRINT "INPUT MEAN TIME-TO-FAILURE FOR A MACHINE";
80 INPUT F1
90 F=1/F1
100 PRINT "INPUT NUMBER OF REPAIRMEN";
110 INPUT M
120 PRINT "INPUT MEAN REPAIR TIME PER MACHINE FOR A REPAIRMAN";
130 INPUT R1
140 R=1/R1
150 PRINT
159 REM -- INITIALIZE VARIABLES
160 FOR I=1 TO N+1
170 Q(I)=0
180 NEXT I
190 Q(1)=1
200 E1=0
210 E2=0
220 E3=0
230 P0=0
239 REM -- LOOP TO CALCULATE PROBABILITIES FOR EACH MACHINE
240 S=Q(1)
250 FOR J=0 TO N-1
259 REM -- K=MIN(J+1,M)
260 K=M
270 IF J+1>M THEN 290
280 K=J+1
290 Q(J+2)=(N-J)*F*Q(J+1)/K/R
300 S=S+Q(J+2)
310 NEXT J
320 IF Q(1)<>1 THEN 350
330 Q(1)=1/S
340 GOTO 240
350 PRINT
360 PRINT "THE SYSTEM IS SAID TO BE 'IN STATE J' IF J MACHINES"
370 PRINT "ARE IN A FAILED CONDITION. THE STATIONARY PROBABILITY
380 PRINT "DISTRIBUTION OVER THE POSSIBLE STATES, 0 THRU";N;","
390 PRINT "AND OTHER CHARACTERISTICS OF INTEREST, FOLLOW."
400 PRINT
410 PRINT "STATE"TAB(8)"PROBABILITY";
420 PRINT "  NO. MACHINES"TAB(35)"NO. MACHINES"TAB(49)
430 PRINT "NO. REPAIRMEN"
440 PRINT TAB(23)"OPERATING"TAB(37)"WAITING"TAB(51)"IDLE"
450 FOR J=1 TO N+1
460 O=N-J+1
470 W=J-M-1
480 IF W>0 THEN 510
490 W=0
```

```
500 PO=PO+Q(J)
510 I=M-J+1
520 IF I>0 THEN 540
530 I=0
540 IF I<M THEN 560
550 I=M
560 PRINTUSING "####"; J-1;: PRINTTAB(9)
570 PRINTUSING ".#######";Q(J);: PRINTUSING "############";O,W,I
580 E1=E1+W*Q(J)
590 E2=E2+I*Q(J)
600 E3=E3+O*Q(J)
610 NEXT J
620 PRINT
630 PRINT "TO CONTINUE, PRESS 'ENTER'";
640 INPUT Z$
650 PRINT
660 PRINT TAB(15);"SYSTEM CHARACTERISTICS"
670 PRINT TAB(15);"----------------------"
680 PRINT "NO. OF MACHINES =";N
690 PRINT "MEAN TIME-TO-FAILURE PER MACHINE =";F1;"TIME UNITS"
700 PRINT "NO. OF REPAIRMEN =";M
710 PRINT "MEAN REPAIR-TIME PER REPAIRMAN =";R1;"TIME UNITS"
720 PRINT "NUMBER OF MACHINES PER REPAIRMAN =";N/M
730 PRINT
740 PRINT "PROB.   (SERVICE SYSTEM IS EMPTY) = ";
750 PRINTUSING ".#######"; Q(1)
760 PRINT "PROB.   (NO MACHINES ARE WAITING FOR SERVICE) = ";
770 PRINTUSING ".#######"; PO
780 PRINT
790 PRINT "EXP. NO. OF MACHINES OPERATING =";E3
800 PRINT "EXP. NO. OF INACTIVE MACHINES =";N-E3
810 PRINT "EXP. NO. OF MACH. IN WAITING LINE =";E1
820 PRINT "EXP. NO. OF MACH. IN A NON-EMPTY 'WAITING LINE' =";
830 PRINT E1/(1-PO)
840 PRINT "MEAN DOWN-TIME PER MACHINE ="(N-E3)*F1/E3"TIME UNITS"
850 PRINT "MEAN WAITING TIME PER MACHINE ="E1*F1/E3"TIME UNITS"
860 PRINT "EXP. NO. OF REPAIRMEN IDLE =";E2
870 PRINT
880 PRINT "TO CONTINUE, PRESS 'ENTER'";
890 INPUT Z$
900 PRINT "'COEFFICIENT OF LOSS' FOR MACHINES = FRACTION OF TIME
910 PRINT "  A MACHINE IS 'DOWN' AS A CONSEQUENCE OF THE SYSTEM"
920 PRINT "  CHARACTERISTICS =";E1/N
930 PRINT
940 PRINT "'COEFFICIENT OF LOSS' FOR REPAIRMEN = FRACTION OF ";
950 PRINT "TIME A"
960 PRINT "  REPAIRMAN IS IDLE AS A CONSEQUENCE OF THE SYSTEM"
970 PRINT "  CHARACTERISTICS =";E2/M
980 PRINT
990 PRINT "TYPE  1  FOR CASH FLOW ANALYSIS"
1000 PRINT "      2  TO HALT"
1010 INPUT Q1
1020 IF Q1=2 THEN 1290
1030 PRINT "THIS ANALYSIS ASSUMES THAT REPAIRMEN ARE PAID 'A'
     MONETARY"
```

```
1040 PRINT "UNITS PER UNIT TIME, THAT THE FIXED COST OF POSSES
SING"
1050 PRINT "EACH MACHINE IS 'B' MONETARY UNITS PER UNIT TIME, AN
D THAT"
1060 PRINT "A MACHINE, WHEN OPERATING, IS CAPABLE OF PRODUCING '
C'"
1070 PRINT "UNITS OF REVENUE PER UNIT TIME."
1080 PRINT
1090 PRINT "INPUT THE REPAIRMEN-COST PER UNIT TIME, 'A'";
1100 INPUT A
1110 PRINT
1120 PRINT "INPUT THE FIXED COST PER UNIT TIME, 'B', OF PROCES
SING"
1130 PRINT "A MACHINE";
1140 INPUT B
1150 PRINT
1160 PRINT "INPUT THE AMOUNT OF REVENUE A WORKING MACHINE PRO
DUCES,"
1170 PRINT "PER UNIT OF (OPERATING) TIME";
1180 INPUT C
1190 PRINT
1200 D=C*E3-A*M-B*N
1210 PRINT "THE AVERAGE CASH FLOW GENERATED BY THE COMBINATION O
F";N
1220 PRINT "MACHINE(S) MAINTAINED BY";M;"REPAIR";
1230 IF M>1 THEN 1260
1240 PRINT "MAN";
1250 GOTO 1270
1260 PRINT "MEN";
1270 PRINT " IS";D;"MONETARY"
1280 PRINT "UNITS, PER UNIT TIME."
1290 END
```

Markov Analysis

This program calculates the future changes, overtime, in a given variable based on its current movement. Management scientists adopted this analysis, using it mostly as a simulation technique for analyzing competitors in the marketplace. Markov analysis has many other applications, however, as illustrated by the examples below.

To use the program, first enter how many states of nature are under consideration. The second entry is optional. If you want to see changes occur over time from stage to stage, you must enter the current population proportion vector. If you are only interested in long-run steady-state equilibrium, the program will seed the vector with equal probabilities. The number of elements in this vector equals the states of nature.

The program then asks you to enter each cell of the transition probabilities matrix (N*N, where N = states of nature). For each cell, enter a transition probability, ranging $0 < = p < = 1$. The sum of the probabilities entered for each row should always add up to 1. Once you have entered the entire matrix, you have the option of looking at each future period or letting the computer calculate the transition matrix at equilibrium.

The program displays the equilibrium vector, the period at which equilibrium was reached, and the first passage times for each state of nature. First passage times will not print for recurrent or null-recurrent states.

Program Notes

This program allows for a maximum of 12 states of nature. You can change this by modifying line 20 of this program:

20 DIM V1(I), T(I,I), V2(I)

Replace I with your maximum (for example, 15, 20, or 25).

If you have large matrices to enter, or if you want to repeatedly run this program with mostly the same data, you can modify the program to accept data through DATA statements, as shown in the "Option" section.

Example

Caffrey's Hardware wants to analyze its accounts receivable in order to estimate its cash flow from credit customers. The company has three aging categories: current, 45-89 days, and 90-plus days past due. Customers in this last category are eventually written off as uncollectable accounts.

The latest aging analysis shows that, for each dollar of accounts receivable outstanding, $0.60 is current, $0.33 is 45-89 days old, and $0.07 is 90-plus days old. Further analysis shows that accounts in the Current category have a 38% chance of being paid in the next month, 45% of all current accounts will remain current, and 17% will be 45-89 days old. Accounts in the 45-89 days category stand a 65% chance of paying all back payments, a 25% chance of paying only the late installment, and a 5% chance of becoming 90-plus days overdue. Of the accounts in the 90-plus category, there is a 25% chance they will be paid and a 75% chance they will become bad debts.

The paid and bad debt categories are "absorbing" states, in that the probability of a paid item remaining paid is assumed to be 100%. The same is true for bad debts. These are called absorbing states because all accounts outstanding now will eventually be paid up or written off. How much of accounts receivable will be collected? How much will be written off?

On the printout below, the paid category and bad debt category have absorbed all outstanding debts. Caffrey can expect about 91% of his accounts to be paid, and 9% to be written off.

MARKOV ANALYSIS

HOW MANY STATES OF NATURE? 5
IS THE POPULATION PROPORTION VECTOR KNOWN (Y/N)? Y

              ENTER VECTOR ELEMENT 1 ? 0
              ENTER VECTOR ELEMENT 2 ? .6
              ENTER VECTOR ELEMENT 3 ? .33
              ENTER VECTOR ELEMENT 4 ? .07
              ENTER VECTOR ELEMENT 5 ? 0

ENTER ELEMENT IN ROW 1 COLUMN 1 ? 1
ENTER ELEMENT IN ROW 1 COLUMN 2 ? 0
ENTER ELEMENT IN ROW 1 COLUMN 3 ? 0
ENTER ELEMENT IN ROW 1 COLUMN 4 ? 0
ENTER ELEMENT IN ROW 1 COLUMN 5 ? 0

ENTER ELEMENT IN ROW 2 COLUMN 1 ? .38
ENTER ELEMENT IN ROW 2 COLUMN 2 ? .45
ENTER ELEMENT IN ROW 2 COLUMN 3 ? .17
ENTER ELEMENT IN ROW 2 COLUMN 4 ? 0
ENTER ELEMENT IN ROW 2 COLUMN 5 ? 0

ENTER ELEMENT IN ROW 3 COLUMN 1 ? .65
ENTER ELEMENT IN ROW 3 COLUMN 2 ? .25
ENTER ELEMENT IN ROW 3 COLUMN 3 ? 0
ENTER ELEMENT IN ROW 3 COLUMN 4 ? .05

ENTER ELEMENT IN ROW 3 COLUMN 5 ? 0
---PROBABILITIES DO NOT ADD UP TO 1.0---
       TRY ENTERING THE ROW AGAIN.
ENTER ELEMENT IN ROW 3 COLUMN 1 ? .65
ENTER ELEMENT IN ROW 3 COLUMN 2 ? .25
ENTER ELEMENT IN ROW 3 COLUMN 3 ? 0
ENTER ELEMENT IN ROW 3 COLUMN 4 ? .1
ENTER ELEMENT IN ROW 3 COLUMN 5 ? 0

ENTER ELEMENT IN ROW 4 COLUMN 1 ? .25
ENTER ELEMENT IN ROW 4 COLUMN 2 ? 0
ENTER ELEMENT IN ROW 4 COLUMN 3 ? 0
ENTER ELEMENT IN ROW 4 COLUMN 4 ? 0
ENTER ELEMENT IN ROW 4 COLUMN 5 ? .75

ENTER ELEMENT IN ROW 5 COLUMN 1 ? 0
ENTER ELEMENT IN ROW 5 COLUMN 2 ? 0
ENTER ELEMENT IN ROW 5 COLUMN 3 ? 0
ENTER ELEMENT IN ROW 5 COLUMN 4 ? 0
ENTER ELEMENT IN ROW 5 COLUMN 5 ? 1

DO YOU WANT TO OBSERVE EACH
PERIOD UNDER ANALYSIS (Y/N)? Y

POPULATION PROPORTION
VECTOR AT PERIOD 2 IS:
                          .4600

```
                                    .3525
                                    .1020
                                    .0330
                                    .0525

POPULATION PROPORTION
VECTOR AT PERIOD   17 IS:
                                    .9058
                                    .0000
                                    .0000
                                    .0000
                                    .0946

EQUILIBRIUM REACHED AT PERIOD 17
VECTOR AT EQUILIBRIUM:
                                    .9058
                                    .0000
                                    .0000
                                    .0000
                                    .0946


DO YOU WANT TO RE-RUN THIS
PROGRAM WITH DIFFERENT DATA (Y/N) ?
READY
```

Practice Problems

1. A survey by Hanley, Ohio, city planners shows recent commuting trends. Citizens were polled to find out if they carpool, take the bus, or drive alone to and from work. Presently, 43% of commuters drive their cars alone, 30% carpool, and 27% take the bus to work. The city wants to know how these patterns will change over the coming months in order to increase or decrease their bus fleet. The survey shows that 65% of those who drive alone will continue to do so. Twenty percent of this group said they would carpool, and 15% would take the bus if gas prices continue to rise. Twenty-five percent of carpoolers say that they find driving alone is preferable, and that they will switch back to it. Fifty-five percent of carpoolers say that they will continue to carpool, and the remaining 20% will switch to the bus.

Twelve percent of bus riders will switch back to driving alone. Thirteen percent of bus riders say they will switch to carpooling, and 75% say they will continue to ride the bus. What will the commuting mix be six months from now? What will it look like at equilibrium?

Answer: In the sixth month, 33.5% will be driving alone, 26.66% will be carpooling, and 39.86% will be taking the bus. At equilibrium, 32.86% will be driving alone, 26.4% will be carpooling, and 40.83% will be riding the bus.

2. Rita's Rent-A-Car competes with two other rental agencies at Manteca Airport. In the past month, Rita's kept 85% of its customers from the previous month, lost 5% of its business to competitor A, and lost 10% to competitor B. Competitor A retained 90% of its customers while losing 10% to Competitor B. Competitor B retained 75% of its customers, while losing 15% to Competitor A, and 10% to Rita's. What are the equilibrium market shares, assuming no known proportion vector? How long, in months, does it take for a customer to return to Rita's to rent a car after having taken his/her business elsewhere?

Answer: Equilibrium shares: Rita's, 19.1%; Competitor A, 52.46%; Competitor B, 28.63%. On the average, it takes about 5.24 months for a patron of either competitor to switch to Rita's.

Program Listing

```
10 CLS
20 DIM V1(12),T(12,12),V2(12)
27 REM V1() ARRAY--POPULATION PROPORTION VECTOR
28 REM  T() ARRAY--TRANSITION PROBABILITIES MATRIX
29 REM V2() ARRAY--SCRATCH FOR VECTOR ARRAY
30 PU$=".####"
40 PRINT "MARKOV ANALYSIS"
50 PRINT
60 N=1
70 PRINT "HOW MANY STATES OF NATURE";
80 INPUT S
90 PRINT "IS THE POPULATION PROPORTION VECTOR KNOWN (Y/N)";
100 INPUT A$
110 IF A$="Y" THEN 160 ELSE IF A$<>"N" THEN 90
118 REM IF VECTOR IS UNKNOWN, ASSIGN EQUAL
119 REM  PROBABILITIES TO EACH STATE
120 FOR I=1 TO S
130 V1(I)=INT((1/S)*1E4+.5)/1E4
140 NEXT I
150 GOTO 210
159 REM LOOP TO ENTER POPULATION PROPORTIONS
160 PRINT
170 FOR I=1 TO S
180 PRINT "           ENTER VECTOR ELEMENT";I;
190 INPUT V1(I)
195 READ V1(I)
200 NEXT I
209 REM ENTER TRANSITION MATRIX (I BY J ARRAY)
210 PRINT
220 FOR I=1 ,TO S
230 K=0
240 FOR J=1 TO S
250 PRINT "ENTER ELEMENT IN ROW";I;"COLUMN";J;
260 INPUT T(I,J)
270 K=K+T(I,J)
280 NEXT J
290 IF K=1 THEN 330
300 PRINT "---PROBABILITIES DO NOT ADD UP TO 1.0---"
310 PRINT "        TRY ENTERING THE ROW AGAIN."
320 GOTO 230
330 PRINT
340 NEXT I
350 PRINT "DO YOU WANT TO OBSERVE EACH"
360 PRINT "PERIOD UNDER ANALYSIS (Y/N)";
370 INPUT A$
380 IF A$="Y" THEN 390 ELSE IF A$<>"N" THEN 350
389 REM LOOP TO MULTIPLY VECTOR (V1) BY TRANSITION MATRIX (T)
390 N=N+1
400 FOR I=1 TO S
410 V2(I)=0
420 FOR J=1 TO S
429 REM ADD MULTIPLIED COLUMNS TO V2 ARRAY
430 V2(I)=V2(I)+INT((V1(J)*T(J,I))*1E4+.5)/1E4
```

```
440 NEXT J
450 NEXT I
459 REM SKIP PRINTING VECTOR IF NOT REQUESTED
460 IF A$<>"Y" THEN 500
470 PRINT
480 PRINT "POPULATION PROPORTION "
490 PRINT "VECTOR AT PERIOD ";N;"IS:"
500 N1=0
510 FOR I=1 TO S
520 IF A$<>"Y" THEN 540
530 PRINT TAB(26) : PRINTUSING PU$; V2(I)
540 IF V2(I)<>V1(I) THEN 560
550 N1=N1+1
560 V1(I)=V2(I)
570 NEXT I
579 REM PRINT EQUILIBRIUM VECTOR VALUES
580 IF N1<>S THEN 390
590 PRINT
600 PRINT "EQUILIBRIUM REACHED AT PERIOD";N
610 PRINT "VECTOR AT EQUILIBRIUM:"
620 FOR I=1 TO S
630 PRINT TAB(26) : PRINTUSING PU$; INT((V1(I))*1E4+.5)/1E4
640 NEXT I
650 PRINT
659 REM PRINT TRANSITIONS NEEDED FOR EACH STATE TO BE REOCCUPIED
660 FOR I=1 TO S
670 IF T(I,I)=1 THEN 710
680 IF V1(I)<=0 THEN 710
690 PRINT "1ST PASSAGE--STATE ";I;":";
700 PRINT TAB(26) INT((1/V1(I))*1E4+.5)/1E4
710 NEXT I
770 END
```

Option

If you plan on entering large matrices, or if you want to run this program repeatedly with the same data, you should use this option. The program will read input from DATA statements, rather than asking you to enter the population proportion vector and the transition probabilities matrix. Make the following changes in the lines shown below. Also delete lines 720 through 760. If you plan to re-run the program without entering the population proportion vector, you must delete lines 180 through 189 if they contain DATA statements for a population proportion vector from a previous run.

```
116 REM IF VECTOR UNKNOWN, YOU MUST DELETE LINES 180-189,
117 REM  OR THE DATA WILL BE READ OUT OF SEQUENCE
 .
 .
159 REM LOOP TO READ POPULATION PROPORTIONS
 .
 .
179 REM PUT PROPORTION VECTOR ELEMENTS HERE
180 DATA 0,.6,.33,.07,0
190 PRINT "                    VECTOR ELEMENT";I;":";
```

```
195 READ V1(I)
200 PRINT V1(I)
205 NEXT I
209 REM READ TRANSITION MATRIX (I BY J ARRAY)
    .
    .
    .
249 REM PUT TRANSITION PROBABILITIES MATRIX HERE
250 DATA 1,0,0,0,0,.38,.45,.17,0,0,.65,.25,0,.1,0
253 DATA .25,0,0,0,.75,0,0,0,0,1
256 PRINT "        ELEMENT IN ROW";I;"COLUMN";J;
260 READ T(I,J)
265 PRINT T(I,J)
```

References

Cabot, A., Victor, and Harnett, Donald L. *An Introduction to Management Science.* Reading, Mass.: Addison-Wesley, 1977.

Levin, Richard I., and Kirkpatrick, Charles A. *Quantative Approaches to Management* (3rd ed.). New York: McGraw-Hill, 1975.

Nonlinear Break-Even Analysis

This program computes the break-even point of a product using a nonlinear method which more closely reflects actual production situations than a linear method. It incorporates a "learning curve" for both costs and prices. This curve means that each time production or sales double, cumulative average costs or revenue per unit will increase or decrease by the amount of the curves. Zero curve values means no change occurs. When you enter different curve values for costs and prices, the program indicates the point of maximum gross profit.

To use the program, enter the unit selling price, the selling price learning curve, the variable costs, the variable costs learning curve, and the fixed costs. Variable costs are those which can be directly ascribed to the production of each unit, such as raw material. Fixed costs, like rent and wages, generally do not vary with each unit produced.

Example

Acme Widget Supply is considering producing and marketing a new widget. New machines, employee training, and all other overhead costs associated with production of this widget total $10,000. Each unit produced requires $5.00 of raw materials, labor, machine depreciation, and so forth, but they will need proportionally more machines and personnel to produce more widgets, and will, therefore, use a 5% cost increase learning curve. The marketing department expects the selling price of $25.00 to decrease on a 5% curve. What is the break-even point on the new widget? What is the maximum gross profit margin that Acme may realize? What are total costs and total revenue at maximum gross profit?

Answer: Break-even will occur at 1,663 units. The maximum gross profit margin is 17.182%. Total costs and revenue at maximum gross profit are $74,134.00 and $89,514.00, respectively.

```
BREAKEVEN ANALYSIS

ENTER THE UNIT PRICE? 25
ENTER UNIT PRICE EROSION RATE
(NEGATIVE VALUE MEANS REVENUE DECREASES AS SALES INCREASE)
? -5

ENTER THE AMOUNT OF VARIABLE COSTS PER UNIT? 5
ENTER VARIABLE COSTS LEARNING RATE
(NEGATIVE VALUE MEANS COSTS DECREASE AS PRODUCTION DOUBLES)
? 5

ENTER THE TOTAL AMOUNT OF FIXED COSTS? 10000

BREAKEVEN POINT = 1663 UNITS
TOTAL REVENUE AT BREAKEVEN =          $24,015

MAXIMUM GROSS PROFIT MARGIN AT 6886 UNITS = 17.183 %

                         TOTAL REVENUE =        $89,515
                            TOTAL COSTS =        $74,134

                           TOTAL PROFIT =        $15,381

WOULD YOU LIKE TO RERUN THIS PROGRAM USING NEW DATA (Y/N) ?
READY
```

Practice Problems

1. The selling price is $30.00, and revenue will decrease by 2.5% each time production doubles. Variable costs are $1.20 per unit, but cumulative average costs will increase by 8% when production quantities double. Fixed costs are $180,000.00. What is the break-even point? What is the maximum gross profit margin?

Answer: Break even at 9,944 units, maximum gross profit margin of 71.186% occurs at 246,753 units.

2. With a unit price of $19.95, variable costs of $4.75, and fixed costs of $6,800, how many units must be sold to break even? (No price or cost changes will occur; use curve values of zero for both revenue and costs.)

Answer: Break even at 447 units.

Program Listing

```
10 CLS
20 PRINT "BREAKEVEN ANALYSIS"
29 REM -- THESE FUNCTIONS COMPUTE THE CURVATURE
30 PU$="$$#####,#####"
40 PRINT
50 PRINT "ENTER THE UNIT PRICE";
60 INPUT U
70 PRINT "ENTER UNIT PRICE EROSION RATE (%)"
80 PRINT "(NEGATIVE VALUE MEANS REVENUE DECREASES AS SALES
   INCREASE)"
90 INPUT L1
100 A1=-LOG(1+((L1)/100))/LOG(2)
110 B1=LOG(1+((L1)/100))/LOG(2)+1
120 PRINT
130 PRINT "ENTER THE AMOUNT OF VARIABLE COSTS PER UNIT";
140 INPUT V
150 PRINT "ENTER VARIABLE COSTS LEARNING RATE (%)"
160 PRINT "(NEGATIVE VALUE MEANS COSTS DECREASE AS PRODUCTION
   DOUBLES)"
170 INPUT L2
180 A2=-LOG(1+((L2)/100))/LOG(2)
190 B2=LOG(1+((L2)/100))/LOG(2)+1
200 PRINT
210 PRINT "ENTER THE TOTAL AMOUNT OF FIXED COSTS";
220 INPUT F
230 PRINT
239 REM INITIALIZE LAST GUESS, LOW GUESS, HIGH GUESS
240 C=0
250 L=1
260 H=1E4
269 REM CALCULATE POINT USING BINARY SEARCH
270 B=INT((L+H)/2)
279 REM IF NEW POINT = LAST GUESS, EXIT
280 IF B=C THEN 380
289 REM SET LAST GUESS TO NEW POINT
290 C=B
299 REM CALCULATE TOTAL REVENUE AND TOTAL COSTS AT QUANTITY B
300 T1=INT((U*B[B1)+.5)
310 T2=INT((V*B[B2+F)+.5)
```

```
319 REM BREAKEVEN POINT FOUND IF TOTAL REVENUE = TOTAL COSTS
320 IF T1=T2 THEN 380
329 REM ADJUST GUESS HIGH OR LOW POINTS, TRY AGAIN
330 IF T1>T2 THEN 360
340 L=B
350 GOTO 270
360 H=B
370 GOTO 270
379 REM BREAKEVEN POINT FOUND, OUTPUT RESULT
380 PRINT "BREAKEVEN POINT =";B;"UNITS"
390 PRINT "TOTAL REVENUE AT BREAKEVEN = ";
400 PRINTUSING PU$; T1
409 REM USE THIS SECTION IF FIGURES ARE LINEAR
410 IF L1<>L2 THEN 450
420 PRINT "COSTS AND REVENUE ARE LINEAR."
430 PRINT "NO MAXIMUM GROSS PROFIT MARGIN POSSIBLE."
440 GOTO 600
448 REM OUTPUT MAXIMUM GROSS PROFIT MARGIN DATA FOR NON-LINEAR
    VALUES
449 REM (SKIP THIS SECTION IF FIGURES ARE LINEAR)
450 B=INT(EXP(LOG((F*(A1-1))/(V*(A2-A1)))/(1-A2))+.5)
460 T1=INT((U*B[B1)+.5)
470 T2=INT((V*B[B2+F)+.5)
480 PRINT
490 PRINT "MAXIMUM GROSS PROFIT MARGIN AT";
500 PRINT B;"UNITS =";: PRINTUSING "###.###"; (T1-T2)/T1*100 ;
510 PRINT " %"
520 PRINT
530 PRINT "                                 TOTAL REVENUE = ";
540 PRINTUSING PU$; T1
550 PRINT "                                  TOTAL COSTS = ";
560 PRINTUSING PU$; T2
570 PRINT
580 PRINT "                                 TOTAL PROFIT = ";
590 PRINTUSING PU$; T1-T2
600 PRINT
610 PRINT "WOULD YOU LIKE TO RERUN THIS PROGRAM USING NEW DATA (
Y/N) ?"
620 Z$=INKEY$ : IF Z$="" THEN 620
630 IF Z$="Y" THEN 40
640 IF Z$<>"N" THEN 600
650 END
```

References

Solomon and Pringle. *An Introduction to Financial Management.* Santa Monica, Calif.: Goodyear
  Publishing Company, 1977.

Texas Instruments. *Programmable 58/59 Calculator Business Decisions Library* (manual), Part number
  1014984-9.

Payoff Matrix Analysis

This program evaluates a set of alternatives, each of which has some measurable benefit, or payoff, subject to varying states of nature. Under different conditions, payoff amounts could be large or they could become losses. To analyze payoffs in conditions of uncertainty, this program employs three criteria: "maximax" (find the alternative with the highest possible payoff), "maximin" (the best alternative under the worst case), and "minimax regret" (the alternative which minimizes opportunity cost).

   To use this program, you should carefully consider your alternatives. They must relate to one another (for example, you have $20,000 and you want to know which of four types of investments is optimal to make given varying states of the economy). You must be able to "guesstimate" what the payoffs will be (positive, negative, or zero) for each alternative under each state of nature, as well as the probability of each state of nature's occurrence.

   The computer will ask you how many states of nature to consider and how many alternatives exist. Then you will enter the payoff matrix row by row, starting with action 1 under state 1, action 2 under state 2, and so on. After you enter the matrix, you will input the probabilities of each state of nature. These probabilities are mutually exclusive, and they must add up to 1.0. The computer will ask you to re-enter them if they do not add up to 1.0.

   The program shows you what choices are best under the maximax and maximin rules. The computer will optionally display the regret matrix. The optimal maximin regret choice displays, followed by the expected payoff values of each alternative.

Program Notes

The program allows for 10 states of nature and 10 alternatives. You can change this by modifying line 20 of this program as follows:

```
20 DIM S(N,A), M(A), R(N), X(A)
```

   Replace the expression N with the maximum states of nature, and A with the maximum number of alternatives.

Example

Fred wants to invest capital in the market. He sees his choices as stocks, Baa bonds or options. These three choices will pay off relative to how the economy behaves:

	State of Economy		
Investment	Recession	Stable	Inflation
Stocks	−20	65	200
Baa Bonds	0	80	80
Options	−300	0	300
Probability	0.3	0.2	0.5

How does Fred run the program?
Answer:

```
PAYOFF MATRIX ANALYSIS


HOW MANY STATES OF NATURE? 3
HOW MANY POSSIBLE ACTIONS? 3
```

```
PAYOFF OF ACTION 1 IN STATE 1 ? -20
PAYOFF OF ACTION 1 IN STATE 2 ? 65
PAYOFF OF ACTION 1 IN STATE 3 ? 200

PAYOFF OF ACTION 2 IN STATE 1 ? 0
PAYOFF OF ACTION 2 IN STATE 2 ? 80
PAYOFF OF ACTION 2 IN STATE 3 ? 80

PAYOFF OF ACTION 3 IN STATE 1 ? -300
PAYOFF OF ACTION 3 IN STATE 2 ? 0
PAYOFF OF ACTION 3 IN STATE 3 ? 300

ENTER PROBABILITY FOR STATE 1 ? .3
ENTER PROBABILITY FOR STATE 2 ? .2
ENTER PROBABILITY FOR STATE 3 ? .5

MAXIMAX PAYOFF OF     300   FROM ACTION    3

MAXIMIN PAYOFF OF       0   FROM ACTION    2

DO YOU WANT TO SEE THE REGRET TABLE (Y/N)? Y

  STATE           1       2       3

ACTION  1       20      15     100   MAX REGRET=    100
ACTION  2        0       0     220   MAX REGRET=    220
ACTION  3      300      80       0   MAX REGRET=    300

MINIMAX REGRET PAYOFF OF     100   FROM ACTION   1

EXPECTED VALUES ARE:
FOR ACTION  1:      107.00
FOR ACTION  2:       56.00
FOR ACTION  3:       60.00

DO YOU WANT TO RE-RUN THIS PROGRAM
AGAIN WITH DIFFERENT DATA (Y/N) ?
READY
```

Practice Problems

1. A business is considering a service agreement for its computer system. The service agreement costs $100 per month, and covers all repairs. Because the system is five years old, it may be necessary to repair it more often than in the past. Downtime for this system can be for minor or major repairs; the minor repairs averaging $140, and major repairs averaging $900. The probability of downtime requiring minor repair is 0.07; for major repairs, 0.08. What are the payoffs?

Answer: Maximax payoff (cost, in this problem): $0. Maximin payoff: $100. Minimax Regret: $100. Expected value (cost) of service agreement: $100. Expected cost of no service agreement: $81.80.

2. A market researcher is interested in gathering responses to an opinion poll in one day. The researcher is paid for each completed survey. The number of responses depends on the weather, as shown below:

	Prevailing Weather		
Location	Sunny	Cloudy	Rainy
Beach	150	30	0
Door-to-Door	40	70	90
Flea Market	80	50	5
Probability of weather:	0.5	0.3	0.2

What are the optimal alternatives under each criterion?

Answer: Under Maximax, option 1 with a payoff of 150; under maximin, option 2 with a payoff of 40; under minimax regret, option 3 with a maximum payoff of 85. Expected values: alternative 1, 84; alternative 2, 59; alternative 3, 56.

Program Listing

```
10 CLS
20 DIM S(10,10),M(10),R(10),X(10)
30 PRINT "PAYOFF MATRIX ANALYSIS"
40 PRINT
50 PRINT "HOW MANY STATES OF NATURE";
60 INPUT N
70 PRINT "HOW MANY POSSIBLE ACTIONS";
80 INPUT A
90 PRINT
100 FOR Q=1 TO A
110 M(Q)=-9E9
120 PRINT
130 FOR P=1 TO N
140 PRINT "PAYOFF OF ACTION";Q;"IN STATE";P;
150 INPUT S(Q,P)
160 NEXT P
170 NEXT Q
179 REM ENTER POSSIBILITIES FOR EACH STATE OF NATURE
180 A1=0
190 PRINT
200 FOR Q=1 TO N
210 PRINT "ENTER PROBABILITY FOR STATE";Q;
220 INPUT P1(Q)
230 A1=A1+P1(Q)
240 R(Q)=0
250 NEXT Q
260 IF A1=1 THEN 320
270 PRINT
280 PRINT "-----PROBABILITIES DO NOT ADD TO 1.0----"
290 PRINT "     CHECK YOUR ENTRIES AND RE-TRY."
300 PRINT
310 GOTO 180
319 REM CALCULATE MAXIMAX AND MAXIMIN VALUES
320 A1=-9E9
330 FOR Q=1 TO A
340 A3=0
349 REM REPLACE A3 WITH THE HIGHEST PAYOFF
```

```
350 FOR P=1 TO N
360 IF A1=-9E9 THEN 380
370 IF S(Q,P)<=A1 THEN 400
380 A1=S(Q,P)
390 A2=Q
399 REM PUT MINIMUM PAYOFF OF EACH ACTION IN M()
400 IF M(Q)=-9E9 THEN 420
410 IF S(Q,P)>=M(Q) THEN 430
420 M(Q)=S(Q,P)
429 REM SAVE HIGHEST PAYOFF FOR REGRET TABLE
430 IF S(Q,P)<=R(P) THEN 450
440 R(P)=S(Q,P)
450 NEXT P
460 NEXT Q
470 PRINT
480 PV$="###" : PU$="##,####"
490 PRINT "MAXIMAX PAYOFF OF";: PRINTUSING PU$; A1;
500 PRINT "  FROM ACTION ";: PRINTUSING PV$; A2
510 PRINT
520 A1=-9E9
530 FOR Q=1 TO A
540 IF M(Q)<A1 THEN 570
550 A1=M(Q)
560 A2=Q
570 NEXT Q
580 PRINT "MAXIMIN PAYOFF OF";: PRINTUSING PU$; A1;
590 PRINT "  FROM ACTION ";: PRINTUSING PV$; A2
600 PRINT
610 PRINT "DO YOU WANT TO SEE THE REGRET TABLE (Y/N)";
620 INPUT A$
630 IF A$="N" THEN 830
640 IF A$<>"Y" THEN 610
650 PRINT
660 PRINT " STATE"; TAB(8);
670 A1=0
679 REM PRINT HEADINGS FOR TABLE
680 FOR P=1 TO N
690 PRINTUSING PU$;   P,
700 NEXT P
710 PRINT
720 PRINT
730 FOR Q=1 TO A
740 PRINT "ACTION";: PRINTUSING PV$; Q;
749 REM PRINT REGRET VALUES
750 A1=0
760 FOR P=1 TO N
770 PRINTUSING PU$; R(P)-S(Q,P),
780 IF R(P)-S(Q,P)<=A1 THEN 800
790 A1=R(P)-S(Q,P)
800 NEXT P
810 PRINT "  MAX REGRET=";: PRINTUSING PU$; A1
820 NEXT Q
830 FOR Q=1 TO A
840 A1=0
850 FOR P=1 TO N
```

```
860 IF R(P)-S(Q,P)<=A1 THEN 890
870 A1=R(P)-S(Q,P)
880 X(Q)=R(P)-S(Q,P)
890 NEXT P
900 NEXT Q
910 A1=0
920 FOR P=1 TO A
930 IF P=1 THEN 950
940 IF X(P)>A1 THEN 970
950 A1=X(P)
960 A2=P
970 NEXT P
980 PRINT
990 PRINT "MINIMAX REGRET PAYOFF OF";: PRINTUSING PU$; A1;
1000 PRINT"  FROM ACTION";: PRINTUSING PV$; A2
1010 PRINT
1020 PRINT "EXPECTED VALUES ARE:"
1030 FOR P=1 TO A
1040 A1=0
1050 FOR Q=1 TO N
1060 A1=A1+(S(P,Q)*P1(Q))
1070 NEXT Q
1080 PRINT "FOR ACTION";: PRINTUSING PV$; P;: PRINT ":";
1090 PRINTUSING PU$+".##"; A1
1100 NEXT P
1110 PRINT
1120 PRINT "DO YOU WANT TO RE-RUN THIS PROGRAM"
1130 PRINT "AGAIN WITH DIFFERENT DATA (Y/N) ?"
1140 A$=INKEY$ : IF A$="" THEN 1140
1150 IF A$="Y" THEN 40
1160 IF A$<>"N" THEN 1110
1170 END
```

Reference

Cabot, A. Victor, and Harnett, Donald L. *An Introduction to Management Science.* Reading, Mass.: Addison-Wesley, 1977.

Bayesian Decision Analysis

This program revises probabilities (given multiple states of nature) according to Bayes's Theorem for conditional events, and further evaluates possible actions by use of a payoff matrix. This technique applies to sampling for quality based on subjective probabilities you enter.

To use this program, first enter how many possible states of nature there are; for example, an outgoing lot of products can have three possible outcomes: 99% good, 90% good, or 85% good. Then enter the number of conditional actions (for example, send out the lot, send out the lot and retool machines to correct defects, or rework the lot and retool the machines). The next set of entries is the payoff matrix. You enter payoffs (or costs as negative numbers) for each action, within each state of nature. Next, enter two probabilities for each state of nature; first, the "prior" probability that each state of nature occurs, and then the "conditional" probability based on the occurrence of that state.

To illustrate, consider the three possibilities above: 99%, 90%, and 85% good. These are conditional probabilities; in other words, "99% good" is a possible outcome of a production run. Therefore, if "99% good" is the present state of nature, then the probability of 99% is conditional based on being in that state of nature. The "prior" probability is the likelihood of that state of nature's occurrence in the first place. Prior probabilities are often "guesstimates" made by production personnel, based on experience.

The last two entries are the size of the sample in question and the actual number of "successes" in the sample taken. In the example above, you may have looked at 50 pieces out of an outgoing lot of 1000, and you find that 5 of them are defective. Enter 50 as the sample size, and 5 as the actual number of successes. The program then prints the expected values of each action, based on revised probabilities. You choose the optimal action from these values, which is usually that action which minimizes costs or maximizes payoff.

After the expected values, the prior probabilities, likelihoods, joint, and posterior probabilities print for each action. A final figure, the marginal probability, prints. This is the "unconditional" or expected success rate. You can go back and re-enter a new sample size (or enter zero to end the program).

Example

The quality control department at Fergis Bolt International estimates that bolts produced fall into three categories; 99% acceptable, 90% acceptable, and 80% acceptable. These three levels of quality occur 70, 20, and 10% of the time, respectively. Roland Fergis II wants to impress his father with a comprehensive study which documents how much the company may lose by not making the right quality control decision. He puts together a payoff matrix which looks like this:

Payoffs / Actions	If 99% good	If 90% good	If 80% good
Send lot out	−1200	−1800	−2400
Retool machines without rework	−1400	−1600	−2200
Retool machines and rework	−2000	−2000	−2000

The cost of producing the lot itself is $1,200. If the lot is sent out and the quality is less than 99%, Fergis will incur costs of returned merchandise. If they decide to retool the machines only, they will incur downtime, but the rate of returned merchandise will be lower for future lots. If the machines are retooled and the bolts are reworked, the lot will be 99% good no matter what; therefore, the cost remains constant. How would Roland Jr. run this program? What will be the optimal strategy based payoffs if 46 of 50 bolts sampled are acceptable?

Answer: The optimal strategy is to retool the machines, at an expected cost of $1,616.75. This sample has a 94.8% probability of being 90% free of defects.

```
BAYESIAN DECISION ANALYSIS

    HOW MANY STATES OF NATURE? 3
HOW MANY CONDITIONAL ACTIONS? 3

  ENTER PAYOFFS FOR:
ACTION 1 UNDER STATE 1 ? -1200
ACTION 1 UNDER STATE 2 ? -1800
ACTION 1 UNDER STATE 3 ? -2400
ACTION 2 UNDER STATE 1 ? -1400
ACTION 2 UNDER STATE 2 ? -1600
ACTION 2 UNDER STATE 3 ? -2200
ACTION 3 UNDER STATE 1 ? -2000
ACTION 3 UNDER STATE 2 ? -2000
ACTION 3 UNDER STATE 3 ? -2000


ENTER PRIOR AND CONDITIONAL POSSIBILITIES:
FOR STATE 1 ? .7,.99
FOR STATE 2 ? .2,.9
FOR STATE 3 ? .1,.8


ENTER SAMPLE SIZE (0 TO END)? 50

ENTER ACTUAL NUMBER OF SUCCESSES? 46

GIVEN 46 SUCCESSES IN A SAMPLE OF 50 ,
THE EXPECTED VALUES ARE:
ACTION 1 : -1809.42
ACTION 2 : -1616.75
ACTION 3 : -2000

PROBABILITY REVISIONS:
STATE   PRIOR   LIKELIHOOD   JOINT    POSTERIOR
  1      .7       .001       .0007     .018
  2      .2       .181       .0362     .948
  3      .1       .013       .0013     .034
ENTER SAMPLE SIZE (0 TO END)? 0
READY
```

Practice Problems

1. In the example above, is the minimum number of acceptable bolts allowable in order to send the lot out without retooling machines? At this point, what is the probability that this lot is actually 99% free of defects? (Hint: Find the answer by trial-and-error. Enter a successively smaller number of successes until you get the answer.)

Answer: The minimum is 48 out of 50, with an expected cost of $1,337.59. At this rate, it is 77.2% likely that the bolts are 99% free of defects.

2. In the example above, does action 3 — rework the lot and retool the machines — become optimal?
   Answer: At 41 acceptable items from a sample of 50, the cost of $2,000 is less than the other two alternatives (send out lot: $2,203.96, send out and retool: $2,003.96). At this point, it is 67.3% probable that the lot is 80% good.

Program Listing

```
10 CLS
20 PRINT "BAYESIAN DECISION ANALYSIS"
30 PRINT
40 DIM P1(4),P2(4),P3(4),P5(4),A(4,4),M(3)
50 PRINT "   HOW MANY STATES OF NATURE";
60 INPUT N1
70 PRINT "HOW MANY CONDITIONAL ACTIONS";
80 INPUT A1
90 PRINT
100 PRINT " ENTER PAYOFFS FOR:"
109 REM ENTER PAYOFF MATRIX
110 FOR I=1 TO A1
120 FOR J=1 TO N1
130 PRINT "ACTION";I;"UNDER STATE";J;
140 INPUT A(I,J)
150 NEXT J
160 NEXT I
170 PRINT
180 X0=0
190 PRINT "ENTER PRIOR AND CONDITIONAL POSSIBILITIES:"
200 FOR I=1 TO N1
210 PRINT "FOR STATE";I;
220 INPUT P1(I),P2(I)
230 X0=X0+P1(I)
240 P3(I)=0
250 NEXT I
260 IF X0=1 THEN 290
270 PRINT "PRIOR PROBABILITIES DO NOT EQUAL 1.0."
280 GOTO 170
290 PRINT
300 PRINT "ENTER SAMPLE SIZE (0 TO END)";
310 INPUT S
320 IF S=0 THEN END
330 PRINT
340 PRINT "ENTER ACTUAL NUMBER OF SUCCESSES";
350 INPUT I1
359 REM CALCULATE EXPECTED COST FOR SAMPLE SIZE
360 M(1)=S
370 M(2)=I1
380 M(3)=S-I1
390 FOR J=1 TO 3
400 IF M(J)=0 THEN 460
410 Z=0
420 FOR K=1 TO M(J)
430 Z=Z+LOG(K)
440 NEXT K
```

```
450 M(J)=Z
460 NEXT J
470 P4 =0
480 FOR H=1 TO N1
489 REM STORE LIKELIHOOD IN P5()
490 P5(H)=INT(EXP(M(1)-M(2)-M(3)+I1*LOG(P2(H))+(S-I1)*LOG(1-P2(H)))
    *1E3+.5)/1E3
499 REM STORE JOINT PROBABILITY IN P3()
500 P3(H)=P5(H)*P1(H)
509 REM SUM JOINT POSSIBILITIES IN P3()
510 P4=P4+P3(H)
520 NEXT H
529 REM CALCULATE EXPECTED MONETARY VALUES
530 FOR I=1 TO A1
540 E(I)=0
550 FOR J=1 TO N1
560 E(I)=E(I)+(A(I,J)*(P3(J)/P4))
570 NEXT J
580 NEXT I
590 PRINT
600 PRINT "GIVEN";I1;"SUCCESSES IN A SAMPLE OF";S;","
610 PRINT "THE EXPECTED VALUES ARE:"
620 FOR I=1 TO A1
630 PRINT "ACTION";I;": ";E(I)
640 NEXT I
650 PRINT
660 PRINT "PROBABILITY REVISIONS:"
670 PRINT "STATE   PRIOR   LIKELIHOOD  JOINT   POSTERIOR"
680 FOR I=1 TO N1
690 PU$=".###" : PV$=".####"
700 PRINTUSING "###"; I;: PRINTTAB(8);P1(I);TAB(17)
710 PRINTUSING PU$; P5(I);: PRINTTAB(27): PRINTUSING PV$; P3(I);
720 PRINTTAB(38): PRINTUSING PU$; P3(I)/P4
730 NEXT I
740 GOTO 300
750 END
```

References

Cabot and Harnett. *An Introduction to Management Science.* Reading, Mass.: Addison-Wesley, 1977.

Economic Order Quantity

The purpose of this program is to determine the economic order quantity of an item. You must enter the number of available price breaks, minimum and maximum quantities and unit price for each level, the inventory holding cost as a percentage of each unit's cost, cost of placing an order (in dollars), and the annual demand quantity. The program will compute the EOQ of each price break and indicate if the quantity is within the minimum and maximum quantities for that level.

Program Notes

It may be more convenient for you to enter holding costs as a fixed dollar amount per unit. Make these changes:

```
130 PRINT
140 PRINT "   ENTER THE UNIT HOLDING COST ($)";
150 INPUT H
   .
   .
180 GOTO 140
190 DELETE 190
200 PRINT "    ENTER THE COST OF PLACING AN ORDER ($)";
   .
   .
270 FOR I=1 TO B
280 E=INT(SQR((2*D*S)/(H)))
290 PRINT E TAB(13) INT(D/E+.9) TAB(23) Q(1,I) ;"-"; Q(2,I) TAB(
40) U(I);
```

Your price breaks may be computed as a percentage discount from a fixed price. Make these changes:

```
60 INPUT B
62 PRINT "ENTER THE BASE UNIT PRICE";
64 INPUT U1
70 PRINT
80 PRINT "ENTER MINIMUM QUANTITY, MAXIMUM QUANTITY, DISCOUNT"
90 FOR I=1 TO B
100 PRINT "AT PRICE BREAK";I;
110 INPUT Q(1,I),Q(2,I),D1
112 U(I)=U1-INT(U1*D1+.5)/100
120 NEXT I
```

Example

Joe Blow, purchasing agent for a small manufacturer, needs to order motor armatures from a machine shop. The machine shop offers three price breaks to Joe's company: 0 to 499 units, $5.00 per unit; 500 to 999, $4.50 per unit; 1000 and up, $3.90 per unit. Joe's company requires 10,000 units each year. $20.00 in clerks' time and forms is needed to place an order. About 20% of each unit's cost is spent on warehousing, shipping, breakage, and so forth. How many orders of how many units should be placed this year in order to minimize costs?

Answer: Joe should place 15 orders of 666 units each.

```
ECONOMIC ORDER QUANTITY

ENTER THE NUMBER OF AVAILABLE PRICE BREAKS? 3

ENTER MINIMUM QUANTITY, MAXIMUM QUANTITY, PRICE
AT PRICE BREAK 1 ? 0,499,5
AT PRICE BREAK 2 ? 500,999,4.5
AT PRICE BREAK 3 ? 1000,99999,3.9

   ENTER THE UNIT HOLDING COST (% PER UNIT)? 20
     ENTER THE COST OF PLACING AN ORDER ($)? 20
ENTER THE DEMAND QUANTITY PER YEAR (0=END)? 10000

 EOQ      # OF ORDERS    QUANTITIES        UNIT PRICE
 632         16          0 - 499           5 -- NOT POSSIBLE
 666         15          500 - 999         4.5
 716         14          1000 - 99999      3.9 -- NOT POSSIBLE

ENTER THE DEMAND QUANTITY PER YEAR (0=END)? 0

DO YOU WANT TO RERUN THIS PROGRAM WITH NEW DATA (Y/N)
READY
```

Practice Problems

1. Three price breaks: $2.50 per unit for 0-999 units; $2.25 each for 1,000-1,999 units; 2,000-9,999 units cost $2.00 each. Cost of placing an order is $50.00, and holding costs represent 10% of an item's cost. What is the EOQ if annual demand is 5,065 units?
   Answer: EOQ is four orders of 1,500 units each.

2. Four price breaks: $89.00 each for 0-9 units; $82.50 per unit for 10 to 19 units; 20 to 29 units are $78.00 each; 30 and up are $75.00 apiece. Cost of placing an order is $75.00. Holding costs are 15%. What is the EOQ if annual use is 50 units?
   Answer: The EOQ is two orders of 25 units each.

Program Listing

```
10 CLS
20 PRINT "ECONOMIC ORDER QUANTITY"
28 REM -- CHANGE SIZE OF ARRAYS Q(2,N) AND U(N) AS NECESSARY
29 REM -- WHERE N = MAXIMUM NUMBER OF PRICE BREAKS YOU WILL USE
30 DIM Q(2,10),U(10)
40 PRINT
50 PRINT "ENTER THE NUMBER OF AVAILABLE PRICE BREAKS";
60 INPUT B
70 PRINT
80 PRINT "ENTER MINIMUM QUANTITY, MAXIMUM QUANTITY, PRICE"
90 FOR I=1 TO B
100 PRINT "AT PRICE BREAK";I;
110 INPUT Q(1,I),Q(2,I),U(I)
120 NEXT I
130 PRINT
140 PRINT "  ENTER THE UNIT HOLDING COST (% PER UNIT)";
```

```
150 INPUT H
160 IF H>0 THEN 190
170 PRINT "HOLDING COST MUST BE GREATER THAN ZERO."
180 GOTO 140
190 H=H/100
200 PRINT "    ENTER THE COST OF PLACING AN ORDER ($)";
210 INPUT S
220 PRINT "ENTER THE DEMAND QUANTITY PER YEAR (0=END)";
230 INPUT D
240 IF D=0 THEN 380
250 PRINT
259 REM -- OUTPUT THE RESULTS
260 PRINT " EOQ" TAB(9) "# OF ORDERS" TAB(24) "QUANTITIES"
    TAB(41) "UNIT PRICE"
269 REM -- CALCULATE EUQ BY FORMULA FOR EACH PRICE BREAK
270 FOR I=1 TO B
280 E=INT(SQR((2*D*S)/(U(I)*H)))
290 PRINT E TAB(13) INT(D/E+.9) TAB(23) Q(1,I) ;"-"; Q(2,I)
    TAB(40) U(I);
299 REM -- SEE IF EOQ FALLS WITHIN ORDER QUANTITY FOR THIS PRICE
300 IF Q(1,I)>E THEN 340
310 IF Q(2,I)<E THEN 340
320 PRINT
330 GOTO 350
339 REM -- PRICE BREAK IS NOT AVAILABLE AT THIS EOQ
340 PRINT "-- NOT POSSIBLE"
350 NEXT I
360 PRINT
370 GOTO 220
379 REM -- RESTART OR END PROGRAM?
380 PRINT
390 PRINT "DO YOU WANT TO RERUN THIS PROGRAM WITH NEW DATA (Y/N)
400 Z$=INKEY$ : IF Z$="" THEN 400
410 IF Z$="Y" THEN 40
420 IF Z$<>"N" THEN 390
430 END
```

References

Chase and Aquilano. *Production and Operations Management.* Homewood, Ill.: Richard D. Irwin, Inc., 1977.

McLaughlin and Pickhardt. *Quantitative Techniques for Management Decisions.* New York: McGraw-Hill, 1975.

Economic Production Quantity

It is often useful to know the optimal quantity of an item to produce in order to minimize expenses. This program computes that quantity for a given item, and incorporates simultaneous sales calculations (where units are being sold while more are being produced).

To use the program, enter the rate of production, the sales or use rate (the average number of units removed from inventory each day), the total number of units sold in a year, the holding cost (in dollars per unit), and the setup cost. The program will output the optimal number of setups per year, and the optimum quantity to produce in each lot. The optimum quantity is that which minimizes setup and carrying costs.

Example

Waldo's Paint Factory produces several different paint colors using a single mixing and filling machine. The machine will produce 300 gallons each day, and currently Waldo ships 125 gallons of each color every day, and 35,000 gallons per year. Holding costs are $0.15 per gallon. For each lot produced, the machine must be completely cleaned, at a cost of $150. How many lots of each color per year should Waldo produce? How many gallons in each lot?

Answer: Each year, Waldo should run three lots of 11,666 gallons each.

```
ECONOMIC PRODUCTION QUANTITY

ENTER THE RATE OF PRODUCTION (UNITS/DAY)? 300
  ENTER THE SALES OR USE RATE (UNITS/DAY)? 125
               ENTER ANNUAL SALES OR USE? 35000
ENTER THE UNIT HOLDING COST ($ PER UNIT)? .15
               ENTER THE SETUP COST ($)? 150

OPTIMAL NUMBER OF SETUPS = 3 PER YEAR
                   EPQ = 11666 UNITS

DO YOU WANT TO RERUN THIS PROGRAM WITH NEW DATA (Y/N)
READY
```

Practice Problems

1. Daily production of 45 units, daily sales of 20 units. Annual sales total 4,000 units. Holding costs are $0.67 per unit. Setup costs are $25.00. What is the EPQ?
Answer: Five lots of 800 unit each.

2. 50 units per day are produced, 35 are sold. Annually, 6,500 units are sold. Holding costs are $0.45 per unit. Setup costs are $60.00 per lot. How many lots are optimum? What size lots?
Answer: Three lots of 2,166 units each.

Program Listing

```
10 CLS
20 PRINT "ECONOMIC PRODUCTION QUANTITY"
```

```
30 PRINT
40 PRINT "ENTER THE RATE OF PRODUCTION (UNITS/DAY)";
50 INPUT R
60 IF R>0 THEN 110
70 PRINT
80 PRINT "PRODUCTION RATE MUST BE GREATER THAN ZERO."
90 PRINT
100 GOTO 40
110 PRINT " ENTER THE SALES OR USE RATE (UNITS/DAY)";
120 INPUT U
130 IF U>=0 THEN 180
140 PRINT
150 PRINT "SALES (USE) RATE MUST BE NON-ZERO."
160 PRINT
170 GOTO 110
180 PRINT "                  ENTER ANNUAL SALES OR USE";
190 INPUT H
200 IF H>=U THEN 250
210 PRINT
220 PRINT "ANNUAL RATE MUST BE HIGHER THAN DAILY RATE"
230 PRINT
240 GOTO 180
250 PRINT "ENTER THE UNIT HOLDING COST ($ PER UNIT)";
260 INPUT J
270 IF J>0 THEN 320
280 PRINT
290 PRINT "HOLDING COST MUST BE GREATER THAN ZERO."
300 PRINT
310 GOTO 250
320 PRINT "                     ENTER THE SETUP COST ($)";
330 INPUT S
340 PRINT
350 IF S>0 THEN 390
360 PRINT "SETUP COST MUST BE GREATER THAN ZERO."
370 PRINT
380 GOTO 320
389 REM OUTPUT THE RESULTS
390 N=INT(SQR(((J*H)/(2*S))*(1-(U/R)))+.5)
400 PRINT "OPTIMAL NUMBER OF SETUPS =";N;"PER YEAR"
410 PRINT "                     EPQ =";INT(H/N);"UNITS"
419 REM RESTART OR END PROGRAM?
420 PRINT
430 PRINT "DO YOU WANT TO RERUN THIS PROGRAM WITH NEW DATA (Y/N)
440 Z$=INKEY$ : IF Z$="" THEN 440
450 IF Z$="Y" THEN 30
460 IF Z$<>"N" THEN 430
470 END
```

Reference

McLaughlin and Pickhardt. *Quantitative Techniques for Management Decisions.* New York: McGraw-Hill, 1975.

Statistical Estimation Theory

Statistical estimation theory is the science of determining unbiased estimates for various statistics from sample figures, establishing confidence interval estimates for those statistics, and determining the number of samples that must be taken to reduce the probability of error in these estimates to stated maxima. This program performs these calculations.

At the start of the program you must enter the size of the sample, the mean of the sample, and the sample variance. The program then prints the unbiased estimate of the population variance and, for both the mean and the standard deviation, each of seven different confidence levels, the confidence interval estimate, and the maximum and minimum values produced thereby. You may then have the program calculate how large a sample you would have to take to reduce the error of your estimate to a given maximum. You enter the desired confidence level, the maximum desired error, and whether you are testing the mean or the standard deviation. The program then calculates the sample size needed.

Example

A government researcher did a study to determine how long people had to wait in line at the post office. He took 100 samples; the mean of the sample was 15 minutes, and the sample variance was 2.02. At each of the seven confidence levels, what is the maximum and mimimum for the mean and standard deviation? How many samples would have to be taken to be 99% confident that the error in the mean was no greater than 0.2?

Answer:

```
STATISTICAL ESTIMATION THEORY

ENTER NUMBER OF SAMPLES TAKEN
? 100
ENTER MEAN OF SAMPLE
? 15
ENTER SAMPLE VARIANCE
? 2.02

UNBIASED ESTIMATE OF SIGMA SQUARED
POPULATION VARIANCE = 2.04040404040404
CONFIDENCE INTERVAL ESTIMATES FOR MEAN:
```

CONFIDENCE LEVEL	PLUS OR MINUS	MAXIMUM	MINIMUM
50	0.0963459973	15.0963459973	14.9036540027
60	0.1202194642	15.1202194642	14.8797805358
70	0.1480469482	15.1480469482	14.8519530518
80	0.1830602661	15.1830602661	14.8169397339
90	0.2349553155	15.2349553155	14.7650446845
95	0.2799665339	15.2799665339	14.7200334661
99	0.3679381272	15.3679381272	14.6320618728

```
CONFIDENCE INTERVAL ESTIMATES
FOR STANDARD DEVIATION:

    50      0.0681269146      1.4965538955      1.3603000664
    60      0.0850080065      1.5134349874      1.3434189745
    70      0.1046850110      1.5331119920      1.3237419700
    80      0.1294431679      1.5578701489      1.2989838131
    90      0.1661385128      1.5945654937      1.2622884682
    95      0.1979662535      1.6263932345      1.2304607274
    99      0.2601715696      1.6885985506      1.1682554113

DO YOU WANT A CALCULATION OF HOW LARGE
A SAMPLE YOU MUST TAKE TO REDUCE
THE ERROR OF THE ESTIMATE TO A
MAXIMUM QUANTITY (Y/N)
? Y
ENTER YOUR CHOSEN CONFIDENCE LEVEL
(FROM ABOVE CHOICES ONLY) : ENTER A
1 FOR 50, 2 FOR 60, 3 FOR 70, 4 FOR 80
5 FOR 90, 6 FOR 95, AND 7 FOR 99
? 7
ENTER MAXIMUM DESIRED ERROR OF ESTIMATE
? .2
ARE YOU TESTING THE MEAN (M) OR
    THE STANDARD DEVIATION (S)
? M

AT THE 99 PERCENT CONFIDENCE LEVEL
IT WOULD BE NECESSARY TO TAKE 339
SAMPLES TO BE SURE THAT YOUR ESTIMATE
OF THE ERROR IN THE MEAN
DID NOT EXCEED .2

DO YOU HAVE
        NO MORE CALCULATIONS (0),
MORE WITH THE SAME SAMPLES (1), OR
            BRAND-NEW SAMPLING (2)
? 0
READY
```

Practice Problems

1. Using the data from the above example, how many samples would have to be taken to reduce the error in the standard deviation to 0.075 at the 99% confidence level?
   Answer: 1,204

2. If all the data is the same as in the above example, how many samples must be taken to reduce the error in the mean to 0.1 at the 95% confidence level?
   Answer: 784

Program Listing

```
10 CLS
20 PRINT "STATISTICAL ESTIMATION THEORY"
```

```
30 PU$="######.##########" : PV$="######"
40 DEFDBL A-Z : DEFINT I
50 DIM C(7),F(7)
59 REM --- READ CONFIDENCE LEVELS AND COEFFICIENTS
60 FOR I=1 TO 7
70 READ C(I),F(I)
80 NEXT I
90 PRINT
100 PRINT "ENTER NUMBER OF SAMPLES TAKEN"
110 INPUT N
120 PRINT "ENTER MEAN OF SAMPLE"
130 INPUT X
140 PRINT "ENTER SAMPLE VARIANCE"
150 INPUT S2
160 S1=S2*N/(N-1)
170 PRINT
180 PRINT "UNBIASED ESTIMATE OF SIGMA SQUARED"
190 PRINT "POPULATION VARIANCE =";S1
200 S=SQR(S1)
210 S3=S/SQR(N)
220 PRINT "CONFIDENCE INTERVAL ESTIMATES FOR MEAN:"
230 PRINT
240 PRINT "CONFIDENCE     PLUS OR"
250 PRINT "  LEVEL"TAB(15)"MINUS"TAB(31)"MAXIMUM"TAB(48)"MINIMUM
260 FOR I=1 TO 7
270 PRINTUSING PV$; C(I);: PRINTTAB(7)
280 PRINTUSING PU$; F(I)*S3; X+F(I)*S3; X-F(I)*S3
290 NEXT I
300 PRINT
310 PRINT "CONFIDENCE INTERVAL ESTIMATES"
320 PRINT "FOR STANDARD DEVIATION:"
330 PRINT
340 FOR I=1 TO 7
350 J=F(I)*S/SQR(2*N)
360 PRINTUSING PV$; C(I);: PRINTTAB(7): PRINTUSING PU$;J;S+J;S-J
370 NEXT I
380 PRINT
390 PRINT "DO YOU WANT A CALCULATION OF HOW LARGE"
400 PRINT "A SAMPLE YOU MUST TAKE TO REDUCE"
410 PRINT "THE ERROR OF THE ESTIMATE TO A"
420 PRINT "MAXIMUM QUANTITY (Y/N)"
430 INPUT B$
440 IF B$="N" THEN 720
450 IF B$<>"Y" THEN 390
460 PRINT "ENTER YOUR CHOSEN CONFIDENCE LEVEL"
470 PRINT "(FROM ABOVE CHOICES ONLY) : ENTER A"
480 PRINT "1 FOR 50, 2 FOR 60, 3 FOR 70, 4 FOR 80"
490 PRINT "5 FOR 90, 6 FOR 95, AND 7 FOR 99"
500 INPUT J
510 PRINT "ENTER MAXIMUM DESIRED ERROR OF ESTIMATE"
520 INPUT M
530 PRINT "ARE YOU TESTING THE MEAN (M) OR "
540 PRINT "  THE STANDARD DEVIATION (S) "
550 INPUT C$
560 IF C$="S" THEN 600
```

```
570 IF C$<>"M" THEN 530
580 N3=INT((S*F(J)/M)[2)+1
590 GOTO 610
600 N3=INT((F(J)*S/M)[2/2)+1
610 PRINT
620 PRINT "AT THE";C(J);"PERCENT CONFIDENCE LEVEL"
630 PRINT "IT WOULD BE NECESSARY TO TAKE";N3
640 PRINT "SAMPLES TO BE SURE THAT YOUR ESTIMATE"
650 PRINT "OF THE ERROR IN THE ";
660 IF C$="S" THEN 690
670 PRINT "MEAN"
680 GOTO 700
690 PRINT "STANDARD DEVIATION"
700 PRINT "DID NOT EXCEED";M
710 PRINT
720 PRINT "DO YOU HAVE"
730 PRINT "      NO MORE CALCULATIONS (0),"
740 PRINT "MORE WITH THE SAME SAMPLES (1), OR"
750 PRINT "        BRAND-NEW SAMPLING (2)"
760 INPUT Y
770 IF Y=1 THEN 380
780 IF Y=2 THEN 100
790 DATA 50, 0.6744902454373
800 DATA 60, 0.8416214285714
810 DATA 70, 1.0364335334476
820 DATA 80, 1.2815515669516
830 DATA 90, 1.6448536821705
840 DATA 95, 1.9599641025641
850 DATA 99, 2.575827586207
860 END
```

References

Harnett. *Introduction to Statistical Methods.* 2nd ed. Reading, Mass.: Addison-Wesley, 1975.

Spiegal. *Statistics.* New York: McGraw-Hill, 1961.

Statistics

This program analyzes grouped and ungrouped data that you enter, and prints as many as 26 statistics: measures of central tendency, variance, skewness, kurtosis, and correlation.

When you run the program, enter the total population (if known), or 0 (if unknown). If the data are grouped, enter G, if ungrouped, enter U. The next step is to enter the frequency, followed by the value observed at that frequency. After the last item, enter a frequency and value of 0. If you are entering ungrouped data, just enter the observations; enter 9E9 after the last one. The program then calculates and prints the statistics, indicating which are not available based on the data entered.

Program Notes

This program accepts a maximum of 250 grouped or ungrouped observations. To change this, modify lines 40 and 50 of the program as follows:

```
40 DIM S(40),X(I),Y(I),Z(I)
50 N1=I
```

Replace the expression I with a constant equal to the maximum number of observations.

Example

Randy Flashpan is a local disk jockey. His weekly show has a segment during which listeners phone in their evaluations of certain songs by rating them on a scale of 1 to 10. One hundred listeners called in their scores on one record, and their scores are listed below:

Score	Number of Listeners
1	13
2	6
3	2
4	4
5	10
6	13
7	22
8	18
9	10
10	2

In Randy's lexicon, a song with a median score of 7 or more is "boss hit-bound." If the median is between 5 and 7, the song is classified as "lukewarm." If the median falls below 4, the record is dropped from the radio station's play-list.

Based on the sample data shown, how should Randy classify the record? Furthermore, how does someone with the intelligence of a disk jockey run this program?

Answer: This song resides in the lukewarm category, with a median of 6.59.

```
STATISTICS

ENTER TOTAL POPULATION (0=UNKNOWN)? 100

ARE DATA (G) GROUPED OR (U) UNGROUPED? G
```

```
ENTER FREQUENCY, THEN VALUE (0,0=END)
PAIR NO. 1 ? 13,1
PAIR NO. 2 ? 6,2
PAIR NO. 3 ? 2,3
PAIR NO. 4 ? 4,4
PAIR NO. 5 ? 10,5
PAIR NO. 6 ? 13,6
PAIR NO. 7 ? 22,7
PAIR NO. 8 ? 18,8
PAIR NO. 9 ? 10,9
PAIR NO. 10 ? 2,10
PAIR NO. 11 ? 0,0
```

```
        RESULTS TABULATED AS FOLLOWS:

                TOTAL POPULATION: 100
                       DATA ARE: GROUPED
                 NO. OF SAMPLES: 100
                 SUM OF SAMPLES: 583
                           MEAN: 5.83
                 SUM OF SQUARES: 4077
                 MEAN DEVIATION: 2.141
                         MEDIAN: 6.59091
                       VARIANCE: 6.78109
             STANDARD DEVIATION: 2.60405
      UNBIASED ESTIM. OF VARIANCE: 6.84959
    STD.DEV. USING THAT VARIANCE: 2.61717
                 PROBABLE ERROR: 1.75641
            STD. ERROR OF MEAN: .261717
            COEFF. OF VARIATION: 44.6664 %
         3RD MOMENT ABOUT MEAN:-11.9467
         4TH MOMENT ABOUT MEAN: 105.99
          MOMENT COEFF. SKEWNESS:-.67655
          MOMENT COEFF. KURTOSIS: 2.30496
  UNBIASED ESTIM. 3RD CENT. MOMENT:-12.3137
  STD. ERR. MEAN WITH FINITE
     POPULATION CORRECTION FACTOR: 0
      PEARSON'S 2ND COEFF. SKEWNESS:-.876606
                          RANGE: 9
  INDEX OF MEAN DEV. TO PRODUCT
          OF M.A.E. AND STD. DEV.: 1.03045
  READY
```

Practice Problems

1. Meter readings from a holding tank at a fuel processing plant are 12.98, 13.001, 18.25, 4.4, 9.8, 11, 14.5, 12.7, 7.2, and 6.1. What are the mean and median meter readings? What is the standard deviation?
Answer: The mean reading is 10.9931; the median is 11.85. The standard deviation is 3.98844.

2. An actuarial clerk wants statistics on the population of Casper County relative to the occurrence of heart disease. The table below shows age brackets and the number of diagnosed heart disease cases for those ages.

Age	Diagnosed Cases (per 1000 people)
0-5	6
6-10	5
11-20	3
21-25	8
26-30	7
31-35	12
36-40	17
41-45	19
46-50	30
51-55	35
56-60	43
61-65	50
66-70	61

What is the median age of the onset of heart disease in Casper County? 1,200 cases were evaluated. What is the measure of skewness for this population, since it appears to be skewed to the right of the mean? What is the standard error of the mean? (Hint: You must increase array sizes on line 40 to 300.)

Answer: The median age is 58.1977 for the onset of heart disease. Skewness −1.26119. The standard error of the mean is 0.903235.

Program Listing

```
10 CLS
20 PRINT "STATISTICS"
30 PRINT
40 DIM S(40),X(250),Y(250),Z(250)
49 REM - N1 = DIMENSION OF X, Y & Z
50 N1=250
60 FOR I=1 TO 40
70 S(I)=0
80 NEXT I
90 S1=0
100 PRINT "ENTER TOTAL POPULATION (0=UNKNOWN)";
110 INPUT T9
120 PRINT
130 PRINT "ARE DATA (G) GROUPED OR (U) UNGROUPED";
140 INPUT U$
150 PRINT
160 IF U$="G" THEN 590
169 REM ---- UNGROUPED DATA ----
170 J=1
180 PRINT "ITEM NO.";J;
189 REM - ENTER 9E9 AFTER LAST ITEM
190 INPUT X(J)
200 IF X(J)<>9E9 THEN 230
210 J=J-1
220 GOTO 280
229 REM - CALCULATES NO. OF ITEMS
230 S(1)=S(1)+1
239 REM - CALCULATES SUM OF ITEMS
240 S(2)=S(2)+X(J)
249 REM - CALCULATES THE SUM OF SQUARES
250 S(4)=S(4)+X(J)*X(J)
```

```
260 J=J+1
270 IF J<N1 THEN 180
279 REM - CALCULATES MEAN
280 S(3)=S(2)/S(1)
289 REM - CAL. DEVIATION FROM MEAN
290 S(5)=ABS(S(3)-X(J))
299 REM - CAL. SUM OF DEVIATIONS
300 S(6)=S(6)+S(5)
309 REM - CALC. 3RD POWER OF DEVIATION
310 S(8)=(X(J)-S(3))[3
319 REM - CALC. SUM OF 3RD POWERS
320 S(9)=S(9)+S(8)
329 REM - CALC. 4TH POWER OF DEVIATION
330 S(10)=(X(J)-S(3))[4
339 REM - CALC. SUM OF 4TH POWERS
340 S(11)=S(11)+S(10)
349 REM - CALC. MEAN DEVIATION
350 S(7)=S(6)/S(1)
358 REM - USE SHELL-METZNER SORT TO
359 REM - ARRANGE DATA IN ASCENDING ORDER
360 M1=S(1)
370 M1=INT(M1/2)
380 IF M1=0 THEN 520
390 K=S(1)-M1
400 J=1
410 I=J
420 L=I+M1
430 IF X(I)<=X(L) THEN 490
440 W=X(I)
450 X(I)=X(L)
460 X(L)=W
470 I=I-M1
480 IF I>=M1 THEN 420
490 J=J+1
500 IF J>K THEN 370
510 GOTO 410
519 REM - CALC. MEDIAN
520 IF S(1)/2=INT(S(1)/2) THEN 560
529 REM - ODD NO. OF ITEMS
530 M=S(1)/2+.5
540 S(12)=X(M)
550 GOTO 1070
560 M=S(1)/2
570 S(12)=(X(M)+X(M+1))/2
580 GOTO 1070
589 REM ---- GROUPED DATA ----
590 PRINT "ENTER FREQUENCY, THEN VALUE (0,0=END)"
600 J=1
610 PRINT "PAIR NO.";J;
619 REM - ENTER 0,0 AFTER LAST ITEM
620 INPUT Y(J),Z(J)
630 IF Y(J)=0 THEN 700
639 REM - CALC. NO. OF SAMPLES
640 S(1)=S(1)+Y(J)
650 S1=S1+1
```

```
659 REM - CALC. TOTAL OF VALUES
660 S(2)=S(2)+Y(J)*Z(J)
669 REM - CALC. SUM OF SQUARES
670 S(4)=S(4)+Y(J)*Z(J)*Z(J)
680 J=J+1
690 IF J<=N1 THEN 610
699 REM - CALC. MEAN
700 S(3)=S(2)/S(1)
710 FOR J=1 TO S(1)
719 REM - CALC. ABSOLUTE DEVIATION
720 S(5)=Y(J)*ABS(S(3)-Z(J))
729 REM - CALC. SUM OF ABS. DEVIATIONS
730 S(6)=S(6)+S(5)
739 REM - CALC. 3RD POWER OF DEVIATIONS
740 S(8)=Y(J)*(Z(J)-S(3))[3
749 REM - CALC. SUM OF 3RD POWERS
750 S(9)=S(9)+S(8)
759 REM - CALC. 4TH POWERS OF DEVIATIONS
760 S(10)=Y(J)*(Z(J)-S(3))[4
769 REM - CALC. SUM OF 4TH POWERS
770 S(11)=S(11)+S(10)
780 NEXT J
789 REM - CALC. MEAN DEVIATION
790 S(7)=S(6)/S(1)
798 REM - USE SHELL-METZNER SORT TO
799 REM - ARRANGE DATA IN ASCENDING ORDER
800 M1=S1
810 M1=INT(M1/2)
820 IF M1=0 THEN 990
830 K=S1-M1
840 J=1
850 I=J
860 L=I+M1
870 IF Z(I)<=Z(L) THEN 960
880 V=Y(I)
890 W=Z(I)
900 Y(I)=Y(L)
910 Z(I)=Z(L)
920 Y(L)=V
930 Z(L)=W
940 I=I-M1
950 IF I>=1 THEN 860
960 J=J+1
970 IF J>K THEN 810
980 GOTO 850
989 REM - CALCULATES MEDIAN
990 T=0
1000 K=1
1010 IF T+Y(K)>S(1)/2 THEN 1060
1020 T=T+Y(K)
1030 K=K+1
1040 GOTO 1010
1050 IF K<=S(1) THEN 1000
1060 S(12)=(Z(K)+Z(K-1))/2+((Z(K)-Z(K-1))/Y(K))*(S(1)/2-T)
1070 N=S(1)
```

```
1080 PRINT
1090 PRINT "      RESULTS TABULATED AS FOLLOWS:"
1100 PRINT
1110 PRINT "                      TOTAL POPULATION:";
1120 IF T9=0 THEN 1150
1130 PRINT T9
1140 GOTO 1170
1150 PRINT "UNKNOWN/NOT INDICATED"
1160 PRINT
1170 PRINT "                          DATA ARE: ";
1180 IF U$="G" THEN 1210
1190 PRINT "UNGROUPED"
1200 GOTO 1220
1210 PRINT "GROUPED"
1220 PRINT "                     NO. OF SAMPLES:";S(1)
1230 PRINT "                     SUM OF SAMPLES:";S(2)
1240 PRINT "                               MEAN:";S(3)
1250 PRINT "                     SUM OF SQUARES:";S(4)
1260 PRINT "                     MEAN DEVIATION:";S(7)
1270 PRINT "                             MEDIAN:";S(12)
1280 S(13)=S(4)/N-S(3)[2
1290 PRINT "                           VARIANCE:";S(13)
1300 IF U$="G" THEN 1330
1310 S(14)=S(13)-(1/12)*(Z(2)-Z(1))[2
1320 PRINT "      VARIANCE WITH SHEP. CORR.:";S(14)
1330 S(15)=SQR(S(13))
1340 PRINT "                 STANDARD DEVIATION:";S(15)
1350 IF U$="G" THEN 1380
1360 S(16)=SQR(S(14))
1370 PRINT "      STD. DEV. WITH SHEP. CORR.:";S(16)
1380 S(17)=S(13)*N/(N-1)
1390 PRINT "      UNBIASED ESTIM. OF VARIANCE:";S(17)
1400 S(18)=SQR(S(17))
1410 PRINT "      STD.DEV. USING THAT VARIANCE:";S(18)
1420 S(19)=.67449*S(15)
1430 PRINT "                     PROBABLE ERROR:";S(19)
1440 S(20)=SQR(S(17)/N)
1450 PRINT "                STD. ERROR OF MEAN:";S(20)
1460 S(21)=S(15)/S(3)
1470 PRINT "              COEFF. OF VARIATION:";100*S(21);"%"
1480 S(22)=S(9)/N
1490 PRINT "             3RD MOMENT ABOUT MEAN:";S(22)
1500 S(23)=S(11)/N
1510 PRINT "             4TH MOMENT ABOUT MEAN:";S(23)
1520 IF U$="G" THEN 1560
1530 R=Z(2)-Z(1)
1540 S(24)=S(23)-.5*(R[2)*S(17)+(7/240)*R[4
1550 PRINT "      4TH MOMENT WITH SHEP. CORR.:";S(24)
1560 S(25)=S(22)/(S(15)[3)
1570 PRINT "            MOMENT COEFF. SKEWNESS:";S(25)
1580 S(26)=S(23)/(S(13)[2)
1590 PRINT "            MOMENT COEFF. KURTOSIS:";S(26)
1600 S(27)=(S(22)*N[2)/((N-1)*(N-2))
1610 PRINT "UNBIASED ESTIM. 3RD CENT. MOMENT:";S(27)
1620 IF T9=0 THEN 1680
```

```
1630 IF N<=.05*T9 THEN 1680
1640 S(28)=S(20)*SQR((T9-N)/(T9-1))
1650 PRINT "STD. ERR. MEAN WITH FINITE "
1660 PRINT "     POPULATION CORRECTION FACTOR:";S(28)
1670 GOTO 1690
1680 PRINT "FINITE POP. CORR. FACTOR N/A"
1690 S(29)=3*(S(3)-S(12))/S(15)
1700 PRINT "    PEARSON'S 2ND COEFF. SKEWNESS:";S(29)
1710 IF U$="G" THEN 1740
1720 S(30)=X(N)-X(1)
1730 GOTO 1750
1740 S(30)=Z(S1)-Z(1)
1750 PRINT "                              RANGE:";S(30)
1760 S(31)=S(7)/(.7978845608*S(15))
1770 PRINT "INDEX OF MEAN DEV. TO PRODUCT"
1780 PRINT "         OF M.A.E. AND STD. DEV.:";S(31)
1790 END
```

References

Mendenhall, William, et al. *Statistics: A Tool for the Social Sciences.* Belmont, Calif.: Duxbury Press, 1974.

Spiegal. *Statistics* (Schaum's Series) New York: McGraw-Hill, 1961.

Unbiased Estimator of Standard Deviation

The concept of an unbiased estimator of the standard deviation is not common among American statisticians. However, according to the Russian mathematician A. A. Sveshnikov, the unbiased estimator of the standard deviation is given by the following formula:

$$\sigma = K_N \sqrt{\frac{1}{N-1} \sum_{J=1}^{N} (x_j - x)^2} \qquad K_N = \sqrt{\frac{N-1}{2}} \left(\frac{\Gamma\left(\frac{N-1}{2}\right)}{\Gamma\left(\frac{N}{2}\right)} \right)$$

Using this symbolism N = sample size, it is easily shown that:

$$K_N = \sqrt{\frac{N-1}{2}} \left(\frac{\frac{2M-3}{2} \cdot \frac{2M-5}{2} \cdots \frac{3}{2} \cdot \frac{1}{2} \sqrt{\pi}}{(M-1) \; (M-2) \cdots 2 \cdot 1} \right) \qquad K_N = \sqrt{\frac{N-1}{2}} \left(\frac{(M-1) \; (M-2) \cdots 2 \cdot 1}{\frac{2M-1}{2} \cdot \frac{2M-3}{2} \cdots \frac{3}{2} \cdot \frac{1}{2} \sqrt{\pi}} \right)$$

To use the program, you must enter the number of samples, and the sum of the squares of the deviations. The program prints out the unbiased estimator of the standard deviation, and asks if you want another calculation.

Example

In a class of 35 seventh-grade students, the sum of the squares of the deviations for their ages is 3.156. What is the unbiased estimator of the standard deviation?
   Answer: 0.30691769

```
UNBIASED ESTIMATOR OF STANDARD DEVIATION

THIS PROGRAM CALCULATES THE UNBIASED
ESTIMATOR OF THE STANDARD DEVIATION
WHEN VARIABLE IS NORMALLY DISTRIBUTED

ENTER THE SUM OF THE SQUARES
OF THE DEVIATIONS
? 3.156
ENTER THE NUMBER OF SAMPLES
? 35
UNBIASED ESTIMATOR OF STANDARD
DEVIATION=  .306918
ANOTHER CALCULATION? (Y/N)
READY
```

Practice Problems

1. If 40 samples are randomly distributed and the sum of the squares of their deviations is 9.63, what is the unbiased estimator of the standard deviation?
Answer: 0.500109

2. In a group of 26 randomly distributed samples, the sum of the squares of the deviations is 34.953. What is the unbiased estimator of the standard deviation?
Answer: 1.1943

Program Listing

```
10 CLS
20 PRINT "UNBIASED ESTIMATOR OF STANDARD DEVIATION"
30 PRINT
40 DEFDBL A-Z : DEFINT N : DEFSNG A,M
50 PRINT "THIS PROGRAM CALCULATES THE UNBIASED"
60 PRINT "ESTIMATOR OF THE STANDARD DEVIATION"
70 PRINT "WHEN VARIABLE IS NORMALLY DISTRIBUTED"
80 PRINT
90 PRINT "ENTER THE SUM OF THE SQUARES"
100 PRINT "OF THE DEVIATIONS"
110 INPUT S
120 PRINT "ENTER THE NUMBER OF SAMPLES"
130 INPUT N
139 REM  COMPUTE K-SUB-N TERM
140 A=SQR((N-1)/2)
150 FOR M = (((N-1)/2)-1) TO 1 STEP -1
160 A = A * M/(M+.5)
170 NEXT M
179 REM SQR(PI)/2 = .8862269255
180 P= .8862269255
190 IF N/2=INT(N/2) THEN 210
200 P=1/P
210 PRINT "UNBIASED ESTIMATOR OF STANDARD"
220 PRINT "DEVIATION= "; CSNG( A * P * SQR(S/(N-1)) )
230 PRINT "ANOTHER CALCULATION? (Y/N)"
240 Y$=INKEY$ : IF Y$="" THEN 240
250 IF Y$="Y" THEN 80
260 IF Y$<>"N" THEN 230
270 END
```

References

National Bureau of Standards. *Handbook of Mathematical Functions.* Washington, D.C., 1966.

Sveshnikov, A. A. *Problems in Probability Theory, Mathematical Statistics and Theory of Random Functions.* New York: Dover, 1968.

Chi-Square

The chi-square test in statistics tests the compatibility of observed frequencies with the expected or theoretical frequencies. For example, suppose we are testing whether a die is fair or biased. We throw the die 60 times, recording the result each time. If the die is fair, we would expect that each of the six sides would come up close to 10 times during the test. But we know that actual events do not always correspond to theoretical expectations. The chi-square test provides the means of determining whether the observed and theoretical results are so divergent that the die cannot be considered fair.

Chi-square is defined as follows:

$$x^2 = \sum_{I=1}^{K} \frac{(O_I - E_I)^2}{E_I}$$

where O represented the observed frequencies and E the expected frequencies. Statisticians have determined what value (the "5% critical value") the chi-square must be below in order that we be 95% positive that two results are compatible. This program tests whether the actual results fall within that level of confidence. It also employs Yates' correction (which some statisticians prefer and some dislike) to test the results. The chi-square formula with Yates' correction is

$$x^2 = \sum_{I=1}^{K} \left(\frac{|O_I - E_I| - .5}{E_I} \right)^2$$

The program also tests whether the results are too good (below the 95% critical value), which makes clinical workers suspicious of the results.

The program first asks if the expected frequency is a constant. In the above example, each face of the die is expected to appear 10 times, so the answer is "Yes" and you would enter 10 as the constant. You then enter the observed frequencies one-by- one; enter 99999 after the last one. If the expected frequencies are not constant, the program will ask for each set of observed and expected frequencies. After the last entry, enter 99999,1 to end the sequence.

The program then will calculate the chi-square statistics, both with and without Yates' correction, and print them out, indicating the degrees of freedom. It then tests each statistic against the 5% and 95% critical values, and prints out the results.

Example

Suppose the results of the 60 throws of the die in the above example are as follows:

Face	Expected	Actual
1	10	9
2	10	8
3	10	12
4	10	10
5	10	13
6	10	8

What are the results of the chi-square test for this data? Can the die be considered fair?

Answer: The die can be considered fair.

```
CHI-SQUARE

IS AMOUNT OF EXPECTED FREQUENCY
CONSTANT? (Y/N)
? Y
ENTER CONSTANT EXPECTED FREQUENCY
? 10
ENTER OBSERVED FREQUENCIES ONE BY
ONE AS REQUESTED BELOW
ENTER 99999 TO END
? 9
? 8
? 12
? 10
? 13
? 8
? 99999
CHI SQUARE FOR THESE
OBSERVATIONS = 2.2
FOR 5 DEGREES OF FREEDOM
WITH YATES' CORRECTION, CHI
SQUARE = 1.35
FIVE PERCENT CRITICAL VALUE OF
CHI SQUARE IS 11.071
THEREFORE THE HYPOTHESIS IS NOT
REJECTED AT THE 5% CRITICAL VALUE
READY
```

Practice Problems

1. A student in a genetics class is performing an experiment to test classical Mendelian theory. That theory predicts that certain biological characteristics should appear in the species under review in the ratios 9:3:3:1. In the 1,600 samples which the student takes, they appear 904, 297, 302, and 97 times, respectively. Are these results compatible with orthodox Mendelian theory?

Answer: The unadjusted chi-square result is 0.151111, and with Yates's correction that result is 0.104444. The 5% critical value for 3 degrees of freedom is 7.8147, so the results are compatible. However, the 95% critical value is 0.35185, so either with or without Yates's correction, the results are "too good," and the instructor must view the student's experiment with suspicion.

2. A Las Vegas pit boss noticed that a particular roulette wheel seemed to be coming up red more often than black. He kept track of the next 100 spins. Red came up 546 times and black 454 times. Is the wheel biased?

Answer: The chi-square without Yates's correction is 8.464, and with it is 8.28101. The 5% critical value is 3.8415, and the hypothesis is therefore rejected. The pit boss should junk that roulette wheel immediately.

Program Listing

```
10 CLS
20 PRINT "CHI-SQUARE"
30 PRINT
40 PRINT "IS AMOUNT OF EXPECTED FREQUENCY"
50 PRINT "CONSTANT? (Y/N)"
```

```
60  INPUT A$
70  IF A$="N" THEN 500
80  IF A$<>"Y" THEN 40
90  PRINT "ENTER CONSTANT EXPECTED FREQUENCY"
100 INPUT Y
299 REM EXPECTED FREQUENCY IS A CONSTANT
300 PRINT "ENTER OBSERVED FREQUENCIES ONE BY"
310 PRINT "ONE AS REQUESTED BELOW"
320 PRINT "ENTER 99999 TO END"
330 INPUT X
340 IF X=99999 THEN 1000
350 N=N+1
360 S=S+(ABS(X-Y)[2)/Y
370 T=T+((ABS(X-Y)-.5)[2)/Y
380 IF A$="N" THEN 530
390 GOTO 330
499 REM EXPECTED FREQUENCY IS NOT A CONSTANT
500 PRINT "ENTER, PAIR BY PAIR, AS REQUESTED, THE"
510 PRINT "OBSERVED, THEN THE EXPECTED, FREQUENCIES"
520 PRINT "ENTER 99999,1 TO END"
530 INPUT X,Y
540 GOTO 340
1000 PRINT "CHI SQUARE FOR THESE"
1010 PRINT "OBSERVATIONS =";S
1020 PRINT "FOR"; N-1; "DEGREES OF FREEDOM"
1030 PRINT "WITH YATES' CORRECTION, CHI"
1040 PRINT "SQUARE =";T
1099 REM BRANCH FOR CALCULATION OF CRITICAL VALUES
1100 IF N>101 THEN 1600
1110 IF N=101 THEN 1500
1120 IF N>31 THEN 1400
1200 FOR I=1 TO N-1
1210 READ C
1220 NEXT I
1230 FOR I=N TO N+29
1240 READ D
1250 NEXT I
1260 GOTO 2500
1400 C=(N-1)*(1-2/(9*(N-1))+1.6449*SQR(2/(9*(N-1))))[3
1410 D=(N-1)*(1-2/(9*(N-1))-1.6449*SQR(2/(9*(N-1))))[3
1420 GOTO 2500
1500 C=124.342
1510 D=77.9295
1520 GOTO 2500
1600 C=.5*(1.6449+SQR(2*(N-1)-1)))[2
1610 D=.5*(SQR(2/(9*(N-1))-1.6449)[2
2500 PRINT "FIVE PERCENT CRITICAL VALUE OF"
2510 PRINT "CHI SQUARE IS"; C
2520 IF T>C THEN 2700
2530 IF S>C THEN 2800
2540 IF S<D THEN 2900
2550 IF T<D THEN 2900
2600 PRINT "THEREFORE THE HYPOTHESIS IS NOT"
2610 PRINT "REJECTED AT THE 5% CRITICAL VALUE"
2620 GOTO 9999
```

```
2700 PRINT "THEREFORE THE HYPOTHESIS IS"
2710 PRINT "REJECTED AT THE CRITICAL VALUE"
2720 GOTO 9999
2800 PRINT "WHILE THE UNADJUSTED CHI SQUARE"
2810 PRINT "VALUES ARE UNACCEPTABLE, THOSE WITH"
2820 PRINT "YATES' CORRECTION ARE NOT; THEREFORE"
2830 PRINT "SAMPLE SIZES SHOULD BE INCREASED OR"
2840 PRINT "SUBSTITUTE MULTINOMIAL DISTRIBUTION"
2850 PRINT "METHODS"
2860 GOTO 9999
2900 PRINT "AGREEMENT IS TOO GOOD AND SHOULD BE"
2910 PRINT "EXAMINED CRITICALLY, BECAUSE EITHER"
2920 PRINT "WITH OR WITHOUT YATES' CORRECTION, THE"
2930 PRINT "CHI SQUARE VALUE IS BELOW THE 95%"
2940 PRINT "CRITICAL VALUE"
5000 DATA 3.8415,5.9915,7.8147,9.4877,11.071,12.592
5010 DATA 14.067,15.507,16.919,18.307,19.675,21.026
5020 DATA 22.362,23.685,24.996,26.296,27.587,28.869
5030 DATA 30.140,31.410,32.671,33.924,35.173,36.415
5040 DATA 37.653,38.885,40.113,41.337,42.557,43.773
5050 DATA .003932,.10259,.35185,.71072,1.1455
5060 DATA 1.635,2.167,2.733,3.325,3.940
5070 DATA 4.575,5.226,5.892,6.571,7.261
5080 DATA 7.962,8.672,9.390,10.117,10.851
5090 DATA 11.591,12.338,13.091,13.848,14.611
5100 DATA 15.379,16.151,16.928,17.708,18.493
9999 END
```

References

Hoel. *Introduction to Mathematical Statistics,* 2nd ed. New York: John Wiley, 1954.

Spiegel. *Statistics* (Schaum's series). New York: McGraw-Hill, 1961.

Data Forecasting Divergence

This program determines the degree to which a forecast diverges from actual data. You enter pairs of actual data and corresponding forecast; after the last data pair, enter 99999,1. The program will then print out the number of pairs of figures, the total error, the total absolute error, the total squared error, the mean error, the mean absolute error (MAE), the mean square error, and the root mean square error.

Example

A statistical forecaster determined the following data having made the following respective forecasts:

Data	Forecast
1	1
2	2.2
3	2.9
4	3.9
5	5.3
6	6.1
7	7
8	7.9

What are the error statistics for these figures?

Answer: Number of pairs = 8; total error = 0.3; total absolute error = 0.9; total squared error = 0.17; mean error = 0.0375; mean absolute error = 0.1125; mean square error = 0.02125; root mean square error = 0.145774.

```
DATA FORECASTING DIVERGENCE

ENTER DATA AND FORECAST
(99999,1 TO END)
? 1,1
? 2,2.2
? 3,2.9
? 4,3.9
? 5,5.3
? 6,6.1
? 7,7
? 8,7.9
? 99999,1

NO. OF PAIRS OF FIGURES= 8
            TOTAL ERROR=-.3
   TOTAL ABSOLUTE ERROR= .9
    TOTAL SQUARED ERROR= .17
             MEAN ERROR=-.0375
    MEAN ABSOLUTE ERROR= .1125
      MEAN SQUARE ERROR= .02125
 ROOT MEAN SQUARE ERROR= .145774
READY
```

Practice Problems

1. The actual and predicted results in a city council race are as follows:

	Vote%	Poll%
Candidate A	40.3	42.7
Candidate B	22.5	21.4
Candidate C	16.3	18.2
Candidate D	10.5	6.0
Candidate E	7.2	7.4
Candidate F	3.2	4.3

How accurate were the polls?

Answer: Number of pairs = 6; total error $\approx$ 0; total absolute error = 11.2; total squared error = 32.08; mean error $\approx$ 0; mean absolute error = 1.86667; mean square error = 5.34667; root mean square error = 2.31229.

2. A new television weatherman lasted only one week at the station. Following are the actual and predicted temperatures during that week:

	Actual Temperature	Predicted Temperature
Monday	74	49
Tuesday	70	62
Wednesday	58	75
Thursday	60	82
Friday	65	37
Saturday	73	58
Sunday	70	92

What statistics were on the dismissal notice?

Answer: Number of pairs = 7; total error = 15; total absolute error = 137; total squared error = 2,955; mean error = 2.14286; mean absolute error = 19.5714; mean square error = 422.143; root mean square error = 20.5461.

Program Listing

```
10 CLS
20 PRINT "DATA FORECASTING DIVERGENCE"
30 PRINT
40 PRINT "ENTER DATA AND FORECAST"
50 PRINT "(99999,1 TO END)"
60 INPUT X,Y
70 IF X=99999 THEN 130
80 T1=T1+1
90 T2=T2+X-Y
100 T3=T3+ABS(X-Y)
110 T4=T4+ABS(X-Y)[2
120 GOTO 60
130 PRINT
140 PRINT "NO. OF PAIRS OF FIGURES=";T1
150 PRINT "          TOTAL ERROR=";T2
160 PRINT "    TOTAL ABSOLUTE ERROR=";T3
170 PRINT "     TOTAL SQUARED ERROR=";T4
180 PRINT "          MEAN ERROR=";T2/T1
190 PRINT "    MEAN ABSOLUTE ERROR=";T3/T1
200 PRINT "      MEAN SQUARE ERROR=";T4/T1
210 PRINT " ROOT MEAN SQUARE ERROR=";SQR(T4/T1)
220 END
```

Reference

Gilchrist. *Statistical Forecasting.* London: John Wiley, 1976.

Newtonian Interpolation

This program applies to Newton's forward difference formula for interpolation of a given function. Newton's formula is intended to work when the arguments you use in the interpolation commence just below the argument for which you are seeking the tabular value.

You first enter the independent variables on either side of the value for which you want the tabular value interpolated, followed by that value (your desired independent variable). The program then asks for the precision (in decimal places) you want in your answer. This should not exceed the accuracy of either your original data, or your computer's Basic. The program will cease calculating differences when they drop below this level of accuracy.

You then enter the tabular values immediately below and above the desired tabular value. The program prints out the difference between these values, called the first difference. The program asks for additional tabular values, printing out the new difference each time, until the new difference drops below the level of precision you entered earlier. To end the entry of tabular values before this, you enter 99999 as the new tabular value, and the program will branch to computation of the answer.

Example

Bill Miller is going to take out a five-year loan at 4¼%. He has a table that shows the factors by which he should multiply the principal of the loan to determine the amount of each monthly payment. Unfortunately, the table only gives figures at half-percent intervals. How should Bill use this program to determine the factor at 4¼%?

Interest Rate	Factor
4%	0.018416522
4½%	0.018643019
5%	0.018871233
5½%	0.019101162
6%	0.019332801
6½%	0.019566148
7%	0.019801198
7½%	0.020037949
8%	0.020276394

Answer:

```
        INTERPOLATION

NEWTON'S FORWARD DIFFERENCE FORMULA

    LOWER INDEPENDENT VARIABLE? .04
    UPPER INDEPENDENT VARIABLE? .045
  DESIRED INDEPENDENT VARIABLE? .0425
PRECISION (IN DECIMAL PLACES)? 9

ENTER TABULAR VALUE AT .04 ? .018416522

ENTER TABULAR VALUE AT .045 ? .018643019


  1 ST DIFFERENCE = 2.26497D-04
ENTER TABULAR VALUE AT .05 ? .018871233


  2 ND DIFFERENCE = 1.717000000000038D-06
```

```
ENTER TABULAR VALUE AT .055 ? .019101162

 3 RD DIFFERENCE =-1.99999999981465D-09
INTERPOLATION IS TO THE ORDER OF
 3 RD DIFFERENCES ANSWER = .018529556
READY
```

Practice Problems

1. Jeanne needs to know the sine of 0.63, using the following table. What is that figure?

X	0.6	0.7	0.8	0.9	1.0
SIN X	0.564642	0.0644218	0.717356	0.783327	0.841471

Answer: The sine of 0.63 is approximately 0.589191.

2. Joe Statistics wants to determine the area under the normal curve at 0.095 standard deviation to the right of the mean. From the following table, what is that area?

Standard Deviations	0.08	0.09	0.1	0.11	0.12
Area	0.53188	0.53586	0.53983	0.54380	0.54776

Answer: The area is 0.53785.

Program Listing

```
10 CLS
20 PRINT "            INTERPOLATION"
30 PRINT
40 DEFDBL A-Z : DEFINT D,I,J
50 PRINT "NEWTON'S FORWARD DIFFERENCE FORMULA"
60 PRINT
70 PRINT "   LOWER INDEPENDENT VARIABLE";
80 INPUT  A(1)
90 PRINT "   UPPER INDEPENDENT VARIABLE";
100 INPUT A(2)
110 PRINT " DESIRED INDEPENDENT VARIABLE";
120 INPUT X
130 IF E>16 THEN PRINT "LIMIT: 16 PLACES" : GOTO 100
140 P=(X-A(1))/(A(2)-A(1))
150 PRINT "PRECISION (IN DECIMAL PLACES)";
160 INPUT E
170 IF E=0 THEN F=0 : GOTO 190
180 F=1/(10[E)
190 J=1
200 PRINT
210 GOSUB 530
220 J=2
230 GOSUB 530
240 IF B(1,J)=99999 THEN 350
250 FOR I=2 TO J
260 B(I,J-I+1)=B(I-1,J-I+2)-B(I-1,J-I+1)
270 NEXT I
```

```
280 PRINT
290 PRINT J-1;
300 GOSUB 560
310 PRINT " DIFFERENCE =";B(J,1)
320 IF B(J,1)<F THEN 350
330 J=J+1
340 IF J<=9 THEN 230
350 Z=0
360 P1=1
370 X=1
380 FOR I=1 TO 8
390 X=X*I
400 P1=P1*(P-I+1)
410 Z=Z+P1*B(I+1,1)/X
420 NEXT I
430 IF A(2)>A(1) THEN 460
440 Z=B(1,1)-Z
450 GOTO 470
460 Z=B(1,1)+Z
470 PRINT "INTERPOLATION IS TO THE ORDER OF"
480 PRINT J-1;
490 GOSUB 560
500 PRINT " DIFFERENCES ANSWER = ";
510 GOSUB 650 : PRINTUSING DP$; Z
520 GOTO 670
529 REM SUBROUTINE TO ENTER TABULAR VALUES
530 PRINT "ENTER TABULAR VALUE AT";A(1)+(J-1)*(A(2)-A(1));
540 INPUT B(1,J)
550 RETURN
559 REM ROUTINE TO PRINT "ST","ND", ETC.
560 IF J<>2 THEN 580
570 PRINT "ST";
580 IF J<>3 THEN 600
590 PRINT "ND";
600 IF J<>4 THEN 620
610 PRINT "RD";
620 IF J<5 THEN 640
630 PRINT "TH";
640 RETURN
649 REM ROUTINE TO SET DECIMAL PLACES
650 DP$="" : FOR DP=1 TO E : DP$=DP$+"#" : NEXT : DP$="."+DP$
660 RETURN
670 END
```

References

Hildebrand, F.B. *Introduction to Numerical Analysis,* 2nd. ed., New York: McGraw-Hill, 1974.

National Bureau of Standards. *Handbook of Mathematical Functions.* Washington, D.C., 1976.

Phillips, G. M., and Taylor, R.J. *Theory and Applications of Numerical Analysis.* New York: Academic Press, 1973.

Scheid. *Numerical Analysis.* New York: McGraw-Hill, 1968.

Lagrangian Interpolation

This program applies Lagrange's formula for interpolation to a given function. For each succeeding tabular value you enter, the program displays the corresponding difference. Starting with the second difference, you may either calculate the interpolated value or proceed to the next order of difference. If you go on, you have one more option at each succeeding order of difference, and that is to back up and calculate the interpolated value on the previous order of difference. This effectively lets you take an uncommitted look ahead to see whether the next order of difference is smaller than the present one. Thus you need not choose the order of difference beforehand. The program permits three-point through ten-point Lagrangian interpolation.

The program first asks you for the central argument, which is the argument immediately *below* the one you want. It also requests the next higher argument listed in the table, and your desired argument. You must then enter tabular values for the central argument and the arguments on either side of the central argument. The program calls these values f_0, f_1 and f_{-1}, respectively.

At this point the program displays the first and second differences. You have the option of stopping here with three-point interpolation, or going on to the higher orders of difference. If you go on you must enter, one at a time, tabular values f_2, f_{-2}, f_3, ..., f_5. As you make each entry, the program displays the next higher difference. You must decide whether to stop to interpolate based on that difference, back up to interpolate on the previous difference, or proceed to enter another tabular value. You can only proceed as far as the ninth difference, since the program calculates at most a ten-point interpolation.

Program Notes

The program employs the algorithm set forth by Pearson for simplifying the Lagrangian coefficients, thus precluding the need for coefficient tables. The program also disregards the remainder term in Lagrange's formula. Finally, the program does not perform two-point interpolation, since it is of little use.

Example

Using the following table, determine the sine of 1.00006 radians.

Angle X in Radians	Tabular Value Sin X	Name of Tabular Value
0.996	0.83930 30496	f_{-4}
0.997	0.83984 62937	f_{-3}
0.998	0.84038 86980	f_{-2}
0.999	0.84093 02619	f_{-1}
1.000	0.84147 09848	f_0
1.001	0.84201 08663	f_1
1.002	0.84254 99058	f_2
1.003	0.84308 81027	f_3
1.004	0.84362 54565	f_4
1.005	0.84416 19667	f_5

Answer: 0.841795035

```
LAGRANGIAN INTERPOLATION

ENTER THE CENTRAL ARGUMENT, NEXT HIGHER
```

```
ARGUEMENT, AND THE DESIRED ARGUMENT
? 1,1.001,1.0006
ENTER F(0)
? .8414709848
ENTER F(1)
? .8420108663
ENTER F(-1)
? .8409302619
DIFFERENCE #1 = 0.000539881500
DIFFERENCE #2 = 0.000000841400
DO YOU WANT FURTHER DIFFERENCES? (Y/N)
? Y
ENTER F( 2 )
? .8425499058
DIFFERENCE # 3 = 0.000000000600
WANT FURTHER DIFFERENCES?
YES(Y), NO(N), ONE LESS(L)
? Y
ENTER F(- 2 )
? .840388698
DIFFERENCE # 4 = 0.000000000200
WANT FURTHER DIFFERENCES?
YES(Y), NO(N), ONE LESS(L)
? Y
ENTER F( 3 )
? .8430881027
DIFFERENCE # 5 = 0.000000000200
WANT FURTHER DIFFERENCES?
YES(Y), NO(N), ONE LESS(L)
? N
LAGRANGIAN 6-POINT INTERPOLATION
PRODUCES A VALUE OF 0.841795035088
READY
```

Practice Problems

1. What is the sine of 1.0001 radians?
Answer: 0.8415250011

2. To ten places, the mantissas of the common logarithms of certain arguments are shown below:

Argument	Mantissa		
6.1242	0.787	0493	652
6.1243	0.787	0564	565
6.1244	0.787	0635	478
6.1245	0.787	0706	390
6.1246	0.787	0777	300
6.1247	0.787	0848	209

What is the common logarithm mantissa for 6.12449?
Answer: 0.7870686855

Program Listing

```
10 CLS
20 PRINT "LAGRANGIAN INTERPOLATION"
30 PRINT
40 DEFDBL A-Z : DEFINT I,J
50 PU$="#.############"
60 DIM D(10,10),E(10),F(10,10),N(4),G(10)
70 G(1)=1
80 F(1,1)=1
89 REM SET UP INITIAL TABLES OF VALUES
90 FOR I=2 TO 10
100 F(I,1)=SGN(I/2-INT(I/2)-.1)
110 FOR J=2 TO I
120 Z=(ABS(F(I-1,J-1))+ABS(F(I-1,J)))
130 F(I,J)=Z*SGN(INT((I+J)/2)-(I+J)/2+.1)
140 NEXT J
150 G(I)=G(I-1)*(I-1)
160 NEXT I
170 PRINT "ENTER THE CENTRAL ARGUMENT, NEXT HIGHER"""
180 PRINT "ARGUMENT, AND THE DESIRED ARGUMENT"
190 INPUT X1,X2,X3
200 P=(X3-X1)/(X2-X1)
210 IF P<=0 THEN 170
220 IF P>=1 THEN 170
230 PRINT "ENTER F(0)"
240 INPUT D(1,1)
250 PRINT "ENTER F(1)"
260 INPUT D(2,1)
270 PRINT "ENTER F(-1)"
280 INPUT D(3,1)
290 D(1,2)=ABS(D(2,1)-D(1,1))
300 PRINT "DIFFERENCE #1 = ";: PRINTUSING PU$; D(1,2)
310 D(2,2)=ABS(D(3,1)-D(1,1))
320 D(1,3)=ABS(D(2,2)-D(1,2))
330 PRINT "DIFFERENCE #2 = ";: PRINTUSING PU$; D(1,3)
339 REM GIVE OPERATOR OPTION OF STOPPING NOW OR CONTINUING
340 PRINT "DO YOU WANT FUTHER DIFFERENCES? (Y/N)"
350 INPUT Y$
360 I=3
370 IF Y$="N" THEN 650
380 IF Y$<>"Y" THEN 340
390 I=I+1
399 REM ENTER FOURTH & SUBSEQUENT TABULAR VALUES
400 PRINT "ENTER F(";
410 IF I/2=INT(I/2) THEN 430
420 PRINT "-";
430 PRINT INT(I/2);")"
440 INPUT D(I,1)
450 FOR J=1 TO I-2
460 D(I-J,J+1)=ABS(D(I-J+1,J)-D(I-J-1,J))
470 NEXT J
480 D(1,I)=ABS(D(1,I-1)-D(2,I-1))
490 PRINT "DIFFERENCE #";I-1;"= ";: PRINTUSING PU$; D(1,I)
500 IF I=10 THEN 590
```

```
510 PRINT "WANT FURTHER DIFFERENCES?"
520 PRINT "YES(Y), NO(N), ONE LESS(L)"
530 INPUT Y$
538 REM OPERATOR MAY STOP NOW, CONTINUE,
539 REM  OR GO BACK TO ONE LESS DIFFERENCE
540 IF Y$="N" THEN 650
550 IF Y$="Y" THEN 390
560 IF Y$<>"L" THEN 510
570 I=I-1
580 GOTO 650
589 REM NO MORE THAN NINE DIFFERENCES POSSIBLE
590 PRINT "WANT NINTH DIFFERENCE (N), OR"
600 PRINT "ONLY EIGHTH DIFFERENCE (E)"
610 INPUT Y$
620 IF Y$="N" THEN 650
630 IF Y$<>"E" THEN 590
640 I=I-1
649 REM LINES 650 TO 710 SET UP VARIABLES USED IN PEARSON'S
    ALGORITHM
650 N(1)=P[3-P
660 N(2)=N(1)*(P*P-4)
670 N(3)=N(2)*(P*P-9)
680 N(4)=N(3)*(P*P-16)
690 FOR J=1 TO 10
700 E(J)=D(ABS(11-(J*2))+SGN(INT(J/6)),1)/(P+5-J)
710 NEXT J
720 FOR J=1 TO I
730 T=T+E(INT((10-I)/2)+J)*F(I,J)
740 NEXT J
750 IF I/2<>INT(I/2) THEN 770
760 T=T*(P-I/2)
770 PRINT "LAGRANGIAN";STR$(I);"-POINT INTERPOLATION"
780 PRINT "PRODUCES A VALUE OF ";
790 PRINTUSING PU$; T*N(INT((I-1)/2))/G(I)
800 END
```

References

National Bureau of Standards. *Handbook of Mathematical Functions*. Washington, D.C., 1966.

Scheid. *Numerical Analysis* (Schaum's series). New York: McGraw-Hill, 1968.

Vega. *Vollstandige Sammlung grosserer logarithmisch-trigonometrischer Tafeln*. 1794. Reprint. New York: Hafner, 1958.

Sums of Powers

This program calculates the sum of the Pth powers (up to the 10th powers) of the first N integers. It will also compute the sums of powers which are not the first N integers, but instead a series of higher integers. For example, if you want the sum of squares of numbers 101 to 1000, subtract the total of the first 100 squares from the total of the first 1000.

Program Notes

Clearly, a simple algorithm exists for computing the sums of powers: a loop with provision for adding the successive powers obtained. When you want the sum of very lengthy series of integers, the methods in this program are more efficient.

Example

What is the sum of the first ten 7th powers?
  Answer: 18,080,425

```
SUM OF POWERS

THIS PROGRAM COMPUTES THE SUM OF THE P-TH POWERS
(LIMIT: 10) FOR THE FIRST N INTEGERS.
ENTER P (1-10) AND N  (ENTER 0,0 TO END)
? 7,10
 THE SUM OF THE  7 TH POWERS OF
THE FIRST  10  INTEGERS IS  18080425

ENTER P (1-10) AND N  (ENTER 0,0 TO END)
? 0,0
READY
```

Practice Problems

1. What is the sum of the first 100 5th powers?
Answer: 17,108,332,500

2. What is the sum of the first six 10th powers?
Answer: 71,340,451

3. What is the sum of the squares of the numbers from 101 to 1000?
Answer: 333,495,150

Program Listing

```
10 CLS
20 PRINT "SUM OF POWERS"
```

```
30 PRINT
40 DEFDBL A-Z
50 ON ERROR GOTO 460
60 PRINT "THIS PROGRAM COMPUTES THE SUM OF THE P-TH POWERS"
70 PRINT "(LIMIT: 10) FOR THE FIRST N INTEGERS."
80 PRINT "ENTER P (1-10) AND N   (ENTER 0,0 TO END)"
90 INPUT P,N
100 IF P=0 AND N=0 THEN END
110 P=INT(P)
120 IF P<1 OR P>10 THEN 60
129 REM -- BRANCH TO PROPER POWER
130 ON P GOTO 140,170,200,230,250,270,300,330,360,390
140 S=N*(N+1)/2
150 PRINT "THE SUM OF THE FIRST POWERS OF"
160 GOTO 440
170 S=N*(N+1)*(2*N+1)/6
180 PRINT "THE SUM OF THE SECOND POWERS OF"
190 GOTO 440
200 S=N*N*((N+1)*(N+1)/4
210 PRINT " THE SUM OF THE THIRD POWERS OF"
220 GOTO 440
230 S=N*(N+1)*(2*N+1)*(3*N*N+3*N-1)/30
240 GOTO 430
250 S=N*N*(N+1)*(N+1)*(2*N*N+2*N-1)/12
260 GOTO 430
270 S1=(2*N+1)*(3*N*N*N*N+6*N*N*N-3*N+1)
280 S=N*(N+1)*S1/42
290 GOTO 430
300 S1=3*N*N*N*N+6*N*N*N-N*N-4*N+2
310 S=N*N*(N+1)*(N+1)*S1/24
320 GOTO 430
330 S1=5*N*N*N*N*N*N+15*N*N*N*N*N+5*N*N*N*N-15*N*N*N-N*N+9*N-3
340 S=N*(N+1)*(2*N+1)*S1/90
350 GOTO 430
360 S1=2*N*N*N*N*N*N+6*N*N*N*N*N+N*N*N*N-8*N*N*N+N*N+6*N-3
370 S=N*N*(N+1)*(N+1)*S1/20
380 GOTO 430
390 S2=3*N*N*N*N*N*N*N*N*N+12*N*N*N*N*N*N*N*N+8*N*N*N*N*N*N*N
400 S1=S2-18*N*N*N*N*N-10*N*N*N*N+24*N*N*N+2*N*N-15*N+5
410 S=N*(N+1)*(2*N+1)*S1/66
420 GOTO 430
430 PRINT " THE SUM OF THE ";P;"TH POWERS OF"
440 PRINT "THE FIRST ";N;" INTEGERS IS ";S
450 PRINT : GOTO 80
460 PRINT "OVERFLOW ERROR: THE ANSWER IS GREATER THAN 1D38,"
470 PRINTTAB(16) "THE LARGEST NUMBER THE TRS-80 CAN HANDLE."
480 RESUME 80
490 END
```

Reference

Chemical Rubber Co. *Handbook of Tables for Mathematicians,* 4th ed. Cleveland: 1970.

Factorials

This program calculates the factorial of an integer. For the factorial of a small number N we recursively multiply the integers from 1 through N. For larger numbers this becomes impractical, and we instead use Stirling's approximation:

$$N! \simeq e^{-N} \, N^N \sqrt{2 \, N \, \pi}$$

This has very high accuracy for large N.

Program Notes

Note that for any given computer there is a theoretical limit beyond which overflow cannot be avoided.

Example

How much is 8!?
   Answer: 40320

```
FACTORIALS

ENTER THE WHOLE NUMBER WHOSE FACTORIAL YOU WANT
(ENTER ZERO TO END)
? 8
THE FACTORIAL OF 8 IS
 40320 COMPUTED RECURSIVELY

ENTER THE WHOLE NUMBER WHOSE FACTORIAL YOU WANT
(ENTER ZERO TO END)
? 0
READY
```

Practice Problems

1. How much is 100!?
Answer: 9.3248×10^{157}

2. What is the factorial of 20?
Answer: $2.43290201 \times 10^{18}$

3. How much is 141!?
Answer: 1.897×10^{243}

Program Listing

```
10 CLS
20 PRINT "FACTORIALS"
30 PRINT
```

```
40 DEFDBL A-Z : DEFINT I
50 PRINT "ENTER THE WHOLE NUMBER WHOSE FACTORIAL YOU WANT"
60 PRINT "(ENTER ZERO TO END)"
70 INPUT N
80 IF N<0 OR N<>INT(N) THEN 50
90 IF N=0 THEN END
100 F=1 : J=0 : I=0 : K=0
110 IF N>69 THEN 190
119 REM CALCULATE USING RECURSIVE ALGORITHM
120 FOR I=1 TO N
130 F=F*I
140 IF F<1E+10 THEN 170
150 F=F/(1E+10)
160 J=J+10
170 NEXT I
180 GOTO 330
189 REM CALCULATE USING STIRLING'S APPROXIMATION
190 K=INT(N/5)
200 I=I+5
210 IF I>K*5 THEN 320
220 F=F*N*N*N*N*N/EXP(5)
230 IF F>1E+30 THEN 260
240 IF F>1E+20 THEN 290
250 GOTO 200
260 F=F/(1E+30)
270 J=J+30
280 GOTO 230
290 F=F/(1E+20)
300 J=J+20
310 GOTO 230
320 F=(F*N[(N-K*5))/EXP(N-K*5)*SQR(N*6.28318530718)
330 PRINT "THE FACTORIAL OF";N;"IS"
340 PRINT F;
350 IF J=0 THEN 370
360 PRINT "TIMES 10 TO THE";J;"TH POWER"
370 IF K>0 THEN 400
380 PRINT "COMPUTED RECURSIVELY"
390 GOTO 30
400 PRINT "COMPUTED BY STIRLING'S APPROXIMATION"
410 GOTO 30
420 END
```

References

Korn & Korn. *Mathematical Handbook,* 2nd ed. New York: McGraw-Hill, 1968.

National Bureau of Standards. *Handbook of Mathematical Functions.* Washington, D.C., 1966.

Temperature Conversion

Chemists, physicists, and other scientists are constantly involved in taking temperatures in one scale and converting them to other scales. In science, temperatures are commonly recorded and manipulated in five scales: Fahrenheit, Celsius (formerly called centigrade), Reaumur, Kelvin, and Rankine. This program takes any temperature (above absolute zero) recorded in any scale and converts it into all four of the other scales.

Example

Convert 98.6° Fahrenheit into the other scales.

```
TEMPERATURE CONVERSION

IN WHAT SCALE WAS THE TEMPERATURE RECORDED?
ENTER 1 FOR FAHRENHEIT
      2 FOR CELSIUS
      3 FOR REAUMUR
      4 FOR KELVIN
      5 FOR RANKINE
? 1

WHAT IS THE TEMPERATURE WHICH
YOU WISH TO BE CONVERTED
(ENTER -999 TO CHANGE SCALE,
      -9999 TO END)? 98.6

  98.6           DEGREES FAHRENHEIT =

  37             DEGREES CELCIUS
  29.6           DEGREES REAUMUR
  310.1          DEGREES KELVIN
  558.18         DEGREES RANKINE

WHAT IS THE TEMPERATURE WHICH
YOU WISH TO BE CONVERTED
(ENTER -999 TO CHANGE SCALE,
      -9999 TO END)? -9999

READY
```

Practice Problems

1. The boiling point of water is 100° Celsius. What is it on the other scales?
Answer: 212° Fahrenheit, 80° Reaumur, 373.1° Kelvin, 671.58° Rankine.

2. Lonna keeps her hot tub at 104° Fahrenheit. How hot is it on the other scales?
Answer: 40° Celsius, 32° Reaumur, 313.1° Kelvin, 563.58° Rankine.

Program Listing

```
10 CLS
20 PRINT "TEMPERATURE CONVERSION"
30 PRINT
40 PRINT "IN WHAT SCALE WAS THE TEMPERATURE RECORDED?"
50 PRINT "ENTER 1 FOR FAHRENHEIT"
60 PRINT TAB(6) "2 FOR CELSIUS"
70 PRINT TAB(6) "3 FOR REAUMUR"
80 PRINT TAB(6) "4 FOR KELVIN"
90 PRINT TAB(6) "5 FOR RANKINE"
100 INPUT S
110 PRINT
120 S=INT(S)
130 IF S<1 OR S>5 THEN 40
140 PRINT "WHAT IS THE TEMPERATURE WHICH"
150 PRINT "YOU WISH TO BE CONVERTED"
160 PRINT "(ENTER -999 TO CHANGE SCALE,"
170 INPUT "          -9999 TO END)";T
180 PRINT
190 IF T=-999 THEN 50
200 IF T=-9999 THEN END
210 REM BRANCH ON TYPE OF SCALE
219 REM BRANCH ON TYPE OF SCALE
220 ON S GOTO 230,270,310,350,390
230 IF T<-459.48 THEN 530
240 T1=T
250 PRINT T, "DEGREES FAHRENHEIT = ":PRINT
260 GOTO 440
270 IF T<-273.1 THEN 530
280 T1=32+T*1.8
290 PRINT T,"DEGREES CELSIUS = ": PRINT
300 GOTO 420
310 IF T<-218.48 THEN 530
320 T1=32+T*2.25
330 PRINT T,"DEGREES REAUMUR = ": PRINT
340 GOTO 420
350 IF T<0 THEN 530
360 T1=32+1.8*(T-273.1)
370 PRINT T,"DEGREES KELVIN = ": PRINT
380 GOTO 420
390 IF T<0 THEN 530
400 T1=T-459.48
410 PRINT T,"DEGREES RANKINE = ": PRINT
420 PRINT T1,"DEGREES FAHRENHEIT"
430 IF S=2 THEN 460
440 PRINT 5*(T1-32)/9,"DEGREES CELCIUS"
450 IF S=3 THEN 480
460 PRINT 4*(T1-32)/9,"DEGREES REAUMUR"
470 IF S=4 THEN 500
480 PRINT 5*(T1-32)/9+273.1,"DEGREES KELVIN"
490 IF S=5 THEN 510
500 PRINT T1+459.58,"DEGREES RANKINE"
510 PRINT
520 GOTO 140
```

```
530 PRINT "TEMPERATURE YOU ENTERED DOES NOT"
540 PRINT "EXIST. PLEASE ENTER A NEW ONE."
550 GOTO 160
560 END
```

Reference

Lange. *Lange's Handbook of Chemistry,* 10th rev. ed. New York: McGraw-Hill, 1967.

Numeric Base Conversion

This program will convert numbers between any two bases 2 through 36. The program will continue to convert values from and to the same bases until you enter zero as the value to convert. Then you can enter a new base to convert to, still using the previously entered base to convert from. If you enter zero as the base to convert to, you must enter a new base to convert from. Enter zero at this point to end the program.

Program Notes

You may convert between a base greater than 36, as long as you define the characters to represent values greater than 35. To do this, add the character(s) you choose between the Z and the closing quotes in line 40. For example, to convert to base 37, we'll represent the number 36 with the character #. Change line 40 so that it reads:

40 N$="0123456789ABCDEFGHIJKLMNOPQRSTUVWXYZ#"

Signs, decimal points, and any other characters you enter as part of the value to be converted that are not included in the chapter representations for the FROM base you selected, are interpreted as zeros wherever they appear.

Note that because the value you enter converted to its base 10 value, which is stored in the numeric variable D, accuracy of the output value is limited by the accuracy of your computer. This is also true because of the repeated division used in the conversion process.

You may encounter problems using this program on your computer because of the use of string variables. See the Appendix of this book for information on conversion of programs which use string variables.

Example

What is the base 16 number ABCD in base 10? What is the base 8 value? What is the base 36 equivalent of the base 10 number 825,062?

Answer: ABCD base 16 is 43,981 base 10. The base 8 value is 125,715. 825,062 base 10 is HOME base 36.

```
NUMERIC BASE CONVERSION

FROM BASE (O TO END)? 16
TO BASE? 10
VALUE? ABCD
ABCD BASE 16 IS 43981 BASE 10
VALUE? O
TO BASE? 8
VALUE? ABCD
ABCD BASE 16 IS 125715 BASE 8
VALUE? O
TO BASE? O
FROM BASE (O TO END)? 10
TO BASE? 36
VALUE? 825062
```

```
825062 BASE 10 IS HOME BASE 36
VALUE? O
TO BASE? O
FROM BASE (O TO END)? O
READY
```

Practice Problems

1. What is the base 16 representation of the base 10 number 45? What is the base 8 representation?
Answer: 45 base 10 is 2D base 16. 45 base 10 is 55 base 8.

2. What is the base 32 representation of the base 18 number 1G6? What is the base 10 value?
Answer: 1G6 base 18 is JA base 32. 1G6 base 18 is 618 base 10.

Program Listing

```
10 CLS
20 PRINT "NUMERIC BASE CONVERSION"
30 PRINT
40 N$="0123456789ABCDEFGHIJKLMNOPQRSTUVWXYZ"
48 REM -- VARIABLE 'M' IS THE HIGHEST BASE
49 REM --   YOU MAY CONVERT FROM / TO
50 M=LEN(N$)
60 PRINT "FROM BASE (O TO END)";
70 INPUT B1
79 REM -- END PROGRAM?
80 IF B1=0 THEN 420
89 REM -- TEST FOR VALID INPUT BASE
90 IF B1>1 THEN 120
100 PRINT "BASES 2 THROUGH";M;"ONLY. SELECT AGAIN."
110 GOTO 60
120 IF B1>M THEN 100
130 PRINT "TO BASE";
140 INPUT B2
150 IF B2=0 THEN 60
159 REM -- TEST FOR VALID OUTPUT BASE
160 IF B2>1 THEN 190
170 PRINT "BASES 2 THROUGH";M;"ONLY. SELECT AGAIN."
180 GOTO 130
190 IF B2>M THEN 170
200 PRINT "VALUE";
210 INPUT V$
220 IF V$="0" THEN 130
229 REM -- FIRST, CONVERT INPUT VALUE TO BASE 10
230 L=LEN(V$)
240 D=0
250 FOR I=1 TO L
260 FOR J=1 TO B1
270 IF MID$(V$,I,1)>MID$(N$,B1,1) THEN 390
280 IF MID$(N$,J,1)<>MID$(V$,I,1) THEN 300
290 D=D+INT((J-1)*(B1[(L-I))+.5)
300 NEXT J
```

```
310 NEXT I
319 REM -- NOW CONVERT BASE 10 VALUE TO DESIRED OUTPUT BASE
320 O$=""
330 X=INT(((D/B2)-INT(D/B2))*B2+1.5)
340 O$=MID$(N$,X,1) + O$
350 D=INT(D/B2)
360 IF D>0 THEN 330
369 REM -- OUTPUT THE RESULT
370 PRINT V$;" BASE";B1;"IS ";O$;" BASE";B2
379 REM -- LOOP BACK TO ENTER ANOTHER VAUE
380 GOTO 200
390 PRINT "INVALID ENTRY:"
400 PRINT "THERE IS NO SUCH NUMBER '";V$;"' (SIC) IN BASE ";B1
410 PRINT : GOTO 60
420 END
```

Musical Transposition

In music, transposition is the art of playing music in a different key from that in which it was written. Some musicians can transpose by sight or by ear; others have to convert each note from one key to another, laboriously, one by one. This program is for those in the latter group. The notes transposed by this program can be used as the roots of harmonies for piano, guitar, and so forth, as easily as they can be used as single notes.

The program first displays all the keys and key signatures, comprising seven flats through seven sharps, with their identifying numbers. You enter the numbers for the keys from and to which you are transposing. The program then displays each of the 12 possible notes, along with their transposed equivalents.

Note that the program will in all cases print out the correct pitch of the note to which it is transposing, and in virtually all cases the correct name as well. However, in those rare cases of some minor keys with multiple accidentals, you may have to supply the alternate name where a double accidental (double sharp or double flat) is called for.

Example

What do notes in the key of B^b become when you transpose to the key of G?
    Answer: G, G#, A, A#, B, C, C#, D, D#, E, F, F#

```
MUSICAL TRANSPOSITION

IN THE FOLLOWING LIST OF KEYS
AND KEY SIGNATURES,
1.  A MAJOR/F-SHARP MINOR-3 SHARPS
2.  B-FLAT MAJOR/G-MINOR-2 FLATS
3.  C-FLAT MAJOR/A-FLAT MINOR-7 FLATS
    B MAJOR/A-FLAT MINOR-5 SHARPS
4.  C MAJOR/A MINOR-NO SHARPS OR FLATS
5.  D-FLAT MAJOR/B-FLAT MINOR-5 FLATS
    C-SHARP MAJOR/A-SHARP MINOR-5 SHARPS
6.  D MAJOR/B MINOR-2 SHARPS
7.  E-FLAT MAJOR/C MINOR-3 FLATS
8.  E MAJOR/C-SHARP MINOR-4 SHARPS
9.  F MAJOR/D MINOR-1 FLAT
10. G-FLAT MAJOR/E-FLAT MINOR-6 FLATS
    F-SHARP MAJOR/D-SHARP MINOR-6 SHARPS
11. G MAJOR/E MINOR-1 SHARP
12. A-FLAT MAJOR/F MINOR-4 FLATS
ENTER THE NO. OF THE KEY FROM WHICH
YOU ARE TRANSPOSING, THEN THE NO. OF
THE KEY TO WHICH YOU ARE TRANPOSING
? 11,8


     TRANSPOSITION TABLE
TRANSPOSED          TRANSPOSED
  FROM                 TO
A                   G-FLAT/F-SHARP
```

```
B-FLAT/A-SHARP        G
B (C-FLAT)            A-FLAT/G-SHARP

C (B-SHARP)           A
D-FLAT/C-SHARP        B-FLAT/A-SHARP
D                     B (C-FLAT)

E-FLAT/D-SHARP        C (B-SHARP)
E  (F-FLAT)           D-FLAT/C-SHARP
F (E-SHARP)           D
G-FLAT/F-SHARP        E-FLAT/D-SHARP
G                     E  (F-FLAT)
A-FLAT/G-SHARP        F (E-SHARP)


DO YOU WANT ANOTHER TRANSPOSITION? (Y/N)
? N
READY
```

Practice Problems

1. In the key of G, the first chords of "My Country 'Tis of Thee" are: G, E^m, C, D, G, E^m, C, G, B^7, E^m. If it is transposed to E, what would these chords be?
   Answer: E, $C^{\#m}$, A, B, E, $C^{\#m}$, A, E, $G^{\#7}$, $C^{\#m}$.

2. Bach's Fifth Brandenburg Concerto, written in D Major, begins: D, D, F#, F#, A, A, D, D, C#, D, C#, B, A, G, F#, E. If he had written it in C Major what would these notes have been?
   Answer: C, C, E, E, G, G, C, C, B, C, B, A, G, F, E, D.

Program Listing

```
10 CLS
20 PRINT "MUSICAL TRANSPOSITION"
30 PRINT
40 DIM A$(12)
49 REM READ TABLE OF NOTES
50 FOR I=1 TO 12
60 READ A$(I)
70 NEXT I
80 DATA "A","B-FLAT/A-SHARP","B (C-FLAT)","C (B-SHARP)"
90 DATA "D-FLAT/C-SHARP","D","E-FLAT/D-SHARP","E  (F-FLAT)"
100 DATA "F (E-SHARP)","G-FLAT/F-SHARP","G","A-FLAT/G-SHARP"
110 PRINT "IN THE FOLLOWING LIST OF KEYS"
120 PRINT "AND KEY SIGNATURES,"
130 PRINT "1.   A MAJOR/F-SHARP MINOR-3 SHARPS"
140 PRINT "2.   B-FLAT MAJOR/G-MINOR-2 FLATS"
150 PRINT "3.   C-FLAT MAJOR/A-FLAT MINOR-7 FLATS"
160 PRINT "     B MAJOR/A-FLAT MINOR-5 SHARPS"
170 PRINT "4.   C MAJOR/A MINOR-NO SHARPS OR FLATS"
180 PRINT "5.   D-FLAT MAJOR/B-FLAT MINOR-5 FLATS"
190 PRINT "     C-SHARP MAJOR/A-SHARP MINOR-5 SHARPS"
200 PRINT "6.   D MAJOR/B MINOR-2 SHARPS
210 PRINT "7.   E-FLAT MAJOR/C MINOR-3 FLATS"
```

```
220 PRINT "8.   E MAJOR/C-SHARP MINOR-4 SHARPS"
230 PRINT "9.   F MAJOR/D MINOR-1 FLAT"
240 PRINT "10. G-FLAT MAJOR/E-FLAT MINOR-6 FLATS"
250 PRINT "    F-SHARP MAJOR/D-SHARP MINOR-6 SHARPS"
260 PRINT "11. G MAJOR/E MINOR-1 SHARP"
270 PRINT "12. A-FLAT MAJOR/F MINOR-4 FLATS"
280 PRINT "ENTER THE NO. OF THE KEY FROM WHICH"
290 PRINT "YOU ARE TRANSPOSING, THEN THE NO. OF"
300 PRINT "THE KEY TO WHICH YOU ARE TRANPOSING"
310 INPUT A,B
320 PRINT
330 IF A>12 THEN 380
340 IF B>12 THEN 380
350 IF A<1 THEN 380
360 IF B<1 THEN 380
370 IF A<>B THEN 400
380 PRINT "ERROR.  PLEASE ENTER AGAIN"
390 GOTO 280
400 PRINT "       TRANSPOSITION TABLE"
410 PRINT " TRANSPOSED";TAB(20);"TRANSPOSED"
420 PRINT TAB(4);"FROM";TAB(24);"TO"
430 P=0
439 REM PRINT TABLE
440 FOR I=1 TO 12
450 D=B-A+I-SGN(INT((B-A+I)/12))*12
460 IF D>0 THEN 480
470 D=12
480 PRINT TAB(1);A$(I);TAB(20);A$(D)
490 P=P+1
500 IF P/3<>INT(P/3) THEN 530
510 PRINT
520 P=0
530 NEXT I
540 PRINT
550 PRINT "DO YOU WANT ANOTHER TRANSPOSITION? (Y/N)"
560 INPUT Y$
570 IF Y$="Y" THEN 110
580 END
```

References

Pistan. *Harmony,* 3rd ed. New York: Norton, 1969.

Priesing and Tecklin. *Language of the Piano.* Boston: Carl Fischer, 1959.

Appendix

In this appendix you will find suggestions for changing the programs to accommodate different output devices.

We describe each of the specific changes listed below in a general way and illustrate wherever possible with an example taken from the book. You must decide how a suggested change would apply to any particular program, if at all. Therefore, you will need some understanding of Basic programming in order to implement these changes.

Pausing With Full Display Screen

Many programs have more lines of output than will fit your 16-line screen. This means the first lines of output flash by quickly and scroll off the top of the screen, leaving you with no idea of what they contained. On the Radio Shack TRS-80, you can press the 'Shift' and '@' keys to freeze the display temporarily. You can then review and record anything on the display. Subsequently pressing any key again sets the computer in motion. More program output appears. You may have to freeze the display several times in order to see all the output.

Alternatively, you can modify a program so it pauses at one or more points during its output, waiting for the user to cue it to continue. To do this, add the following subroutine to the program, and call the subroutine at suitable intervals during the output phrase of the program.

```
5799 REM WAIT FOR OPERATOR CUE
5800 PRINT "ENTER 'C' TO CONTINUE"
5810 INPUT W$
5820 RETURN
```

This technique is used in the Income Averaging program. In programs where some or all of the output occurs inside a loop (for example, between FOR and NEXT statements), you may not be able to merely place calls to this subroutine between appropriate PRINT statements, as we did in the Income Averaging program on lines 1910, 1960, 2070, and 2180. In this case, use the subroutine below, which counts the number of lines displayed since the last pause. Each time you call this subroutine, it increments a counter, and tests to see if the new count exceeds the size of the display. If so, it pauses for the operator cue. Otherwise, it simply returns to the calling point in the program. Therefore, you would insert a call to this subroutine immediately after every PRINT statement that causes a line of output (that is, a PRINT statement not ending with a comma or semicolon).

```
5757 REM SUBROUTINE CHECKS LINE COUNT
5798 REM WAITS FOR CUE IF DISPLAY IS FULL
5799 REM FIRST INCREMENT AND CHECK LINE COUNT
5800 L9 = L9 + 1
5810 IF L9 < 15 THEN 5850
5819 REM SCREEN IS FULL — —
5820 PRINT "ENTER 'C' TO CONTINUE";
5830 INPUT W$
5839 REM RESET LINE COUNT
5840 L9 = 0
5850 RETURN
```

Printer Output

Viewing program output on the display screen is perfectly acceptable when you are using a program as an experimental or investigative tool. But sooner or later, you will probably tire of continually copying program output from the display by hand. The solution, of course, is to direct program output to a printer. You can modify any program to use a printer. By replacing 'PRINT' with 'LPRINT' the programs will output to a printer. Input parameters however will not be printed unless a

```
LPRINT X1 ; X2 ; X3
```

line is inserted after each

```
INPUT X1 , X2 , X3
```

where X1, X2, X3 are the input variables requested.

Frequency of Compounding Interest

Several of these programs base their computations on interest compounded annually. This is acceptable in most cases. But you can have the calculations compound interest more frequently. Perhaps the easiest way to do this is to convert the annual interest rate to the effective interest rate, based on the number of compounding periods per year. Then enter this effective rate when the program asks for an interest rate. The general formula for this is

$$E = \left(1 + \frac{1}{N}\right)^{NY}$$

where E is the effective interest rate, I is the annual interest rate expressed as a decimal fraction, N is the number of compounding periods per year, and Y is the number of years. The formula for continuous compounding is

$$E = e^{IY}$$

where E is the effective interest rate, e is 2.718281828... (the base of natural logarithms), I is the nominal interest rate, and Y is the number of years.

Of course, you can change a program to accept the nominal interest rate and convert it automatically to the effective interest rate. The program would have to ask for the number of compounding periods per year in order to make the conversion. Alternatively, you could restate the interest compounding calculation in the program so that it compounds at the desired frequency. For example, this calculation occurs in the Future Value of an Investment program on line 200. If you restate line 200 as shown below, the program will compute the future value of an investment at growth rate R, compounded continuously.

$$200\ T = T + INT(C * EXP(R*(N-5)) * 100 + 0.5)/100$$

Other OSBORNE/McGraw-Hill Publications

An Introduction to Microcomputers: Volume 0 — The Beginner's Book
An Introduction to Microcomputers: Volume 1 — Basic Concepts, 2nd Edition
An Introduction to Microcomputers: Volume 2 — Some Real Microprocessors
An Introduction to Microcomputers: Volume 3 — Some Real Support Devices
Osborne 4 & 8-Bit Microprocessor Handbook
Osborne 16-Bit Microprocessor Handbook
8089 I/O Processor Handbook
CRT Controller Handbook
68000 Microprocessor Handbook
8080A/8085 Assembly Language Programming
6800 Assembly Language Programming
Z80 Assembly Language Programming
6502 Assembly Language Programming
Z8000 Assembly Language Programming
6809 Assembly Language Programming
Running Wild — The Next Industrial Revolution
The 8086 Book
PET and the IEEE 488 Bus (GPIB)
PET/CBM Personal Computer Guide, 2nd Edition
Business System Buyer's Guide
Osborne CP/M® User Guide
Apple II® User's Guide
Microprocessors for Measurement & Control
Some Common BASIC Programs
Some Common BASIC Programs — PET/CBM Edition
Some Common BASIC Programs — Atari Edition
Some Common BASIC Programs — TRS-80™ Level II Edition
Some Common BASIC Programs — Apple II Edition
Practical BASIC Programs
Payroll with Cost Accounting
Accounts Payable and Accounts Receivable
General Ledger
8080 Programming for Logic Design
6800 Programming for Logic Design
Z80 Programming for Logic Design